BIRDS
OF PREY

BIRDS
OF PREY

CONSULTING EDITOR
Dr. Ian Newton

EDITORIAL ADVISOR
Penny Olsen

ILLUSTRATIONS BY
Tony Pyrzakowski

Lon Lauber/Oxford Scientific Films

MEREHURST
LONDON

Published 1990 by Merehurst Press
Ferry House, 51/57 Lacy Road, Putney, London, SW15 1 PR

By arrangement with Weldon Owen
Produced by Weldon Owen Pty Limited
43 Victoria Street, McMahons Point NSW 2060, Australia
Telex 23038; Fax (02) 929 8352
Weldon Owen Inc.
90 Gold Street, San Francisco CA 94133, USA
Fax (415) 291 8841
Members of the Weldon International Group of Companies
Sydney • San Francisco • Hong Kong • London • Paris

President: John Owen
Publishing Manager: Stuart Laurence
Project Coordinators: Jane Fraser, Beverley Barnes
Editor: Daphne Rawling
Picture research: Annette Crueger
Final picture edit: Brigitte Zinsinger
Illustrations research: Kathy Gerrard
Captions: Penny Olsen
Designer: Andi Cole, Andi Cole Design
Series design: Sue Burk
Assembly: Ingrid Padina
Maps and diagrams: Greg Campbell
Index: Dianne Regtop
Production Director: Mick Bagnato

Typeset by Keyset Phototype
Printed by Kyodo Printing Co. (S'pore) Pte Ltd
Printed in Singapore

A Weldon Owen Production

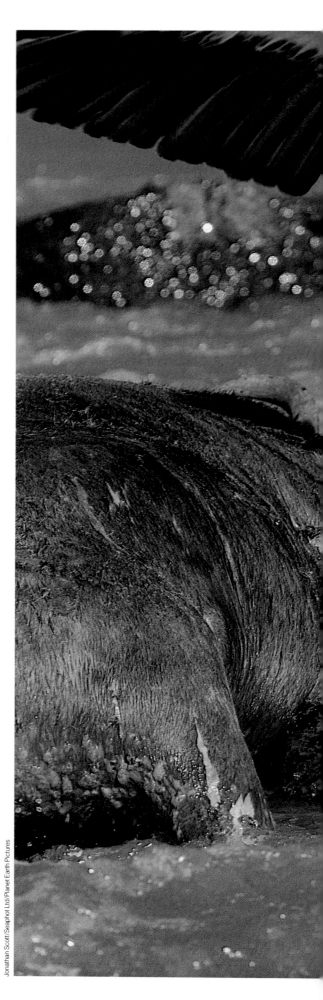

Cover:
A magnificent White-bellied Sea Eagle in Sri Lanka
Photo by Joanna Van Gruisen/Ardea London

Endpapers:
The Osprey makes dramatic dives into the water for fish, and often choses equally spectacular
settings to nest: here a coastal rock pinnacle in the Sea of Cortez, Mexico.
Photo by François Gohier/Ardea London

Page 1:
In striking combination, the red face, raised ebony head feathers and rich chestnut cape signal
maturity and emotion to other Bateleurs.

Page 2:
The archetypic eagle: perched on a rock, a majestic Golden Eagle surveys its remote territory.

Page 3:
Thousands of Bald Eagles flock annually at river mouths near the Alaskan coast to feast on salmon,
returned from the sea to spawn and die.

Pages 4—5:
A Ruppell's Griffon and African White-backed Vulture arrive, competitively, at an ungulate carcass.
Little will remain in an hour or so.

Page 7:
Eurasian Buzzards squabble; feet and talons are many raptors' most powerful weapon.

Pages 8—9:
A Brahminy Kite breaks its rippled reflection to snatch a fish from the surface. Specialized to forage
in aquatic habitats, it frequents estuaries and coasts, rice fields and marshlands.

Pages 10—11:
With red-skinned, puppet-like head and massive bill, the huge Lappet-faced Vulture is strong enough
to open a carcass and tear coarse tissue.

Jonathan Scott/Seaphot Ltd/Planet Earth Pictures

Morten Strange/NHPA

D iurnal birds of prey include the various eagles, buzzards, kites, harriers, vultures, falcons and other raptors which hunt in the daytime. They are some of the world's most graceful and spectacular predators.

Being meat eaters, they can be recognized by their hooked beaks, adapted for tearing flesh, and by their powerful feet and sharp claws, adapted for seizing and holding prey. Despite this common design, birds of prey span an enormous range of sizes, from small falconets to huge vultures and condors. They are found on all continents except Antarctica, and in all habitats from forest to desert, and from farmland to cities. They eat a wide range of prey from fish to birds, and snails to insects. Carrion feeders, such as vultures, find their motionless food by keen sight or smell, while large falcons catch their avian prey in a spectacular chase or stoop.

Being top predators, raptors live at low densities compared to most other birds, and are extremely sensitive to human-induced changes in their environment. Any alteration of land use or other action that reduces wildlife populations will inevitably affect raptors, which depend on other wildlife for food. Any persistent chemical pollutant that can enter the bodies of animals will eventually concentrate in the bodies of raptors. It was this vulnerability to pollutants that resulted in sudden population crashes in several species over large parts of the developed world in the 1950s and 1960s, following the large-scale use of DDT and other organochlorine pesticides in agriculture. An ecological catastrophe of unprecedented scale and suddenness, it helped to focus attention on birds of prey, and their role as environmental monitors, as never before.

This book is concerned with all aspects of the biology of raptors: the factors that affect their numbers and breeding, the main threats and conservation successes, and their importance to people. It is an international effort, drawing on the lifetime knowledge and experience of more than 50 biologists and other experts from around the world. We hope that the book will impart some feeling for the variety and beauty of these birds, for their importance in human culture, and for the inspiration they have given to people everywhere.

Ian Newton
CONSULTING EDITOR

Peter Davey/Bruce Coleman Ltd

Largest living raptor, with a wingspan approaching 3 meters (10 feet), the Andean Condor soars over slopes and coastal plains but returns to roost and nest in the mountains, from Venezuela to Patagonia.

RAPTORS OF

THE WORLD

WHAT IS A RAPTOR?

ALAN KEMP

▲ Both eagle and symbolism unmistakable, the names of the crew members of one of America's space exploration missions crown a NASA (National Aeronautical and Space Administration) badge. The American national emblem, a Bald Eagle, carries the mission skyward with power, determination, and absolute mastery of the air.

The word raptor comes from the Latin word for a plunderer, stemming from *raptare* "to seize and carry away." The term conjures up visions of predatory birds grasping, bodily carrying away and consuming their prey, and it is no coincidence that the grasping and cutting organs of raptors are among their most recognizable features. The strong legs and powerful feet, armed with sharp curved talons, together with the hooked bill set in a bare fleshy cere, make raptors immediately separable from most other birds. Parrots have a similarly hooked beak, but only one species regularly uses this to rend flesh, and none have powerful grasping feet like a raptor. Other birds with powerful feet, such as gamebirds, do not have the grasping ability of raptors nor the curved, sharp claws that are such an integral part of the weaponry of raptors.

The eyesight and powers of flight of raptors are other attributes for which they are recognized, embodied in such sayings as "hawk-eyed," "far-sighted as a vulture," "the vision of an eagle," "swift as a falcon," "soars like an eagle" and "hovers like a kite." These abilities so impress humans that raptors have become incorporated into the emblems of many societies, and allusions to their prowess, often with special terms acquired from the ancient practice of falconry, have been integrated into many different languages.

▲ In perfect miniature, an African Pygmy Falcon (*Polihierax semitorquatus*) displays all the attributes for which raptors are renowned. Weighing less than 100 grams (3.5 ounces), it shares a hooked beak, strong toes, sharp talons, and rapid, agile flight with many of its larger, better-known relatives.

▶ One of the largest actively hunting raptors in the world and the largest in Africa, the impressive 6-kilogram (13 pound) Martial Eagle (*Hieraaetus bellicosus*) can overcome an Impala calf but prefers smaller prey, particularly gamebirds.

Living birds that are classed as raptors include some 292 species of diurnal birds of prey and 162 species of owls. Within such an abundance of species it is to be expected that some fit the typical image of a raptor better than others. Diurnal raptors range in size from thrush-sized falconets, which feed mainly on insects, to turkey-sized eagles which catch live monkeys, and large vultures which tear into carcasses of dead antelope. Between these extremes exist species that specialize in eating wasps, snails, bats, snakes or bones, others that are expert fishers, high-speed aerialists that capture flying birds or bats, and hikers that walk along in search of small animals. One species, the Egyptian Vulture (*Neophron percnopterus*), even uses stones as tools to break open Ostrich eggs. The smaller species overlap in their predatory ability with birds such as shrikes, drongos, vangas, tyrant-flycatchers and antbirds. However, the larger species of raptors have no avian equivalents in the strength and agility with which they overcome prey often much larger than themselves.

The different types of raptors fall into six major groups, each recognizable by a unique combination of anatomical, behavioral and biological features. The ancestry of the groups, and therefore their relationships to one another, remains a matter of conjecture, since traditional groupings of birds have been made more on superficial overall similarities than on details of anatomy and biology. Such an approach is likely to stress common features, such as the hooked bill and powerful feet, even though these similarities are often convergent—that is, common designs

evolved to meet the same ends but developed from different ancestral stocks. However, there is widespread agreement on which species of raptor fall into which group.

The owls (strigids), those raptors specialized for crepuscular and nocturnal predation, are immediately identifiable by many anatomical, physiological and developmental peculiarities but are not included in this book. They are distinguished from other raptors by, among other details, lacking a crop, having an arch on the radial bone in the forearm, possessing long cecal sacs on their intestine, and differing in the sequence, structure and molt of their plumage. They have, in addition, an advanced design to their eyes, ears and soft plumage which adapt them well to their nocturnal habits. They are the group thought to be least related to other raptors, are classified in the avian order Strigiformes among other groups of arboreal birds, and are usually allied with such other nocturnal specialists as the nightjars, oilbirds, potoos, frogmouths, and owlet-nightjars, in the order Caprimulgiformes.

The diurnal birds of prey, which are the majority of raptors, have been grouped together traditionally in one big order, the Falconiformes, more on the basis of their gross similarity of appearance than on details of their anatomy and behavior. They do share a different type of feather lice to those found on owls, and details of their chromosome and DNA structure show diurnal and nocturnal raptors to be quite independent developments. The affinities of diurnal raptors to other birds are not certain, but growing evidence, based on anatomical and DNA studies, points to

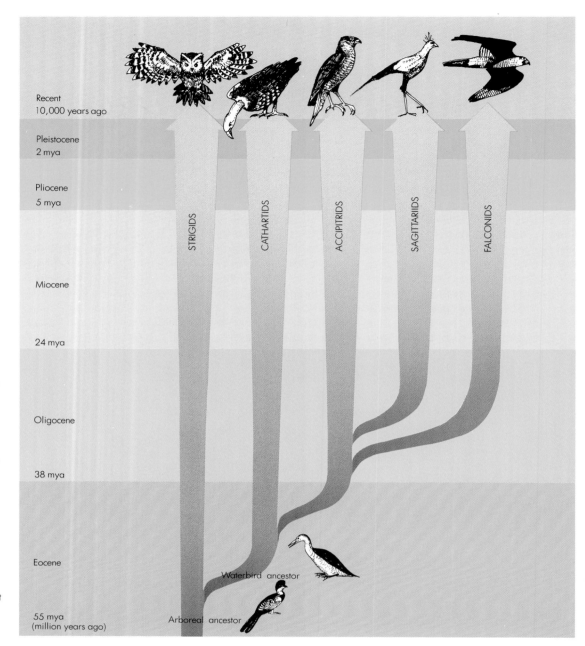

► The origins and affinities of the five main groups of raptorial birds are uncertain. Owls (Strigids), thought to be least closely related to the other raptors, are most likely allied to the nightjars and frogmouths. As this proposed family tree shows, the remaining four groups may well share a waterbird ancestor, some more distantly than others. Cathartid or New World Vultures are the group most similar to waterbirds, particularly the storks, and seem to be the earliest of the diurnal raptors.

▼ Competing for carrion, an uneasy Ruppell's Griffon (*Gyps rueppellii*) reluctantly shares Africa's Masai Mara with a Marabou Stork. Storks are thought to be among the nearest relatives of the diurnal raptors and have much in common with the New World Vultures.

Recent
10,000 years ago

Pleistocene
2 mya

Pliocene
5 mya

STRIGIDS

CATHARTIDS

ACCIPITRIDS

SAGITTARIIDS

FALCONIDS

Miocene

24 mya

Oligocene

38 mya

Eocene

Waterbird ancestor

55 mya
(million years ago)

Arboreal ancestor

various waterbirds—plovers (order Charadriiformes), pelicans (order Pelecaniformes), storks (order Ciconiiformes) and seabirds (order Procellariiformes)—as their nearest relatives. The five groups of diurnal birds of prey are each so distinctive that they have all, at times, been given ordinal ranking of their own.

All are immediately recognizable by their hooked beaks, strong feet and large eyes, but the adaptive significance of their other features in common is less obvious. The base of the bill is saddled by a fleshy cere through which the nostrils open. The crop (in which freshly eaten food is stored) is well developed, but only minute cecal sacs lead off the intestine. The ovary and oviduct, which are well developed only on the left side in most birds, are equally developed and functional on both sides in diurnal raptors. The young hatch in a fine first down, growing from the follicles that will later produce the true feathers. This is supplanted by a denser second down which grows from the follicles that will produce the down layer over the whole body surface under the final plumage. All diurnal raptors, once feathered, have 10 functional primary wing feathers, 11–25 secondaries and 12 or 14 tail feathers. In most species, the flank feathers on the tibia (upper leg) are elongated, and in many are distinctively colored and used in display. Most species adopt a characteristic posture when drying out after rain or sunbathing, with the wings fully extended and the body upright. Further details for each group of diurnal raptors, given later, together with background on their biology and relationships, will reveal the extent to which exceptions exist to this fundamental raptorial design.

◄ The diurnal raptors share a number of physical and behavioral characteristics. Most adopt a striking, heraldic pose when sunbathing or drying their feathers. Here, with wings fully outstretched and body upright, an immature Sea Eagle (*Haliaeetus leucogaster*) dries itself after fishing.

▼ Raptors have a number of anatomical features in common. Apart from the characteristic beak and feet, distinctive characters include a fleshy cere straddling the beak, a crop between the chin and the breast, for the short-term storage of food, 10 primary wing feathers, 12 or 14 tail feathers, and a functional alula which helps prevent stalling when braking in flight. The diagram shows the main external features.

Joanna Van Gruisen/Ardea London

OLD WORLD AND NEW WORLD VULTURES

DAVID C. HOUSTON

Vultures are distinctive, with several features that separate them from other raptors. They do not usually kill their own prey, but rely on finding dead animals. They use soaring flight more than other birds of prey, and have characteristic bare areas of skin around the head and neck. Most species show no sexual dimorphism, so that both sexes are almost identical in size and appearance. Many species are also found at far higher densities than any other kind of raptor, congregating in hundreds at sources of food, and some species nesting in large colonies.

Despite the fact that all vultures look very similar, these birds come from two quite separate stocks. The 15 species of Old World vultures, living in Africa, Asia and southern Europe share a common ancestry with the eagles and hawks. But the seven species of New World vultures are probably descended from the same line as the storks. They are a textbook example of convergent evolution: two quite unrelated groups of animals that look alike because they have developed the same adaptations for a similar way of life. The similarities between these two groups are remarkable.

The largest species are the Andean Condor (*Vultur gryphus*) and the Himalayan Griffon (*Gyps himalayensis*) both of which weigh up to 10 kilograms (22 pounds). The Condors and Griffon Vultures feed on muscle and viscera from large carcasses, are dull in coloration, with a prominent white neck ruff and long neck, and both species forage widely in search of food and congregate in large numbers at food sites.

Both Old and New World vultures have medium-sized species, weighing 4–6 kilograms (9–13 pounds) and which are often brightly colored around the head. These species take the skin, tendons, sinews and other tough tissues, and do not forage widely but usually feed within a known feeding range, and do not collect in large numbers.

Then finally both vulture guilds contain small species, weighing only 1–2 kilograms (2–4 pounds) which specialize in taking small scraps that the other birds leave behind. Between them they can deal efficiently and quickly with most carcasses, and in both Old and New Worlds these birds are often the main scavengers in undisturbed wildlife communities.

▲◄ Vultures are a fascinating example of convergent evolution. Only distantly related, Old World and New World Vultures are remarkably similar in appearance because they have adapted to similar lifestyles. Perforated nostrils, open from one side of the beak to the other, immediately identify the Turkey Vulture (above) as a New World vulture, descended from an ancestral stork. Dark brown, with patchily feathered head and neck, broad wings and straight stubby claws, superficially it is not unlike the Old World Cinereous Vulture (*Aegypius monachus*), at left. Here the similarity ends as the huge Cinereous Vulture is most closely related to the hawks and eagles.

CATHARTIDS

The seven species of cathartid vultures, classified in the family Cathartidae and including condors and Turkey Vultures (*Cathartes aura*), show the most similarity to their waterbird relatives. Indeed, recent studies, of anatomy, behavior and genetic material, suggest that cathartids are so similar to storks that they belong alongside them in classification, maybe even within the same family. Such vultures are now found only in North and South America. They are immediately recognizable by their open nostrils, such that one can look right through the tops of their beaks, and by the first joint of the inner toe being elongated, both features in common with storks. Less obvious characteristics that distinguish them include the fused maxillo-palatine bones, special consolidation of the plantar tendons in the feet, absence of a sound-producing syrinx, the lack of a slender aftershaft alongside each feather, long cecae on either side of the intestine, and a naked oil gland. They show particular similarity to storks in their habit of defecating on their legs to cool themselves and in the development of the fluffy down and pattern of emergence of feathers in the chicks. Their vulturine appearance comes from their bare head and neck, from the ruff of feathers or down around the neck, from their broad wings and soaring flight, from the reticulated leg scales, from the hind toe raised off the ground, and from the long toes with webs of skin in between and straight stubby claws at their ends. All these characteristics are also found in the unrelated vultures of the Old World, and must therefore be convergent features, evolved independently in both groups, to suit the scavenging habit.

ACCIPITRIDS

The largest and most diverse group of raptors are the 223 species in the family Accipitridae, one of the largest avian families. Its members occur on all continents except Antarctica and include those species known colloquially as hawks, buzzards and eagles, together with more specialized species such as kites, Old World vultures, cuckoo-hawks, harriers, sparrowhawks and goshawks. They are rather uniform in structure, despite showing a wide range of sizes, designs, flying abilities and predatory habits, yet the accipitrids are not obviously characterized by any one feature.

Most have 14 neck vertebrae, whereas other raptors have 15, but they are unique among raptors in the number and form of their chromosomes, in having eggshells with an outer crystalline layer interspersed with vacuoles (holes), and in the proportion of soluble nitrogen in the shells.

Anatomically, accipitrids have a well-developed oil gland, lack the expansor secondarium muscle in the wing and have broad muscular tongues. Most also show good

Francois Gohier/Ardea London

Jonathan Scott/Planet Earth Pictures

▲ Common, conspicuous and widespread in the Americas, the bare-faced Turkey Vulture scavenges for carrion and other waste. It is one of a group of vulturine species, the cathartids, now found only in the New World. They have an elongated inner toe and a habit of defecating on their legs to keep cool, characteristics that ally them with the storks rather than the other raptors.

◄ With 223 representatives worldwide, the accipitrids are the largest and most diverse group of raptors. Members include the hawks, eagles, kites and Old World vultures and are all modifications of the same basic design. They range from generalists to more specialized species like this Pale Chanting Goshawk (*Melierax canorus*), a long-tailed and long-legged hunter of lizards and other terrestrial prey.

development of the supra-orbital process of the frontal bone that forms a shield over the eye. Their wing molt usually starts with the inner primary and proceeds outwards or in descending order. Their secondaries molt inwards from centers at the outermost and fifth-from-outermost feathers, with a third center at the eighth-to-ninth-from-outermost, up to the seventeenth-from-outermost in species with long wings. The sequence of molting of the tail feathers is less consistent, both between and within species. In the larger eagles and vultures a complete molt is not possible within a year, and a second or even third wave of molt starts before the first has finished. In some species this is further modified by suspension of

▼ The impressive, hooked beak of the Golden Eagle (*Aquila chrysaetos*) identifies it as a raptor, but it is the broad, muscular tongue and bony brow ridge protecting the eye that characterize it as an accipitrid.

Kevin Schafer/Tom Stack & Associates

▲ Similar to the accipitrids and sometimes placed with them, the cosmopolitan Osprey is the sole representative of the Pandionidae. A spectacular diver for fish, it has many specialized features of its own and some in common with the accipitrids, cathartids, falconids and even owls.

features distinguish it from them and suggest connections to other groups. It is a cosmopolitan species that is highly specialized for the capture of fish by diving into the water, and what resemblance it does show to accipitrid species is mostly to the kites and honey buzzards. It shares with them the same proportion of soluble nitrogen in the eggshell, with them and falconids the lack of a ridge of bone above the eyes, and with falconids and some kites the ochre-colored lining to the eggshells. It is the only raptor other than the cathartid vultures lacking the slender aftershaft beside each feather on the underparts and with long cecal sacs leading from the intestines; it has the largest and most tufted oil gland; and it does not show the spread-winged sunning posture. Its feet are very powerful and it has bony bridges over the tendons behind the "knee" most like owls. The layout of feathers on the body is again most like cathartid vultures, as is the arrangement of tendons in the feet.

molt during breeding or migration. Behaviorally, accipitrids kill their prey primarily with the feet; they also squirt out their droppings rather than just letting them fall, and they build their own nests. They also have eggshells with a green lining.

PANDIONIDS

Two groups of raptors are each represented now by only a single well-defined species, allied to the Accipitridae but sufficiently distinct from them to deserve placement in their own families. The Osprey (*Pandion haliaetus*), sole representative of the family Pandionidae, is superficially much like the accipitrid raptors, but numerous anatomical

SAGITTARIIDS

The Secretarybird (*Sagittarius serpentarius*), sole member of the Sagittariidae, is restricted to Africa. It looks much like a stork with its long legs, short toes and habit of walking over savanna in search of food. Aspects of its breeding biology are also stork-like, such as both parents alternating care of the eggs and chicks, and both delivering food and water to the young by regurgitation. However, most of the anatomy, green-lined eggshell with vacuoles, calls and displays, are similar to eagles and place the Secretarybird as an early offshoot from the accipitrid raptors. It is superficially similar to other long-legged birds of the South American savannas, the two species of seriemas (family Cariamidae), but differs from them and is like

► Hiking across savanna and woodland and stamping on its prey, the 1-meter tall Secretarybird resembles no other raptor. Like the Osprey it is the lone representative of a group, the Sagittariidae, but its affinities are clearer. It shares features with both accipitrids and storks and is thought to be an early offshoot from the Accipitridae.

accipitrids in the feathered thighs, among other features. The similarities apparently result from convergence to the same terrestrial lifestyle, but the seriemas are more closely related to cranes and rails.

FALCONIDS

The falcon family, Falconidae, is the most distinctive and divergent within the diurnal birds of prey. The family occurs throughout the world, but shows its greatest diversity in South America where each of the major subdivisions—caracaras, forest falcons, and true falcons—is well represented. The falconids share with the accipitrids a similar center from which molt of their secondaries starts, the wishbone free of the other shoulder bones, and the same feather lice. All 60 members of the family differ from other raptors in their primary molt pattern, which always starts at the fourth primary counting from the inside of the wing and proceeds in both directions. They differ from accipitrids in the composition of their egg white, in the proportion of soluble nitrogen in their eggshells and in the ochre color of the inside of their shells. They are also distinctive in details of the skull, including the bony tubercle in the nostril, in the form of their breastbone, in the extra pair of tail vertebrae fused into the pygostyle to support the tail, and in the solid construction of the vertebrae within the thorax. They lack the supra-orbital process above the eyes, their tongues are short and fleshy, and their syrinx is quite elaborate with a large tympanic membrane in the gap between the first and second bronchial semi-rings.

Their jaw musculature and the nerves that are connected to it show striking convergence with owls, as do aspects of behavior and breeding biology, such as using the bill as well as the feet to dispatch prey, holding prey in one foot while eating, building no nest structure, the young hissing in threat, bobbing the head when nervous, and letting fall rather than squirting out their droppings. Falconids also appear to differ from other raptors in laying relatively large eggs, and in regularly eating small stones, termed wrangle, to assist in digestion and nutrition.

▼ Small to medium-sized and perhaps the most distinctive and discrete group of raptors, about 60 species of Falconidae occur throughout the world. They differ anatomically and behaviorally from the accipitrids and include the forest falcons, falconets and true falcons. Two Striated Caracaras (*Phalcoboenus australis*), perched on a Falkland Island clifftop, are among the least typical of the falconids—they build their own nest and scavenge like vultures.

Rod Allin/Tom Stack & Associates

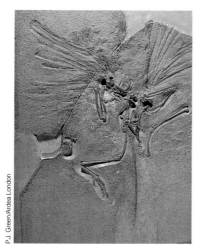

P.J. Green/Ardea London

▲ The discovery of the first skeleton of Archaeopteryx (shown), the earliest-known fossil bird, in 1861, lent considerable support to the theory of evolution. It provided a link between birds and reptiles. Feathers clearly show it to be a bird, and most scientists believe that it was weakly flighted. Yet it has teeth, and they are of the type found in crocodilians. Archaeopteryx was a small predator, probably catching insects and lizards, but not an ancestor to the raptors. Nor is it likely that it was a direct precursor to modern birds; rather, on a side branch of avian evolution. Fossilized raptors are quite abundant, and their study shows that they evolved early in fossil history, from an ancient group of birds that may have been contemporaries of Archaeopteryx.

FOSSIL EVIDENCE

Fossils of raptors, which might shed some light on the origins and relationships of the different groups, are widespread and quite abundant. Their interpretation suffers from a problem which still plagues an understanding of relationships in the whole group, namely that detailed skeletal and other studies of living species are still awaited. Fossil remains, representing all five major groups of diurnal raptors, are first known from the early Tertiary, 30–50 million years ago ("mya"), indicating that raptors must stem from an ancient group of birds. Such remains become more frequent nearer to the present.

The cathartid vultures were first known from fossil beds in France that were laid down in the late Eocene or early Oligocene (35–40 mya). Surprisingly, the presence of cathartids in the New World, to which they are now confined, was first evident in California and Kansas only during the Pliocene, 2–5 mya. Such fossil evidence offers a special caution to those trying to understand the geographical origins of living birds. Some of the extinct condors were most stork-like in their appearance, with long legs and barely hooked bills. Their extinct stork-like relatives, the teratorns (Teratornithidae), were huge soaring birds, of which at least four species are recognized. The earliest known species, discovered from late Miocene deposits in Argentina from 10 mya, was the largest of all, and probably had a wing span of over 7 meters (23 feet) and a mass of about 120 kilograms (264 pounds). All species were as large as, or larger than, any condors living today. They appear to have originated in South America and led the lives of active and awesome predators, rather than passive scavengers. The last of the teratorns survived right up until the Pleistocene Ice Ages only 1.8 mya.

The earliest accipitrids first appear in late Eocene or early Oligocene deposits in France, from about 35 mya, and are thought to be buzzard-like, although not much like modern buzzards. Remains of vultures very like modern species of the Old World, especially the Egyptian Vulture, are known from deposits in North America, warning once again against the risk of assuming geographical origins for a group based on their present distribution.

Fossil relatives of the Osprey are known from the Oligocene of Egypt and the middle Miocene of California, suggesting a wide distribution for the group from early in its evolution. A rather different lineage appeared in Florida in the late Miocene. Remains of two species related to Secretarybirds, one as big as the modern form but both with relatively shorter legs, are known from France, although the family is now confined to Africa. They are dated back to the Upper Oligocene, 25–30 mya, and to the Miocene, and were contemporaneous with cathartid vultures in the Old World.

Early falconids, most similar to caracaras, are known from the early Miocene in the Americas, only about 20 mya, but support the suggestion that this particular group may have radiated most widely in the New World.

SPECIAL ATTRIBUTES

Having surveyed the more obvious features by which raptors may be recognized, and the basic diversity shown by these birds, we can now examine in more detail some of the special attributes of diurnal birds of prey.

► A recent fossil species by archaeological standards, Haast's Eagle (Harpagornis moorei) inhabited the then forest-clad islands of New Zealand from at least 30,000 years ago until less than 1000 years ago. It probably preyed on large, flightless geese and moas until the Polynesians colonized the islands, destroyed habitat by turning forest and shrub to grassland, and hunted the birds to extinction. Thought to be larger than any living eagle, it had robust legs, and talons the size of tiger claws. Its fossilized skull (bottom) is similar to the smaller skull of a contemporary Wedge-tailed Eagle.

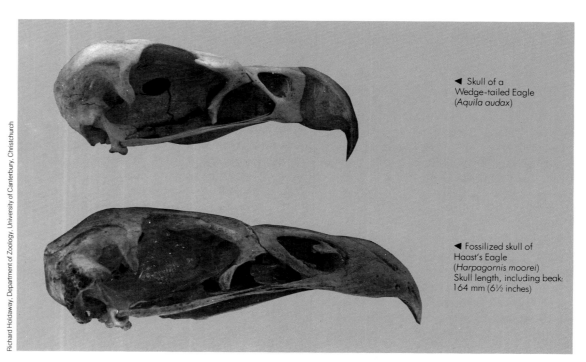

Richard Holdaway, Department of Zoology, University of Canterbury, Christchurch

◄ Skull of a Wedge-tailed Eagle (Aquila audax)

◄ Fossilized skull of Haast's Eagle (Harpagornis moorei) Skull length, including beak: 164 mm (6½ inches)

EYES

Their remarkable vision is the result of one of the most advanced designs developed by the vertebrate eye. The eyes of most birds are large relative to their skull, but in raptors this reaches its extreme, especially in owls, and the eyes of larger raptors are as big as those of humans. This provides as large an area as possible for capture of light through the cornea, enhanced by its sharp curvature, and also sets the lens as far as possible from the sensitive retinal area, thus providing long focal length and some telescopic vision. The retinal surface is more tightly packed with sensory cells than in any other vertebrate, and especially with color-sensitive cones in the two retinal fovea or pits. Together with the long focal length, this makes for maximum resolution of the image cast on the retinal surface by the lens. Furthermore, the nerve connections behind the sensory cells are well developed and permit complex neural processing of the image. Raptors have up to 50° of binocular vision with their forward-facing eyes, and this allows them good judgment of depth and distance, as well as enhancement of their vision through integration of overlapping images in the brain. The low density of light-sensitive but color-insensitive rods in the retina means that diurnal raptors have limited night vision. Apart from slow dark adaptation, they can probably see as well as humans at night. The net result is that birds of prey have excellent all-round vision, and some large eagles achieve a visual acuity twice that of humans.

The bony structures around the eyes provide secure anchorage for muscles operating the pupil apertures, lens curvature and fine eye movements, and all contribute to fast tracking, accurate focusing and wide accommodation to different light intensities. The large eyes of raptors include

Frithfoto/Australasian Nature Transparencies

Wendy Shattil & Robert Rozinski/Tom Stack & Associates

▲ The orange eye of the Black-mantled Goshawk (*Accipiter melanochlamys*) is a sign of maturity in this species.

◄ The gentler, brown eye of the Rough-legged Hawk (*Buteo lagopus*) is probably functionally similar. Both have color vision and relatively forward-facing eyes which allow good judgment of depth and distance.

▼ With excellent visual acuity, a Wedge-tailed Eagle can detect a rabbit 1.6 km (1 mile) distant. In the same situation, a human would have to approach to within 500 meters (546 yards) before being barely able to distinguish the rabbit.

What the raptor sees

The equivalent human view

▲ As well as an upper and a lower eyelid, which close to meet mid-eye, raptors have a third eyelid. Tough and opaque, the nictitating membrane of this Bald Eagle helps to clean and moisten the cornea and is often closed on impact with prey to protect the eye.

▶ Hooked bill contrasting with colourful cere and facial skin, a Crested Caracara (*Polyborus plancus*) claims a carcass.

▼ The deep, sturdy, strongly hooked beak of this Bonelli's Eagle (*Hieraaetus fasciatus*) enables it to dissect its prey.

the largest pectens of any birds; the pleated protrusion from the retina is filled with blood vessels and provides the eye fluids with nutrients and possibly assists in detection of movement. The surrounds of the eyes also contribute to the fierce appearance of many species of raptor, through the bony eyebrows that project above the eyes. This may assist in protecting this vital and sensitive organ from damage when subduing prey. The transparent nictitating membrane, or third eyelid, is also well developed and is drawn over the eye during such encounters.

HOOKED BILL

The hooked bill is the other obvious feature of the head and shows a variety of forms suited to the exact role it plays in the feeding of each species. The most common form is a well-curved hook on the tip of the upper mandible, which drives into flesh like a knife point. The cutting edges along the side then shear off the flesh forced against them by the lower jaw. The lower jaw, often notched at the tip to aid in cutting, provides the force for rending the food, assisted by twisting the head and pulling with the neck and back while the prey is anchored between the feet. In falcons and a few other species the cutting edges of the bill are themselves notched, as an aid in cutting and to help with dislocating the neck vertebrae of prey. A few species have the curved point of the upper bill greatly extended, as with snail kites, and this serves as a probe to sever the shell-closing muscles of mollusks and extract them from their shells.

In some species the bill probably serves a secondary role in display, being brightly colored or extraordinarily large as in some big eagles. It may also serve a role in flight, working together with the head as an anterior aerofoil. The bill is accentuated by the naked fleshy cere which covers the base of the upper mandible, and in which the nostrils are situated. This naked area often extends onto the face and rims the mouth and is usually brightly colored, most often yellow. The lining of the gape is a conspicuous feature, as most raptors have a wide mouth to ingest large pieces of prey, especially large in such species as the Bat Hawk (*Machaerhampus alcinus*) which swallows bats whole while in flight.

LEGS AND FEET

The legs and feet of raptors show wide variation in design. They are exceptionally powerful, and studies have shown that the blow delivered by the feet during a strike is at least as important as the grip of the feet or piercing of the talons in incapacitating prey. The lower leg or tarsus is, in most species, a channel for tendons from muscles in the upper leg that operate the toes and claws. In a few of the larger eagles these muscles extend into the lower leg, adding to the awesome power that

Jeff Foott/Bruce Coleman Ltd

◀ Spicules on the bottom of a Bald Eagle's toes help it to grasp slippery fish. As anyone who has handled a raptor will testify, a raptor's feet are its most powerful weapon. They are used to capture prey and to kill by squeezing or through sheer force of impact.

▼ The size, thickness and curvature of a raptor's talons and the length and thickness of its legs and toes are matched to its hunting habits. The scrounging vulture has chicken-like, walking feet and no need of a strong grip. At the other extreme, the powerful, grasping feet of the Harpy Eagle (*Harpia harpyja*), with dagger-like rear talon and extraordinary grip, can subdue large prey not already killed by the impact of the eagle's strike. Long, sinewy toes allow sparrowhawks to snare small birds in the air, while the spiny feet of the Osprey, and reversible outer toe, help it grasp slippery, writhing fish and eels.

can be supplied to the foot for crushing prey. In most species the tarsus is covered in scales, varying in form from small nodules to large sheets of keratinous tissue arranged in specific patterns, but in true eagles and two buzzards the tarsus is feathered over its whole length. Species dealing with robust prey tend to have short and stout tarsi; those capturing fast aerial prey have long thin tarsi to enhance their reach; and at the extreme the Secretarybird has long stork-like legs with stubby toes which it uses to disable its prey with effective well-aimed kicks.

The structure of the foot shows most variation in the length and stoutness of the toes, details of the pads under the toes, and length, curvature and cross-sectional form of the talons. The inner and hind toes are invariably the most powerful and armed with the longest talons, which work in opposition to apply the main grip to prey. Scavenging species, such as vultures, have long slender toes with relatively slight gripping ability, no special development of the toe pads, and claws that are stubby and almost straight. Predators of robust prey, such as mammals, have thick toes and well-curved talons, the latter probably serving as much to provide anchorage for the powerful squeeze of the toes as to serve as daggers for incapacitating the prey. Sparrowhawks and falcons that catch dextrous aerial prey, such as flying birds, have long slender toes, especially the center one, needle-sharp and well-curved claws and toe pads with protrusions that match the claw tips, offering maximum reach and grasping ability. Species that

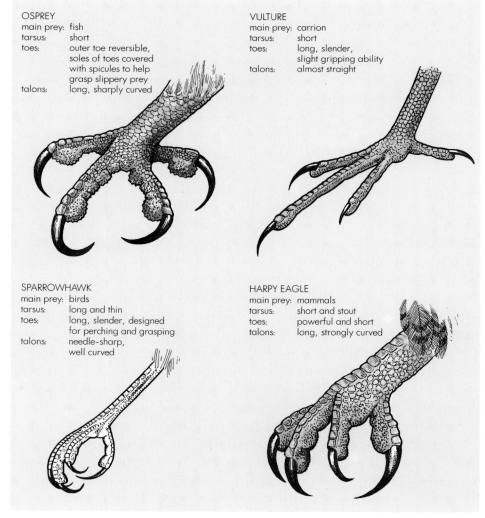

OSPREY
main prey: fish
tarsus: short
toes: outer toe reversible, soles of toes covered with spicules to help grasp slippery prey
talons: long, sharply curved

VULTURE
main prey: carrion
tarsus: short
toes: long, slender, slight gripping ability
talons: almost straight

SPARROWHAWK
main prey: birds
tarsus: long and thin
toes: long, slender, designed for perching and grasping
talons: needle-sharp, well curved

HARPY EAGLE
main prey: mammals
tarsus: short and stout
toes: powerful and short
talons: long, strongly curved

catch fish, regardless of their relationships, have the longest and most recurved talons which, together with the spiny scales of the toe pads, serve as perfect organs for securing their slippery prey.

WINGS

Most raptors require good powers of flight to cover the relatively large home ranges that they occupy, and to allow them to pursue their prey. Larger and heavier species have long broad wings which enable them to make use of rising air currents, either winds rising off slopes or hot air in thermals, to soar relatively effortlessly for long periods. Raptors of densely wooded habitats, such as hawk-eagles and goshawks, have broad wings and long tails, and this provides them with the good lift and dexterity needed to wend their way at speed through vegetation. Raptors of open air

Hans & Judy Beste/Auscape

▶ An Australian Kestrel (*Falco cenchroides*), landing at its nest, displays the long, pointed wings of the larger true falcons, so admired for their powers of flight. Kestrels have been clocked cruising at a respectable 32 km/h (20 mph) in calm conditions and are also light enough to hover with great skill.

▶ The effortless soaring flight of some of the larger raptors is much esteemed; it allows them to traverse immense distances with ease. A Bearded Vulture (*Gypaetus barbatus*), at home in its mountain wilderness, is incapable of sustained flapping flight, but its long, fingered wings carry it to great height on rising air currents.

Eric Dragesco/Ardea London

spaces, such as kestrels and falcons, have the long narrow wings and muscular bodies necessary for high-speed aerial maneuvers or, used in combination with a long tail, for hovering motionless above the ground.

HEARING

The extent to which raptors use other senses and attributes in locating and capturing prey is less well documented. All species are sensitive to sound and are able to detect its direction, by both angle and elevation, and this is especially well developed in owls. Good hearing serves to locate prey, mates, neighbors and enemies, but the ears of most diurnal raptors are not obviously specialized. The forest falcons, and even more so the harriers, are exceptions, with a ruff of feathers behind the ears and enlarged ear openings to enhance detection of both intensity and direction of sound—these developments again being taken to their extreme in owls.

SENSE OF SMELL

All birds have a sense of smell but in only a few species is the dorsal chamber of the olfactory bulb elaborated by folding into an extensive surface for detecting chemicals in the air. This chamber is well developed in some cathartid vultures, which can locate food by smell. For most raptors, however, the role of smell is unstudied and they are likely to rely more on sight and sound to locate their prey.

PLUMAGE

The plumage of most raptors is not particularly colorful, being white when unpigmented or colored with various forms of melanin granules to produce black, and shades of gray, brown, rufous and chestnut. The lack of variety in pigments does not mean that raptors are unattractive, and many have striking plumages, jet black or snow white at the extremes, with a variety of lovely shades in between, and of handsome patterns, either in bold areas of pure color or in fine detail of intricate streaking, barring or banding. Some of the more recurrent patterns among raptors include pale patches on the rump, pale bars of different widths across the breast, abdomen, wings or tail, and a pair of pale nuchal spots at the back of the head. Little is known of the function of these colors and patterns, and they are usually different in adult and immature plumages of the same species, and sometimes in the sexes of adults. In many species the females are slightly duller and browner (that is, more camouflaged) than the males, and the juveniles have the undersides streaked, only to become barred when adult with broader wing and tail bars.

In a few species the plumage is elaborated into special structures. The most common of these are long and distinctively colored flank feathers which

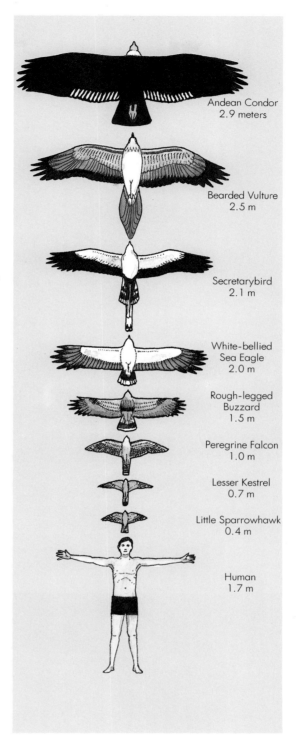

Andean Condor
2.9 meters

Bearded Vulture
2.5 m

Secretarybird
2.1 m

White-bellied
Sea Eagle
2.0 m

Rough-legged
Buzzard
1.5 m

Peregrine Falcon
1.0 m

Lesser Kestrel
0.7 m

Little Sparrowhawk
0.4 m

Human
1.7 m

◄ Most raptors depend on their powers of flight to find and catch prey, for various aspects of breeding and, for some, to migrate. Some of the largest and some of the smallest of flying birds can be found among the raptors. Their wing and tail shape and proportions reflect their lifestyle. Raptors with large, broad wings soar with ease; those with long, pointed wings fly at speed through open country; and those with short rounded wings make short, buoyant flights through forest.

M. P. Kahl/Bruce Coleman Ltd

◄ Rich, subtle hues of brown and gray, jet black or crisp white—while not colorful, the plumage of raptors is often strikingly attractive. The graceful Swallow-tailed Kite (*Elanoides forficatus*), with distinctive deeply forked tail, combines hard black flight feathers with soft white body feathers.

can be revealed or concealed like semaphore flags. Other structures include voluminous undertail coverts, elongated tail feathers and prominent head feathers that can be erected as crests of different shapes. Several species show regular color morphs—that is, distinct plumage shades that are retained throughout the life of the individual. The most extreme of these are all-black melanistic morphs or albinistic all-white morphs, but most morphs are essentially darker or lighter versions of the most common plumage color. Several species also show regular individual variation in plumage color and pattern.

All these variations in plumage are presumed to fulfill two main functions—making the raptor less obvious to its prey and enhancing communication between individuals of the same and of different species. Other factors may influence plumage colors, and within the raptor fauna of every continent there are species which resemble one another so closely that mimicry may be involved. Thus the predatory Zone-tailed Hawk (*Buteo albonatatus*) may mimic the scavenging Turkey Vulture (*Cathartes aura*) in order to lull the prey into complacency. In other cases, such as the juvenile African Cuckoo Hawk (*Aviceda cuculoides*) resembling the young African Goshawk (*Accipiter tachiro*), the advantages to either are unclear. This is even more so when the hawks resemble other non-raptorial birds, such as parrots and cuckoos.

Other environmental or nutritional factors may also be involved in the predominance of certain color combinations in different areas, such as pied hawks and eagles in Africa and slate and orange falcons in South America.

▲ A resemblance to an early lawyer's clerk carrying a bunch of quill pens behind his ears gives the Secretary Bird (*Sagittarius serpentarius*) its name. Twenty plumes cascade down the back of its head until the bird raises them in emotion. An orange-pink face passively communicates the information that this is an adult—immatures are yellow.

▶ A lack of plumage, except for a few black bristles, may help keep this Lappet-faced Vulture (*Aegypius tracheliotos*) cool as well as reduce fouling during feeding inside a carcass. The bright folds (lappets) signal maturity—young birds have gray heads.

S. C. Bisserot

COLOR OF SOFT PARTS

What raptors lack in color of plumage they make up for with the bare skin of their face, crop, legs, feet or glaring pupils. Colors of these areas range from bright red, orange, chrome, green or cerulean through to delicate shades of rose, buttercup, lime and sky-blue. In a few species, such as the Gymnogene, these colors can be temporarily intensified by suffusions of blood below the skin, allowing them to blush or pale instantly and at will. The colors of the soft parts, as with the plumage, often change with age, and in a few species they develop distinctively for each sex. Vulturine species, with their bare heads and necks, have particularly brightly colored areas of bare skin, elaborated in some species into loose lappets on the neck or special protrusions on the cere or head. These bright colors, in combination with the plumage, serve as important signal areas, highlighting the age, sex, status and individual identity of a raptor and being shown to best advantage in the various movements and positions presented during display.

Leonard Lee Rue III/Bruce Coleman Ltd

▲ Variations in the bizarre corrugated face of vivid colors, set on a neck trimmed with a furry ruff, signal age, status, health and individual identity to other King Vultures (*Sarcoramphus papa*). The bare-skinned crop, bulging with recently eaten food, may also play a role in display.

◄ Slight variations in the much more understated tones of a Tawny Eagle (*Aquila rapax*) also distinguish individuals and ages.

M. P. Kahl/Auscape

Leonard Lee Rue III/Tom Stack & Associates

► Vision and visual signals figure prominently in raptor communication and, in general, raptors tend not to be noticeably vocal except around the breeding season. Nevertheless, they use a variety of basic sounds to communicate and augment visual signals. Whistling Kites (*Haliastur sphenurus*) throw back their heads and give a loud, clear aggressive whistle; a long, descending "seeo" followed by "si si si si si" ascending upwards through the scale.

► Less melodic, the Bald Eagle's harsh "kark kark kark" carries well across its watery habitat.

► Now in the last half of their time in the nest, these Golden Eagles (*Aquila chrysaetos*) can be left while the female hunts. By the time they leave the nest they will be almost full sized. With few exceptions, most raptors conform to a standard pattern of breeding—in solitary pairs within a defended territory. The male tends to do most of the hunting while the female incubates, broods and feeds the chicks. Parental care often extends well past fledgling, until the young disperse.

CALLS

The visual signals are augmented by auditory ones, both vocal and mechanical. The cathartid vultures, lacking special development of the syrinx, can only make simple hissing and croaking sounds, but most raptors have a wide range of vocalizations and many are noisy, at least near the onset of breeding. In no raptor is the syrinx particularly specialized, and their calls are mainly screams, whistles, croaks, mews, barks, yelps, cackles and other basic sounds. Calls begin with the soft sounds made by young chicks, even from within the egg, but later young of many species become extremely vociferous in their cries for food. The parents do not usually make much vocal response to such demands, but they are often noisy in defense of their young, making loud cries as they attack intruders or rushing past and clapping their wings in threat. The start of the next breeding cycle is usually marked by the pair soaring high above their territory, often calling loudly to one another as they circle and continuing their conversation more quietly when they descend to busy themselves in the vicinity of the nest. Occasionally, the vocalizations may be given in conjunction with conspicuous visual displays, many of which have aggressive components. The most common include circling high over the breeding area and complex rituals while perching and calling near the nest. The flight displays are most obvious and have been best described, including such elaborations as sky-dancing in harriers, pothooks, pendulums and cartwheels in many eagles, flutter-stalls in honey buzzards and slow-flapping or undulating in sparrowhawks. Displays around the nest are less well studied, but a regular and spectacular component in most species is the passing of food by the male to his mate, most often at a perch but sometimes in spectacular fashion in mid-air.

SIZE

Raptors range in size from cathartid condors, accipitrid vultures and some eagles with wingspans of 3 meters (10 feet) and weights of 8–12 kilograms (18–26 pounds), through the larger falcons and caracaras at 4 kilograms (9 pounds), down to the tiny kites and sparrowhawks and ending with the 45 gram (1.6 ounce) falconets. Size, per se, has a wide range of effects on the biology of raptors, as it does on all animals. Small species have higher food requirements per unit weight than large species. They lay proportionately, but not absolutely, larger eggs than large species, with more eggs in a clutch but with a shorter laying interval between each egg. Incubation takes less time for small eggs than large ones. Chicks take a shorter time to grow to fledging size in small species, remain dependent on their parents for less time and reach maturity quicker. These and many other effects of size are not absolute determinants of the biology of each species, but body size is the major influence across a group with such a wide range of body sizes. It is the deviations from these basic patterns that highlight the special adaptations within a species.

The female is larger than the male in the majority of raptor species, across the whole spectrum of body sizes, but the size difference is not consistent with absolute body size or with relatedness. This difference in size between the sexes is known as sexual size dimorphism, and in most raptors, including owls, it is the reverse of most other birds where the male is the larger sex. Scavenging species, including both cathartid and accipitrid vultures, show little or no sexual dimorphism, and both sexes share fully the roles of incubation and of feeding themselves and the young. At the other extreme, as in some sparrow-hawks and falcons, the female is twice as heavy as the male and, while she undertakes the incubation and care of the young, the male does all the hunting for himself, his mate and his offspring. The difference in size between the sexes correlates best with the agility of the prey favored by each species, being most extreme for those species that catch agile aerial prey such as small birds. Why this should be so, why the female and not the male is largest, and what effect this has on other aspects of the biology of the sexes is one of the most debated issues in raptor biology and is considered later in further detail.

BREEDING PATTERNS

Raptors show marked uniformity in breeding biology, despite the wide variation in sexual dimorphism and dietary habits. Most species breed as pairs within a defended territory, although their hunting activities may extend out of this area into common hunting grounds. As predators, they can be expected to be more sparsely distributed than prey animals of equivalent size, and areas over which pairs hunt may range from less than 1 square kilometer (0.4 square mile) for pigmy falcons to more than 300 square kilometers (116 square miles) for Martial Eagles (*Hieraaetus bellicosus*).

Both sexes take part in the selection and preparation of the nest, but the male is more active in display and carries single items of food to its mate, initially in courtship feeding but continuing through incubation and the early nestling period. The female stays at the nest area, laying and incubating the eggs, brooding and feeding the chicks and initiating defense of the nest. To feed the chicks, she tears off small morsels of flesh and passes them, one at a time, to the young. The extent to which the female leaves the nest to hunt for herself, and to which the male shares her role in caring for the eggs and chicks, varies according to the species and to the food available to the pair. As the breeding cycle progresses, the female takes an increasing role in feeding herself and helping to provision the chicks.

The annual molt usually commences during or immediately after breeding, except for those species which undertake long post-breeding migrations, in which case molt may be suspended or interrupted until after arrival on the non-breeding grounds. Completion of molt, often several months later, marks the end of the annual cycle in most species.

Exceptions to this basic pattern of breeding occur in scavenging vultures, honey buzzards and the Secretarybird where the sexes share incubation more or less equally, taking turns off the nest to feed themselves, and bringing back food to the chicks, which they carry in their crops.

A few species of small falcon nest colonially, usually in response to a concentrated food source, but even here they breed as pairs and maintain a territory around the nest, albeit of only a few square meters. A few species breed polygynously, where one male has more than one female, or polyandrously, where each female has more than one male, but these unusual social systems are discussed in later chapters.

W. Perry Conway/Tom Stack & Associates

KINDS OF RAPTORS

ALAN KEMP

Living raptors are traditionally all included in the single avian order Falconiformes. This order consists of four major divisions or families. One of these, including the seven species of vultures in the Cathartidae, seems least closely related to the others and may belong in a separate order with the storks. The Secretarybird constitutes a single species within its own family the Sagittariidae. The two families with the most species, the 224 species of Accipitridae and 60 species of Falconidae, contain some clear subgroups of species. However, since the exact limits of these subgroups are not agreed upon, and since the placement of several little-known species is equivocal, formal subfamilial groupings are not presented here.

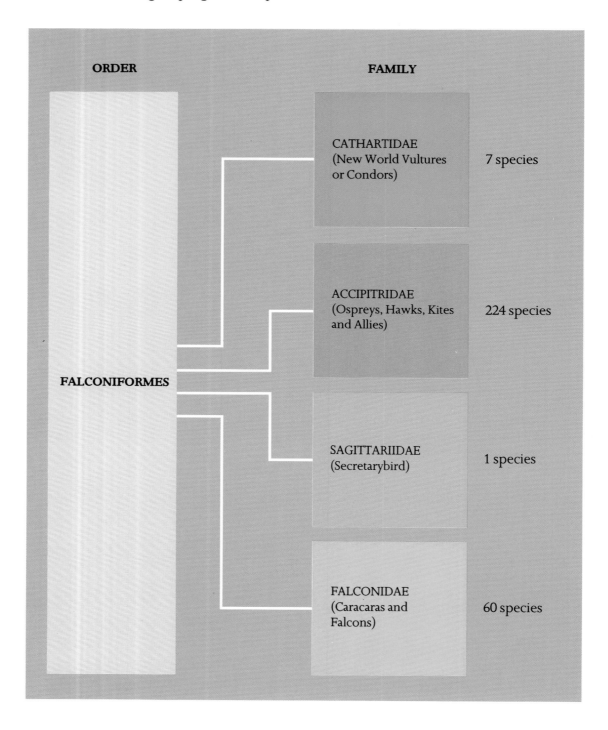

ORDER

FAMILY

FALCONIFORMES

CATHARTIDAE
(New World Vultures or Condors)

7 species

ACCIPITRIDAE
(Ospreys, Hawks, Kites and Allies)

224 species

SAGITTARIIDAE
(Secretarybird)

1 species

FALCONIDAE
(Caracaras and Falcons)

60 species

FAMILY CATHARTIDAE

Seven species

Andean Condor
Vultur gryphus

APPEARANCE A very large raptor, predominantly black with a ruff of white downy feathers at the base of the neck and with the white upper wing coverts and upper surface of the secondary flight feathers appearing as light patches on the wing. The naked head and neck are deep reddish-purple; in adult males the skin is extended into folds and there is a comb-like wattle on top of the head and bill. The bill and eyes are yellow, and the legs black but often washed with white droppings. Immatures are brown all over with dark brown eyes and a horn-colored bill. Silent but for low hisses and croaks at close quarters.
SIZE Length about 105 centimeters (42 inches), probably the largest raptor in terms of wingspan and overall body dimensions. The female is noticeably smaller than the male.

HABITAT AND DISTRIBUTION Andean mountains to the highest elevations and adjacent deserts and plains, from Venezuela south to Tierra del Fuego, in all non-forested habitats.
REPRODUCTION The male displays to the female with wings spread and neck arched and inflated, showing off the comb and the white shoulders to good effect. A single egg is laid on a ledge or in a cave and the parents share the 54-58 days of incubation and up to a year of caring for the chick until it becomes independent.
DIET Carrion, usually of larger mammals such as guanacos, located while soaring effortlessly on the huge wings. Numbers may also congregate at seabird colonies, where eggs and young nestlings are consumed.

FAMILY ACCIPITRIDAE

Two hundred and twenty-four species

Osprey
Pandion haliaetus

APPEARANCE A medium-sized raptor, predominantly white below with long gull-like wings and rather short barred tail. Above dark brown, except for the white crown of the head. The dark stripe across the sides of the face, crossing the yellow eye, is distinctive. There is brown streaking on the upper breast, especially in immatures which also have brown eyes. The bill is black, and the cere and large, strong feet are blue-gray. Utters a variety of high yelping calls.
SIZE Length about 56 centimeters (22 inches), the female about 13 per cent heavier than the male.
HABITAT AND DISTRIBUTION Rivers, lakes and coasts that provide ice-free and relatively calm waters, almost cosmopolitan but mainly only as a migrant to the southern hemisphere except for Australasia where it breeds.
REPRODUCTION Nest area advertised and defended by undulating sky-dancing and calling flight display, especially by the male. Both sexes build the large stick-nest, placed on trees, rock pinnacles, man-made structures or (on islands) even the ground depending on available sites. The female takes the main role in incubating the beautiful cream and brown clutch of two or three eggs for 34-40 days, fed by the male on fish carried to the nest. The female also does most of the brooding of the chicks which fledge at 49-57 days.
DIET Fish, caught after a plunge into the water from the air, including a wide range of species, mostly of 100-250 grams (3-9 ounces) but up to 3 kilograms (6.6 pounds) in weight.

Crested Baza
Aviceda subcristata

APPEARANCE A medium-sized hawk with a pointed crest at the back of the head, light gray above and on the upper breast, with a wash of cinnamon over the back and broad brown bars on the white underparts. The underwing and undertail coverts are pale cinnamon, contrasting with the white undersides and broad black and white bars of the long broad wings and long tail. The eyes are yellow, the cere and bill black, the latter with two tooth-like notches at the sides, and the feet are light blue-gray. Juveniles are browner above with brown streaks on the upper breast, finer bars on the underparts, a yellow cere and dark brown eyes. There is inter-island variation in details of plumage coloration and markings. Call is a two-syllable whistle.

SIZE Length about 40 centimeters (16 inches), with no noticeable difference in size between the sexes.

HABITAT AND DISTRIBUTION Favors woodland and forest edge, from eastern and northern Australia through New Guinea to the Solomon, Mollucca and Lesser Sunda Islands.

REPRODUCTION Breeds in early summer after tumbling courtship flight displays. Lays usually two or three white eggs in a shallow stick-nest placed on a horizontal fork of a tree. Incubation proceeds for 33 days and the nestlings develop for a further 32-35 days. Both sexes take part in nest building, incubation and feeding young but the male takes the major role in capturing prey and bringing it to the female and nestlings.

DIET Insects and small vertebrates, especially tree frogs and stick insects; occasionally figs and other plant matter.

Hook-billed Kite
Chondrohierax uncinatus

APPEARANCE A small raptor with stubby wings and a long tail, highly variable in plumage colors, markings and in the size of the heavy and very hooked bill. Adult males are most often gray above with fine white bars on the gray underparts. Adult females are usually dark brown above with a gray head, the underparts rufous with fine white bars and the rufous extending around the back of the neck as a collar. All adults have white eyes set in greenish-yellow facial skin and the feet are deep yellow. Immatures have brown eyes and most are sooty-brown above with pale brown feather tips and white below that extends into a collar round the neck. An uncommon melanistic form occurs, black all over but for a broad white bar across the tail and white tips to the tail and upper tail coverts.

SIZE Length about 40 centimeters (16 inches), with no obvious difference in size between the sexes.

HABITAT AND DISTRIBUTION Inhabits dense undergrowth in forest and woodland of tropical South America, from Mexico south to northern Argentina and Paraguay and including certain islands in the West Indies.

REPRODUCTION Pairs soar, call and dive at one another in the nest area. Both sexes build a small stick-nest in the outer branches of a tree, breaking off twigs with their bills to carry up to one kilometer (0.6 mile) to the nest. Two eggs are laid, well marked with brown and cream, but further details of the nesting cycle are lacking.

DIET Feeds primarily on arboreal and terrestrial snails, sometimes hanging upside down by its feet while foraging, and congregating in flocks of up to 25 birds. The shells, showing characteristic damage, accumulate under favorite perches. Also eats amphibia and insects when necessary.

Black-shouldered Kite
Elanus caeruleus

APPEARANCE This small raptor is white except for the delicate dove-gray upperparts, crown and flight feathers and for the prominent black patches on the upperwing coverts and wrists. The cere and legs are yellow, the bill black and the eyes a brilliant ruby red, accentuated by a narrow rim of black feathers. The sexes are similar but males have slightly deeper gray wing coverts. Immature birds are quite different, having the head and upper breast washed with russet, the feathers of the upperparts tipped with russet and eyes brown. Call with a harsh screech or soft chipping notes and may display from a perch with exaggerated wagging of the tail.
SIZE Length about 35 centimeters (14 inches), the sexes similar in size.
HABITAT AND DISTRIBUTION Semi-open country, from Spain to Southern China, Indonesia and Papua New Guinea.
REPRODUCTION Female solicits courtship feeding with high screams and male makes fluttering displays to possible nest sites. The nest is a flimsy platform of sticks and weeds, on which two to six well-marked cream and brown eggs are laid. The female undertakes most of the 30-32 days of incubation and the early care of the young, fed at the nest by the male. Both parents hunt for larger chicks but before they fledge at 30-38 days of age the female may leave the family to start another attempt with a new mate. In this way the species is capable of very high productivity when food is abundant. It also forms communal roosts and may nest at high densities.
DIET Largely rodents, taken either from a perch or after bouts of hovering, but also some small birds, lizards and a few insects.

Snail Kite
Rostrhamus sociabilis

APPEARANCE The sexes of this medium-sized raptor are quite different in color. The male is black with a gray cast over the upperparts, only the basal half of the tail, the tail coverts and the tail tip being white. The female is sooty-brown above and dusky below, the underparts are mottled and the flight feathers barred with light brown. The tail has the same white areas as the male and the forehead and throat are also white. In both sexes the eyes are red, and the cere, bare facial skin and legs are bright orange. The immature resembles the adult female but has a buff eye stripe, the underparts are buff streaked with dark brown, and the bare areas of the face and legs are yellow.
SIZE Length about 38 centimeters (15 inches), the sexes indistinguishable in size.
HABITAT AND DISTRIBUTION Restricted to marshland throughout its wide range, from Florida and eastern Mexico south to the pampas of Argentina and Uruguay, and extending to the islands of Cuba and Isle of Pines.
REPRODUCTION Pairs soar and plunge with folded wings over the breeding area and nests are often placed close together in loose colonies of as many as 100 nests. The nest is an untidy platform of grass and weeds, usually low over water in marsh grass or bushes. Both sexes build the nest and take part in incubation of the two to four eggs and care of young during the 30-day nestling period.
DIET Largely freshwater snails of the genus Pomacea, caught with the feet and extracted while perched by using the elongated and thin upper mandible to prise off the operculum that shields the body of the snail.

Swallow-tailed Kite
Elanoides forficatus

APPEARANCE Unmistakable medium-sized raptor with snowy white head and underparts, including underwing coverts, and glossy black upperparts and flight feathers. The wings are long and slender and the tail elongated and forked, both contributing to its graceful and dextrous flight. The eyes are dark reddish-brown, and the cere and legs are blue-gray. Utters high whistling and twittering calls.
SIZE Length about 60 centimeters (24 inches), including long outer tail feathers. The sexes are similar in size.
HABITAT AND DISTRIBUTION Prefers forest but ranges widely over adjoining grasslands and savanna, extending from the southeastern United States of America down to southern Argentina. All populations migrant or nomadic, often in company with Plumbeous Kites.
REPRODUCTION A social species, even when breeding, with dramatic aerial maneuvers a prelude to nesting and several nests placed in close proximity to one another. Both sexes build the flimsy stick-nest high in a tree, breaking off sticks with their feet in flight. The female does most of the 28 days of incubation of the two to four eggs, fed on items delivered by the male. She will also forage for herself and later in the 40-day nestling period helps the male to feed the chicks.
DIET Mainly large insects and tree frogs but also eggs, nestlings, reptiles, wasp grubs and fruit, all taken in the air or from foliage with the feet while in flight. Also drinks in flight, by dipping low over the water like a swallow.

Pearl Kite
Gampsonyx swainsonii

APPEARANCE This very small raptor is handsomely marked, predominantly white below and black above but offset with russet forehead, cheeks and thighs, white edging to the flight feathers, a white collar with a chocolate posterior and black feathers forming a yoke on the upper breast. The eyes are deep red, the bill and cere black and the feet chrome. The sexes are alike. Immatures commonly have more russet on the flanks, brown edges to the dorsal feathers and brown eyes.
SIZE Length only 22 centimeters (9 inches), no obvious difference between the sexes.
HABITAT AND DISTRIBUTION Occupies savanna and open woodland in central South America from Colombia south to Paraguay and northern Argentina and west to Peru and Bolivia.
REPRODUCTION A small stick-nest is built in the outer fork of a tree and as many as three eggs are laid, but further details of the breeding cycle are undescribed.
DIET Small vertebrates and insects are recorded, and the strong legs and feet suggest strongly rapacious habits.

White-bellied Sea Eagle
Haliaeetus leucogaster

APPEARANCE A very large and striking raptor, the upperparts blue-gray and the underparts, together with the head and neck, pure white. The flight feathers rim the broad wings in black and there is a broad white band at the tip of the short tail. Immatures are quite different, brown except for a white area at the base of the primaries and the white base to the tail, both marks best seen when in flight. Braying cries and yelps are uttered in flight or from a perch with the bill open and head thrown back.

SIZE Length about 80 centimeters (32 inches) and wingspan about 2 meters (6.5 feet), the female slightly larger than the male.

HABITAT AND DISTRIBUTION Mainly along coasts and estuaries but extending far up larger rivers and occupying lakes well away from the sea. Extends around the periphery of India and Sri Lanka, through southeast Asia and Indonesia to New Guinea, the Bismarck Archipelago and all round Australia.

REPRODUCTION Pairs call, soar and cartwheel together prior to breeding at one of their traditional nest sites. The nest is a huge structure of sticks placed on a cliff or in a tree, even on the ground on offshore islands. Two dull white eggs are laid but often only one chick is raised. The female does the bulk of incubation and brooding of the young chicks, the male bringing food to the nest, joined by his mate later in the cycle. The chicks spend at least 70 days in the nest but disperse within a few weeks of flying.

DIET Catches fish, waterbirds and sea-snakes, usually from a perch, but also patrols beaches for carrion and is notorious for robbing other birds of their prey.

Brahminy Kite
Haliastur indus

APPEARANCE The white head, neck and upper breast contrast sharply with the rich chestnut color of the remainder of the plumage of this medium-sized raptor. The pale yellow bill, cere and legs are not as obvious as the dark brown eyes, and in flight the black primary feathers give dark tips to the flexed wings and the rounded tail is tipped white. Immature birds appear quite different, basically brown with lighter brown streaks on the underparts and pale edges to the feathers of the upperparts. Utters mewing and wailing calls.

SIZE About 43 centimeters (17 inches) long, females only marginally larger than males.

HABITAT AND DISTRIBUTION Most common around the shores and along estuaries from India and Sri Lanka through the islands of southeast Asia to the northern coast of Australia.

REPRODUCTION The breeding territory is demarcated by fast plunging flights and wailing contact calls. The substantial stick-nest is built over a fork within the foliage of a tall tree, and the female takes the major role in affairs at the nest, feeding herself and the chicks on food delivered by the male. One or two sparsely marked eggs are laid but further details of the nesting cycle are undescribed.

DIET Mainly small vertebrates, including many fish, and much of it taken as carrion. Dextrous at snatching food in flight from the ground or in the air.

Black Kite
Milvus migrans

APPEARANCE This medium-sized raptor has dark brown upperparts and more rufous underparts, all feathers streaked in the center with black. The long wing feathers and deeply forked tail are dark brown barred with lighter brown and the forehead and face are washed with pale gray in some forms. The cere and legs are yellow but the eyes may be dark brown or cream and the bill yellow or black according to which population the individual belongs. Immatures are similar to adults but have the underparts streaked with pale brown, the upperparts tipped with rufous and the tail less deeply forked.
SIZE Length about 55 centimeters (22 inches), females only slightly larger than males.

HABITAT AND DISTRIBUTION Prefers open woodland but will occupy habitats ranging from forest to desert if food available. Occurs throughout the warmer parts of Europe, Africa and Asia, extending to Japan and south through Indonesia to New Guinea and Australia. Only a migrant to some areas.
REPRODUCTION Mates pursue one another in dextrous weaving flights and utter mewing calls prior to nesting. Both sexes build the flimsy stick platform in the fork of a tree, and two or three eggs, varying in size within clutches, are laid on a lining of rubbish and debris. The female does most of the 29-35 days of incubation, fed by the male but also gathering some of her own food. The nestling period lasts about six weeks and the female is most attentive to the chicks during the early stages.
DIET A most catholic feeder, dextrous in flight at catching small animals or scavenging scraps. Readily takes carrion, including fish, and eats some snails and palm nuts when available.

Lappet-faced Vulture
Aegypius tracheliotos

APPEARANCE One of the largest raptors, sooty-brown above but white below, including the downy ruff at the base of the neck, with dark brown streaks down the centers of the breast feathers. The naked head and neck, with loose skin formed into pendent lappets, are deep red and the massive bill is colored pale horn. The cere and legs are blue-gray and the eyes dark brown. In flight the narrow white line along the forearm and voluminous white leggings are prominent. Immatures are all brown, but for white edgings to the breast feathers, white dappling on the mantle and the dirty flesh-color of the bare head skin.
SIZE Length about 110 centimeters (44 inches) and the sexes are indistinguishable by size.

HABITAT AND DISTRIBUTION Open woodland, savanna and desert from the Sahara and Negev Deserts south to northern South Africa.
REPRODUCTION Usually seen singly or in pairs and probably occupies widely spaced territories. The pairs perform high coordinated soaring in courtship, build a stick platform almost 2 meters (6.5 feet) across on the crown of a tree and line it with grass tufts. A single egg is the normal clutch, laid during the dry season, both parents alternating at the nest during the 56-day incubation period. Both also alternate in care of the chick, feeding it by regurgitations from the crop when they return to the nest. The chick is left alone once well-feathered and about two months old, the parents only returning to feed it during the rest of the 120-day nestling period.
DIET Carrion, including many small animals, but the heavy bill can also rend the skin and sinew of the largest carcasses. Suspected to occasionally kill its own prey.

Eurasian Griffon
Gyps fulvus

APPEARANCE A very large sandy-brown raptor with a long neck covered in short white down and emerging from a ruff of fluffy white feathers. The flight feathers and tail are dark brown and the underparts streaked with dark brown. The eyes and bill are yellow and the cere and legs gray. Utters hisses, croaks and cackles at close quarters.

SIZE Length about 100 centimeters (40 inches), females slightly smaller than males.

HABITAT AND DISTRIBUTION Prefers mountains for nesting, roosting and soaring, but will move to open plains to feed. Extends across Eurasia from southern Europe to western China, south to northwest Africa, Sinai and Bombay, and even further south on winter migration.

REPRODUCTION Breeds in colonies of 5-50 pairs on cliff ledges, pairs soaring close together above the colony before nesting. The nests are platforms of sticks and debris, partly lined with green leaves to receive the single egg. The parents relieve one another for incubation, brooding and feeding the chick, allowing each to locate its own food and later to return with food to regurgitate for the chick. Incubation lasts for 48-54 days and the nestling period for 110-115 days, after which the young learn to locate their own food supplies.

DIET Carrion, mainly from large mammals, located after soaring to great heights and often after covering more than 100 kilometers (62 miles).

Bateleur
Terathopius ecaudatus

APPEARANCE A large and handsome eagle, jet black with white under the wings, gray on the shoulders, a rufous tail and back, bright crimson face and legs, yellow cere and black bill. The female can be distinguished at rest by the gray bar across her secondaries and in flight by the narrow black border to the underwing. An uncommon cream-backed form occurs. The immature is brown, with cere and face blue-green and legs cream. The short tail and upturned wing tips produce a distinctive shape in flight. A challenging bark is uttered in flight with the feet dropped and head thrown back or the wings are clapped in bursts of aggressive flapping.
SIZE Length about 60 centimeters (24 inches), the female slightly larger than the male.
HABITAT AND DISTRIBUTION Tree and bush savanna throughout Africa south of the Sahara and extending into Arabia.
REPRODUCTION Mates chase one another in spectacular fashion prior to nesting in a large stick-nest placed in the upper fork of a large tree. Both sexes take part in nest building but the female sits most on the single egg during its 55 days of incubation. The young chick, attractively clad in cream and chocolate down, is brooded and fed mainly by the female. The male brings food to the nest occupants, assisted later by his mate. The nestling fledges after 95-120 days in the nest but remains dependent on its parents for a further four months; thereafter it ranges widely until mature at about seven years old.
DIET Mammals, from small antelope to mice, birds, and reptiles as large as monitor lizards, form the bulk of the diet, some of it obtained as carrion.

Palmnut Vulture
Gypohierax angolensis

APPEARANCE This large raptor is strikingly colored black and white. The black tail with its white tip, black scapulars, black secondaries and their coverts, and black tips to the primaries produce a striking pattern against the rest of the white plumage when in flight. The eyes, bill and legs are yellow, the cere gray, and the bare skin on the face and throat is deep pink. The immature is quite different, brown in plumage and eye color with the bare skin areas dull yellow.
SIZE Length about 60 centimeters (24 inches), the female indistinguishable in size from the male.
HABITAT AND DISTRIBUTION Forest and moist savannas of tropical Africa south of the Sahara Desert where oil palms (*Elaeis*) and raffia palms (*Raffia*) are found.
REPRODUCTION Pairs roll and dive together in flight before nesting and both contribute to the large stick-nest in a tree that may be used in successive seasons. The female undertakes the incubation of the single egg for about 44 days and the chick develops in the nest for at least a further 90 days. Further details of the breeding cycle are undescribed.
DIET The husks of oil and raffia palm nuts are the staple food, but mollusks, crabs and fish, taken alive or as carrion, are also consumed in the marshes and coastal swamps favored by its food plants.

Bearded Vulture
Gypaetus barbatus

APPEARANCE A very large and spectacular raptor, the cere covered in long black bristles that project down like a beard and are connected to a mask of black feathers that surround the yellow red-rimmed eyes. The head, neck and underparts are rufous, the latter underlain by powder down patches that help absorb the mineral dust that causes the coloration. The upperparts are dark brown with cream streaks and the flight feathers charcoal. The elongate bill is horn-colored and the legs gray. The immature is browner with pale brown edges to the feathers of the upperparts and a sooty-brown head and neck. The long pointed wings and diamond-shaped tail form a distinctive falcon-like silhouette in flight.
SIZE Length about 100 centimeters (40 inches) with a wingspan of 2.5 meters (8 feet) and the sexes similar in size.
HABITAT AND DISTRIBUTION Mountains and high grasslands from southern Europe to South Africa and east to China.

REPRODUCTION Performs undulating dives in display and each pair builds a deep nest of stick and debris on a ledge or in a pot-hole high on a cliff. One or two eggs are laid on the lining of fur and wool but only one chick is ever raised. The parents alternate during the 55-58 days of incubation and both share in the raising of the chick during the 110 days that it remains in the nest, feeding it from prey carried to or regurgitated onto the nest.
DIET Carrion, especially large bones broken by being dropped in flight onto rocks, the marrow extracted with the scoop-like tongue and the fragments swallowed with the wide gape. It will scavenge scraps around human dwellings, gather insects and may sometimes kill its own prey, having more grasping feet and curved claws than most other vultures.

African Harrier Hawk
Polyboroides typus

APPEARANCE A medium-sized raptor whose broad wings, long tail and slender legs make it appear larger. It is a gray bird with fine white bars on the breast and underwing coverts, black spots on the back, black ends to the flight feathers and a black tail with a white bar across the center. The cere, bare facial skin and legs are yellow but the face can blush deep pink at will. The black spots on the back are more extensive in males. Immatures are dark brown, with different amounts of light brown edging to the feathers, have yellow legs and a greenish-yellow face.
SIZE Length about 55 centimeters (22 inches), the female slightly larger than the male.
HABITAT AND DISTRIBUTION Forest, woodland and savanna throughout Africa south of the Sahara. A very similar species occurs on Madagascar.
REPRODUCTION In spring performs shallow undulating flights with whistling calls. Both sexes construct the large stick-nest on a rock ledge or, more often, in a tree on a hillside or by water. One or two beautifully marked eggs are laid on the bed of leaves lining the nest and the female performs most of the 35 days of incubation. The first chick to hatch may attack its sibling which often succumbs. Once its cream down, with long filaments on the head, is replaced by feathers, the female leaves the chick to help the male bring food to the nest. The juvenile fledges after about 50 days and soon joins its parents to search for food.
DIET Small animals, especially nestlings, bats and squirrels extracted from holes with either the narrow bare-faced head or the long double-jointed legs. Also floats slowly past vegetation on its broad wings in search of prey, including insects and lizards.

Eastern Chanting Goshawk
Melierax poliopterus

APPEARANCE This medium-sized gray raptor has the underparts and ends of the secondary coverts finely barred with white. In flight the black primaries and pale undersides to the secondaries form a distinctive pattern from below, and the black-and-white barred tail and white rump are obvious from above. The cere and legs are bright orange and the eyes red-brown. The immature is brown above and white below, the upper breast streaked and the lower breast barred with brown. The white rump remains a conspicuous feature but the eyes, cere and legs are yellow.
SIZE Length about 50 centimeters (20 inches), the female slightly larger than the male.
HABITAT AND DISTRIBUTION Dry open woodland and semi-desert of eastern Africa from Somalia south to Tanzania.
REPRODUCTION Nocturnal display flights may enhance territoriality, and bouts of loud singing from a perch in the mornings herald the onset of breeding. A small stick-nest is built in the outer fork of a tree by both sexes. One or two white eggs are laid on the lining of dung and debris, and the female performs most of the 36-38 days of incubation. The newly hatched chick has a halo of long wispy down on the head and remains in the nest for about six weeks before flying. Most food is brought to the nest by the male, assisted later in the nesting period by the female.
DIET Lizards and insects are the main prey, taken after still-hunting from a perch or, rarely, while walking about on its long legs. Small mammals and birds are also taken when available, sometimes after a dashing pursuit.

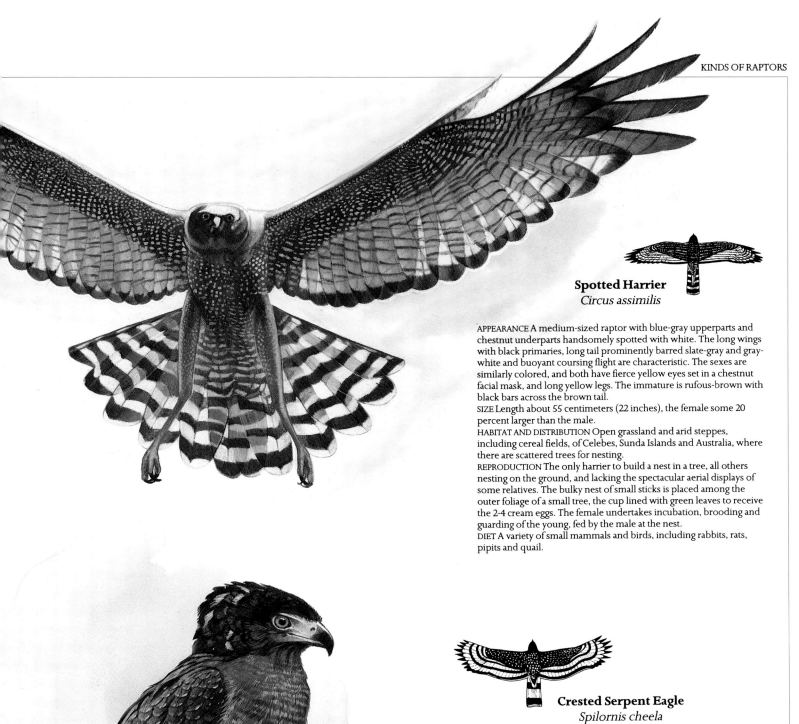

Spotted Harrier
Circus assimilis

APPEARANCE A medium-sized raptor with blue-gray upperparts and chestnut underparts handsomely spotted with white. The long wings with black primaries, long tail prominently barred slate-gray and gray-white and buoyant coursing flight are characteristic. The sexes are similarly colored, and both have fierce yellow eyes set in a chestnut facial mask, and long yellow legs. The immature is rufous-brown with black bars across the brown tail.
SIZE Length about 55 centimeters (22 inches), the female some 20 percent larger than the male.
HABITAT AND DISTRIBUTION Open grassland and arid steppes, including cereal fields, of Celebes, Sunda Islands and Australia, where there are scattered trees for nesting.
REPRODUCTION The only harrier to build a nest in a tree, all others nesting on the ground, and lacking the spectacular aerial displays of some relatives. The bulky nest of small sticks is placed among the outer foliage of a small tree, the cup lined with green leaves to receive the 2-4 cream eggs. The female undertakes incubation, brooding and guarding of the young, fed by the male at the nest.
DIET A variety of small mammals and birds, including rabbits, rats, pipits and quail.

Crested Serpent Eagle
Spilornis cheela

APPEARANCE This raptor varies from medium-sized to large across its wide range and some of the local color variants may prove to be distinct species. The head and nape are sooty-brown, the broad feathers of the latter mottled by white bases to the feathers. The upperparts are dark brown, flecked with white on the wing coverts, and the underparts deep cinnamon with white spots on lower breast and thighs. The flight feathers are dark brown, the wings with white bars and the tail with a broad white patch in the center. The immature is much paler, the feathers of the upperparts edged with white and the cream underparts finely streaked with dark brown. The eyes, cere and legs are yellow at all ages.
SIZE Length about 40-75 centimeters (16-30 inches), the female slightly larger than the male.
HABITAT AND DISTRIBUTION Forest and tall woodland from India east to southern China and south to Bali and the Philippines.
REPRODUCTION Soars and utters ringing screams over the nest area prior to building the relatively small stick-nest high in a tree. Both sexes build but only the female incubates the single egg, for about 36 days. The chick fledges after about 60 days, brooded and fed by the female for the first half of this period with food brought by the male. Thereafter both parents bring food to the nest.
DIET Tree snakes and other reptiles, many taken on the ground, are the favorite prey, but small mammals and birds are taken at times.

Slate-colored Hawk
Leucopternis schistacea

APPEARANCE This medium-sized raptor is gray all over but for the blackish wing tips and tail, the latter with a broad white bar across the center, narrow white tip and a second white bar concealed at the base. The eyes, cere, facial skin and legs are orange. The immature has the underparts finely barred with white and the eyes are yellow.
SIZE Length about 44 centimeters (17 inches), the female only slightly larger than the male.
HABITAT AND DISTRIBUTION Tropical forests of Amazonia from southern Venezuela to Ecuador, Colombia, Peru and Bolivia.
REPRODUCTION Undescribed.
DIET The remains of a snake and a frog have been found in the stomachs of specimens collected for research.

Rough-legged Hawk
Buteo lagopus

APPEARANCE This large raptor is very variable in plumage color and pattern. Generally dark brown above and lighter below, variously streaked with darker brown on the head, breast and thighs and mottled with white on the back and upper wing coverts. In most birds the flanks are sooty-brown, the tail is whitish with a broad black terminal bar and a white tip, and the undersides of the long broad wings are pale gray with black tips and a black patch under the wrists. Some individuals are almost entirely sooty-brown. Immatures are more streaked below and have streaks rather than blotches on the thighs. The eyes are dark brown and the cere and feet yellow. This is one of only two buzzards with feathered legs, like a true eagle.
SIZE Length about 55 centimeters (22 inches), females only some 5 percent larger than males.
HABITAT AND DISTRIBUTION Open tundra straddling the Arctic Circle in North America, Europe and Asia, migrating south in winter.
REPRODUCTION A stick-nest is built on a rock ledge, or in a tree if available. As many as seven eggs are laid in the deep, well-lined nest cup and the female incubates for 28-31 days. The chicks leave the nest when about 40 days old, remaining in the area for a further four to six weeks before starting their first migration south.
DIET Lemmings are the staple food, their abundance determining the success and productivity of nesting attempts. Rodents are also the staple food outside the breeding season, with other small vertebrates only rarely taken. Much hunting is done on the wing, often by hovering.

Great Philippine Eagle
Pithecophaga jefferyi

APPEARANCE This very large eagle is among the most powerful raptors. The feathers of the upperparts are dark brown edged with buff. The underparts are off-white, streaked with rufous on the throat, thighs and underwing coverts. The head is surmounted by a crest of long pale rufous feathers streaked with dark brown. The eyes are blue-gray, the cere blue-green and the massive bare legs and feet are pale yellow. The black bill is exceptionally deep and prominent. Immatures resemble the adults, and the sexes are similar.

SIZE Length about 95 centimeters (38 inches), the female noticeably larger than the male.

HABITAT AND DISTRIBUTION Tropical forest on the largest Philippine islands of Luzon, Mindanao, Samar and Leyte.

REPRODUCTION A huge nest high in a forest tree is used over successive years and the pair may soar in the area of the nest before breeding. Both sexes line the nest with green leaves and a single egg is incubated, mostly by the female, for about 60 days. The male delivers food to the nest throughout the breeding cycle until assisted by the female in the latter half of the 105-day nestling period. The young only try to catch their own prey four or five months after leaving the nest and, with such a prolonged cycle, successful breeding may only occur in alternate years.

DIET Arboreal mammals, such as flying lemurs and squirrels, are the most important food. Monkeys, deer, palm civets, bats, snakes, monitor lizards and large birds, such as hornbills and young owls, are also taken at times.

Ornate Hawk Eagle
Spizaetus ornatus

APPEARANCE This spectacular large raptor has a black crown with a long crest, black upperparts and white underparts boldly barred with black. The sides of the head and neck are chestnut but for the white throat rimmed with black-tipped feathers. The flight feathers are marked with broad black and white bars. The cere and feet are yellow and the eyes orange. The immature is quite different, dark brown on the upperparts with the head, neck and underparts pure white but for black tips to the crest feathers and black bars on the flanks. The eyes are pale yellow.
SIZE Length about 60 centimeters (24 inches), the female some 25 percent larger than the male.
HABITAT AND DISTRIBUTION Tropical forest from Mexico south to northern Argentina and Paraguay and including the islands of Trinidad and Tobago.
REPRODUCTION The male performs an undulating diving display and the pair often soar together in the nest area, sometimes with high screaming calls. A huge stick-nest is built in the upper fork of a large tree. Only a single chick is raised, but further details of the nesting cycle are undescribed.
DIET Mainly medium-sized to large birds, such as guans and parrots, but also some small mammals.

Bonelli's Eagle
Hieraaetus fasciatus

APPEARANCE A large raptor, black above with some mottling where white feather bases are exposed. The underparts are white streaked with dark brown especially on the upper breast, thighs and undertail coverts. Females tend to be more heavily streaked than males. The eyes, cere and feet are yellow. The immature is brown above and russet below, the breast streaked with dark brown feathers and the eyes brown.
SIZE Length about 70 centimeters (28 inches), the female some 12 percent larger than the male.
HABITAT AND DISTRIBUTION Broken and wooded terrain, from southern Europe and northern Africa east to China, southeastern Asia and the Lesser Sunda Islands.
REPRODUCTION The pair soar over the nest area and perform undulating flight displays prior to breeding. The large stick-nest is built on a cliff ledge or in a tall tree and the same site may be used in successive years. Two eggs are usually laid but the first chick to hatch kills its sibling. The female performs most of the 43 days of incubation and cares for the chick during the early part of its 65-day nestling period. The male provides the female and chick with food, only rarely helping with duties at the nest.
DIET Game birds, such as partridges, and mammals as large as hares form the basis of the diet, but occasionally snakes and lizards are included.

FAMILY SAGITTARIIDAE

One species

Secretary Bird
Sagittarius serpentarius

APPEARANCE An unmistakable very large raptor, the only living species with long legs like a stork. It has gray plumage but for the black flight feathers, black tips to the elongate crest feathers on the nape, black leggings on the thighs and a black band across the tail. The belly and underwings are white and produce a distinctive pattern against the black flight feathers when flying with neck and legs outstretched and the elongated central tail feathers projecting. Each brown eye is set in a patch of bare red skin, the cere is gray and the legs are pink. The immature has gray bars on the thighs and underwing coverts, gray eyes and yellow facial skin.
SIZE Length about 120 centimeters (48 inches), the male slightly smaller than the female.
HABITAT AND DISTRIBUTION Steppe, grassland and open woodland throughout Africa south of the Sahara.
REPRODUCTION Undulating flight displays and croaking calls are performed prior to breeding and a 2 meter (6.5 feet) diameter stick-and-weed platform on the crown of a low tree may form the nest for several successive attempts. Both sexes build and both alternate incubation of the one to three white eggs and care of the chicks. Mates usually bring billfuls of grass during nest changeovers and are greeted by a deep bowing display and croaking calls. Incubation proceeds for about 43 days and the nestling period for 65-106 days. The young are fed from cropfuls of prey regurgitated onto the nest floor and from a liquid trickled from the bill of the parent.
DIET Rodents, reptiles and locusts form the bulk of the diet but any small animals close to the ground, that can be brought down by swift kicks from the long legs and stubby toes, are taken.

FAMILY FALCONIDAE

Sixty species

Lined Forest Falcon
Micrastur gilvicollis

APPEARANCE A small raptor, gray above and pale gray on the head but white below with fine gray bars, especially on the upper breast. The flight feathers are sooty-brown, the tail with one or two narrow white bars. The cere, bare facial skin, eyes and legs are yellow. The immature is chocolate brown above and ochre below and the eyes are dark brown. A noisy bird that utters high yapping calls when perched well up in the forest foliage, especially for about 20 minutes at dawn and dusk. Recognized as a full species, separate from the Barred Forest Falcon (*Micrastur ruficollis*), only in 1972.
SIZE Length about 32 centimeters (13 inches), the female slightly larger than the male.
HABITAT AND DISTRIBUTION Dense tropical rainforest and secondary growth of the Amazon Basin, from Venezuela and Colombia to Ecuador and Amazonia in Brazil.
REPRODUCTION The breeding is undescribed although the species is common, sedentary and occurs at densities of 30-50 hectares (74-123 acres) per pair. The first nest of any forest falcon was observed by ornithologists only in 1978, an unlined natural hole in a tree in which a single chick was raised. Earlier, a captive female had laid two buff eggs that were blotched with chocolate.
DIET Lizards and insects, sometimes disturbed by army ant colonies, probably captured after short dashes through the undergrowth. Will also attack small birds entangled in nets.

African Pygmy Falcon
Polihierax semitorquatus

APPEARANCE The sexes of this very small raptor are separable even when in immature plumage. The birds are light gray above and white below, including the forehead and face, but in females the back is a deep chestnut color. The flight feathers and tail are black, traversed by lines of white spots. The eyes are dark brown and the cere and legs orange. Immatures have the plumage washed with light brown.
SIZE Length about 20 centimeters (8 inches), the sexes indistinguishable in size.
HABITAT AND DISTRIBUTION Semi-arid savanna with scattered trees in southwest and northeast Africa.
REPRODUCTION Courtship includes the male feeding his mate. Copulation may be preceded by exaggerated tail-wagging displays by the female. A chamber in the nest of a weaver bird is adopted for breeding, Sociable Weaver (*Philetairus*) in southwest Africa and Buffalo Weaver (*Dinemellia*) in northeast Africa. The female does most of the 30 days' incubation of the two to four white eggs and also broods and feeds the young chicks. The nestling period lasts about 29 days and the male provides most of the food to the nest throughout breeding. Pairs and families usually roost together in a chamber, in part to counter the effects of cold desert nights.
DIET Small lizards and insects form the bulk of the diet but rodents and birds are also taken by this bold little predator.

Striated Caracara
Phalcoboenus australis

APPEARANCE A large black raptor, the somber color relieved by white streaks on the neck and breast, by chestnut thighs and underwing coverts, by a white band across the tail and by the bright yellow cere, facial skin, naked crop (when distended) and legs. The eyes are dark brown. The immature is sooty-brown with pale brown flight feathers and flecks on the neck, and the bare skin areas are light gray. It takes about five years to assume full adult plumage. Utters prolonged high-pitched screeches with the head thrown back.
SIZE Length about 60 centimeters (24 inches), females slightly larger than males.
HABITAT AND DISTRIBUTION The sea shore and adjacent interior of the Falkland Islands and small islands off the southern tip of South America.
REPRODUCTION A small nest of grass is constructed on the ground among clumps of tussock grass or on rocky ledges. The eggs, richly marked in shades of brown, number two to four, and are laid on a lining of fine material including wool. Pairs may nest in close proximity to one another. Breeds during the austral summer.
DIET Scavenges around summer breeding colonies of penguins and other seabirds and for the rest of the year combs the beaches for scraps or digs out insects with its strong legs. Attacks weak sheep, introduced to the islands, for which it is persecuted.

White-eyed Kestrel
Falco rupicoloides

APPEARANCE A small red-brown raptor, barred with dark brown on the back, wing coverts and thighs and streaked with brown on the head and upper breast. The flight feathers, tail and rump are sooty-brown with broad bars of pale gray across the feathers. The eyes are cream and the cere and legs yellow. The immature has the flanks streaked not barred, the rump and tail red-brown barred with dark brown, the eyes brown and the cere pale blue.
SIZE Length about 33 centimeters (13 inches), the sexes indistinguishable in size.
HABITAT AND DISTRIBUTION Grassland, steppe and semi-desert with scattered trees from Somalia south to South Africa.
REPRODUCTION Pairs perch prominently near the nest and proclaim their territory by high screams and fast rocking flights, flashing their silvery underwings. The old stick-nest of another bird, often a crow, is adopted for breeding and two to five eggs, marked with shades of brown, are laid. The female performs most of the 32 days of incubation, relieved briefly by the male when he brings her prey. The female also does most of the brooding and feeding of the chicks but, later in their 30-35 days nestling period, leaves them to help the male supply food to the young. Juveniles remain for about eight weeks in the parental territory before dispersing.
DIET Lizards, birds, rodents, locusts, and termites are the most important prey but any small animals may be taken either from a perch or during bouts of hovering.

Gregarious at all times, whether breeding, roosting or feeding, Asian White-backed Vultures gather around slaughterhouses and villages where they feed on carrion and refuse.

RAPTOR

BIOLOGY

HOW RAPTORS ARE STUDIED

ANDREW VILLAGE

To the biologist trying to understand the ecology and behavior of birds, raptors offer both advantages and disadvantages. Raptors often nest in the same restricted locations from year to year and, once these are known, the breeding population can be monitored fairly easily thereafter. Most species are large enough to carry permanent visual markers or radio-transmitters that last for months or even years. Individuals can thus be recognized and followed for long periods.

However, their large size and positions near the tops of food chains also make raptors more difficult to study than other birds. Populations can be at extremely low densities, and simply finding nests can be a major task. Reaching nests may be practically impossible if they are on huge, dead trees or towering cliffs. Catching raptors can also be difficult, and samples of marked birds are often small, especially for the larger species.

Because of these problems, the study of raptors has, until recently, been confined to those aspects on which information can be most easily collected—nesting behavior and diet. Population studies have mainly involved the monitoring of breeding numbers and breeding success, with little attention paid to the non-breeding element or the winter population.

Interest in raptors has grown in recent years, and there have been great advances in the way they are studied. Scientists are now beginning to understand the detailed ecology and behavior of an ever wider range of species.

▼▶ Much interest in raptors is due to their powers of flight, characteristics that can make them at once highly visible and inaccessible. The impressive Verreaux's Eagle (*Aquila verreauxii*) (below) nests on towering cliffs, while the huge Bearded Vulture (*Gypaetus barbatus*) (opposite) is dwarfed by its mountainous habitat. Biologists study such raptors for their own curiosity, and for the sake of the birds. A desire to identify these fascinating birds often becomes a compelling pursuit.

Peter Steyn

Guy Robbrecht/Bruce Coleman Ltd

IDENTIFYING RAPTORS

A first step in studying any group of animals is to be able to identify the species within the group. Accurate identification of raptors is especially important where counts are made on migration routes, because many similar species may pass simultaneously over the same point. The major raptor families can be distinguished by their size, shape or flight. Identification to the species level poses more problems, especially if all that can be seen is a distant silhouette. Fortunately, most species have unique features of shape, flight pattern or markings that aid their identification, and these have been published in several excellent field guides. These guides allow even novice raptor-watchers to become reasonably proficient, and enhance the accuracy of species counts. Even so, some species remain difficult to identify, even when handled, especially those that exist in several subspecies or color morphs.

The taxonomy of raptors is by no means fully understood, because the relatedness of species is difficult to judge solely from their size, shape or color. Anatomy is strongly influenced by lifestyle, and convergent evolution can make unrelated groups look superficially similar. Recently developed biochemical techniques, which compare particular enzymes or DNA fragments common to many species, are throwing new light on the taxonomy of raptors, and may soon make it possible to infer the course of their evolution.

▲► Having found your raptor you must identify it, not always an easy task. Good binoculars and a copy of one of the better field guides are necessities. Major groups can be distinguished by size, shape, flight and habitat. Recognizing species can be more difficult. To the untrained eye, the Western Honey Buzzard (*Pernis apivorus*) (above) and Eurasian Buzzard (*Buteo buteo*) (right) are both just brown hawks. Closer examination reveals distinguishing features. The Honey Buzzard has more variegated plumage and a yellow eye; in flight other distinguishing features become more obvious.

Michael Leach/NHPA

WATCHING RAPTORS

Because raptors are widely dispersed, they can be difficult to find, and may be seen only sporadically by casual bird-watchers. The best opportunities to watch raptors are during migration or at nests. The important concentration points on migration routes in Europe and North America have become major tourist attractions, giving many people a unique chance to watch raptors in numbers.

Nest-watching is a more solitary pursuit, usually confined to scientists, keen amateurs or photographers. There are notable exceptions, however, such as the pair of Ospreys (*Pandion haliaetus*) that breed at Loch Garten, Scotland, and are viewed from hides by thousands of visitors each year. Although every care must be taken when erecting hides at nests, many raptors are less likely to be disturbed than some other birds, and their relatively long nestling stage makes the effort particularly worthwhile. Much of the early information on raptors came from amateur naturalists or photographers who spent many hours meticulously recording the behavior of birds at nests.

But first you must find your nest. This can be hard work, and unrewarding. There is nothing quite so satisfying as marking the location of another pair on the map, and nothing so depressing as searching all day without success. Before beginning, it is especially useful to know the raptor's preferred nesting habitat and most likely nesting sites.

Looking directly for nests is possible in species such as Ospreys and some eagles, which build large, conspicuous structures. Nests near the tops of large trees can be spotted from aircraft, which are invaluable in covering large, remote areas. Species that have small, well-hidden nests must be searched for on foot, and the first indication of a breeding pair may be a displaying bird or signs such as droppings, prey remains or molted feathers. Even secretive, woodland raptors, such as Western Honey Buzzards (*Pernis apivorus*), often have striking breeding displays, and these may be the most effective way of locating their hidden nesting places.

Ground-nesting raptors, such as harriers, hide their nests in rank vegetation. Often the only way to find them is to watch the adults delivering food, or to walk in the vicinity of the nest until a sitting bird is flushed. Pairs with young will often dive and call at human intruders who approach the nest, and this can give away its position.

Once a nest is found, a hide can be built gradually. Disturbance is more likely to affect large raptors than small ones, particularly during the early stages of breeding. Nest watches give useful information on parental behavior and prey delivery rates, and they have been used to good effect for many species. Feeding rate may be expressed as the number of items delivered per

day, but this may have to be converted to prey-weight if items differ widely in size. In some studies, the number of food morsels given to each chick was recorded and used to relate growth rates to food intake.

▼▲ Finding nests can be challenging. They are not always as substantial as that of the African Crowned Eagle (below), nor as accessible as the ground nest of the desertion-prone Northern Harrier (above). Any disturbance must be circumspect.

Arthur Butler/Oxford Scientific Films

Peter Steyn

Watching nests is a labor-intensive task. One way to reduce the effort needed is to use time-lapse photography, with frames taken at fixed intervals or whenever adults arrive at the nest. A carefully placed camera may show what items are delivered and when, as well as rare events such as visits by predators. Other remote-sensing devices used at raptor nests include "telemetric eggs" (electronic sensors placed in a lifelike dummy egg which record the nest temperature, and hence incubation routine) and electronic balances, which record automatically the weight of the adults or chicks.

▼ Estimates of the density of nesting pairs over several years and between habitats can yield vital information about the viability and status of populations. Dense vegetation may hinder accurate estimates. Nevertheless, survey techniques based on a sound knowledge of the species can make census less daunting. In mangroves, nests of the Whistling Kite (*Haliastur sphenurus*) are often near the water's edge and are fairly evenly spaced, and breeding pairs call loudly and behave quite conspicuously.

COUNTING RAPTORS

Many studies measure variations in raptor density over time or between habitats. This has become particularly important following the post-1950 population decline in some species. Estimating the exact number of raptors in an area can be extremely difficult, and the usual technique is to count the number of active nests, although this excludes the large number of individuals that do not attempt to breed. However, regular counts of breeding pairs can reveal long-term changes in the abundance of a species, as can transect counts and counts of migrating raptors.

To get an accurate estimate of density, it is necessary to find a reasonable number of pairs, so the area searched will vary according to the species being studied. For small species, 100 square kilometers (40 square miles) may be sufficient, but this would hold only one or two pairs of the larger eagles, which therefore require huge study areas. Searching large areas thoroughly is a major problem, particularly in remote wilderness. Fortunately, many large raptors are confined to particular types of nesting site, so whole sections of land with no suitable sites can be discounted.

Another useful feature that helps in locating pairs is the regular spacing of nesting territories in some species. Few raptors will tolerate pairs of the same species in close proximity, and there is usually a minimum distance between pairs in a particular environment. The spacing pattern becomes apparent once several adjacent pairs have been found, and searching can then be concentrated where there are gaps in the distribution. Some gaps may be due to lack of suitable nesting sites, but this is usually obvious from a quick inspection of the terrain. Not all species space their nests regularly, however, and for these there may be no alternative to laboriously searching the whole study area.

Care must be taken to ensure that all the breeding pairs are located, and that the study area gives a representative density. Pairs that fail early in their breeding cycle may abandon a territory and remain undetected, so searching must be started early in the nesting season, before such pairs fail. In some species, pairs may move to another site if they fail and be recorded as a new pair unless their origin is known.

Problems can also arise if the study area is too small. Raptors that space their nests unevenly may breed at high densities in restricted localities, but these local densities are not representative of a wider area. At the other extreme, trying to search too big an area will increase the chances of missing pairs, and lead to density being underestimated. Transect or "roadside" counts of raptors are usually done from a vehicle and work best for conspicuous species such as kestrels and buteos, which perch in the open. Roadside counts can be

Jean-Paul Ferrero/Auscape

converted to actual densities by calibration against known densities found from marked birds, or by estimating the area searched along the transect and the visibility of each species. They are useful in detecting changes in numbers over time and may also reveal which habitats are preferred by a particular species. Roadside counts of American Kestrels (*Falco sparverius*) gave the first positive indication that the sexes segregated into different habitats in winter.

Transect counts are prone to errors if the visibility of birds varies. Some species are easier to see than others, giving a distorted picture of their relative densities. Weather may cause day-to-day variations because raptors seek shelter in heavy rain or winds, and soar out of sight if it is hot. Seasonal changes in visibility may be due to growth of vegetation, or because birds behave differently in winter than when breeding. Counts must therefore be made in similar conditions, preferably by the same observers.

Counts of migrating raptors are often made at points of concentration on migration routes, though they may sample only a fraction of the total birds moving to and from the wintering grounds. Some species are less dependent on thermals

David A. Ponton

◄ Counts of raptors as they pass over points of concentration on their regular migration routes can monitor populations, reflecting changes in breeding populations, and revealing sex and age differences in migrants and their routes. Each winter, Zone-tailed Hawks (*Buteo albonatatus*) leave the badlands of southwestern USA to follow narrow migration routes to South America.

▼ Young Eurasian Griffons (*Gyps fulvus*) and millions of other raptors migrate over Israel, endangering military aircraft operating in the limited airspace. A coordinated study using ground crew, motorized glider and radar to follow the migrants resulted in regulations that successfully keep aircraft away from raptor flight paths during critical times.

Angelo Gandolfi

during migration, so they move over a broad front and many will not even pass through the usual concentration points. Those that do may be missed because they are invisible from the ground, or because migration is spread over many more days than there are counts made. Weather also influences the passage of migrants, and this can produce spurious year-to-year fluctuations that are not related to changes in numbers.

Nonetheless, counts of migrating raptors do give some idea of the numbers of some species on passage, which may run into thousands or even millions at a single place. At Falsterbö, Sweden, long-term declines in the number of Eurasian Sparrowhawks (*Accipiter nisus*) seen on migration coincided with their decline as a breeding bird during the period when organochlorine pesticides were heavily used.

BREEDING PERFORMANCE

Monitoring the breeding success of raptors has taken on a special significance since it was realized that pollutants can seriously depress productivity. Poor breeding success may be the result of many different factors, and only careful recording of the timing and cause of nesting failures will indicate if the losses are natural or due to human influence.

Checking nests can be time-consuming, difficult and sometimes dangerous. Birds nesting

▼ A biologist monitors a Red-tailed Hawk (*Buteo jamaicensis*) nest. Sometimes dangerous but often rewarding, such studies of breeding success are vital to the understanding of raptors. Evidence gained from careful documentation of unnatural breeding losses has helped save species.

Erwin & Peggy Bauer/Bruce Coleman Ltd

on high cliffs or on the top of large, dead trees may have totally inaccessible nests which cannot be reached even to band the young. It is usually possible to tell if such pairs are successful, however, by looking for fledged young or for droppings under the nest.

One way of easing the task of checking nests is to encourage pairs to breed in accessible, artificial sites. These may be simple platforms on which a nest can be built, as for Ospreys or Bald Eagles, or nestboxes for hole-nesting species. Artificial sites not only make finding and checking nests easier, they can also increase the density of breeding pairs in the study area—sometimes in dramatic fashion. In the Dutch polders, for example, boxes placed on tall poles in open areas increased the density of Old World Kestrels (*Falco tinnunculus*) more than fivefold in one year.

The information usually collected at nests is the date that laying starts, the number of eggs laid, the number that subsequently hatch and the number of young that fledge. In any population, a proportion of nests will fail to raise young: deciding the cause of failure in each case requires careful detective work at the nest and its surroundings. Predators may leave tell-tale signs if the nest is robbed. Crows usually punch holes in eggs, while owls or other avian predators may leave feathers or plucked remains. Mammals chew rather than pluck feathers, and may leave hair, footprints, droppings or a characteristic odor. Predation may sometimes be a secondary event, because predators often take eggs only after the female has already deserted them. Robbing by humans may be obvious if climbing spikes are used on the nest tree, but not all thieves leave such distinct clues.

Since the advent of DDT, egg breakage has become common in some species, and fragments of shell in the nest during incubation may indicate that not all the clutch survived until hatch. Again, caution is needed in interpreting such signs, because shell can also come from eggs that hatched or were smashed by predators.

These scattered clues build into a pattern that shows how most breeding losses and failures occur. If egg breakage is common, or fully incubated eggs fail to hatch, high pesticide levels are likely to be found in any eggs analyzed. Alternatively, late laying, small clutches, many clutch desertions and frequent deaths among nestlings all point to a shortage of food. Sudden inexplicable failure of nests is unusual, but can often be traced to human activity.

The performance of pairs can also be assessed by the growth rates of their chicks, normally quantified by regular measurements of weight, tarsus length and wing length. Slow growth, compared to the norm for the species, indicates poor food supply, and young chicks that fail to gain weight usually die.

◄ By banding young Peregrine Falcon (*Falco peregrinus*) nestlings, Alaskan biologists have learned that some females return to breed in the area when they are about three years old. Others have been trapped or recovered dead en route to South America, revealing information about migration routes and times.

◄ Adult Peregrine Falcons, caught at the nest or on migration, are banded, weighed and measured. The length of the wing can give clues to the origins of migrants.

◄ An index of shell thickness, calculated using measurements of the length, breadth and weight of blown Bald Eagle eggs, clearly shows which have been thinned through exposure of adults to significant amounts of DDT. The study of eggs collected before persistent pesticides were introduced to agriculture gives comparative, baseline data on natural thickness and its variation.

RAPTOR DIETS AND ABUNDANCE OF PREY

The amount of food available is often a key factor affecting raptor population density and breeding performance. In species with varied diets, it is important to know the most frequent prey, as these will have the most influence on the predator.

The techniques used to assess raptor diets vary according to the species and its main prey. Raptors that eat mammals swallow some fur and bones, and these indigestible parts are regurgitated as pellets. Diet can then be quantified by counting the number of each prey type found, or the proportion of pellets that contain remains of a particular type. Counting items may be possible by matching jaws or other parts of the skeleton, but this is difficult for insect remains.

Raptors digest their prey more thoroughly than do owls so their pellets usually contain fewer bones. Soft-bodied prey, such as earthworms, may be completely digested, leaving no obvious remains in pellets. Variations in the digestibility of different prey items means that their frequency in pellets is not the frequency with which they were eaten by the raptor. Pellet analysis is nonetheless a useful way of measuring variations in diet over time or between habitats for raptors such as eagles, buteos, harriers and kestrels.

S. Roberts/Ardea London

► Once or twice a day, most raptors regurgitate a pellet of compacted fur, feathers and other indigestible material. Collected from beneath roosts or around nests, not only do they indicate the presence of a raptor but a careful inspection of their contents is a useful way to determine diet. Bald Eagle pellets can be identified to prey type and, in some cases, an estimate can be made of the number of different items eaten.

▼ The pellets of Brown Snake Eagles (*Circaetus cinereus*) contain scale and bone from the snakes they eat. These and prey remains can be collected from and around nests to determine breeding diet, often quite different from that during the non-breeding season and critical to successful reproduction.

Peter Steyn

N. N. Birks

Some bird-eating raptors normally pluck the feathers from their prey, so they swallow less indigestible matter and produce small, insignificant pellets. Diet in these species can be assessed from the plucked feathers of kills brought to the nest area during the breeding season. Accipiters often use regular plucking perches, at which masses of feathers can accumulate. Sorting out how many of each prey species are represented in these piles of feathers can require a certain amount of guesswork. Biases may also affect results if some prey remains are more visible or last longer than others, or if the male brings only larger items to the nest.

Recording prey items on nests is widely used to assess raptor diets during the breeding season. Remains accumulate during the nestling stage because the young are unable to eat the larger bones and feathers of their prey. Bias is again likely if only large items are delivered to the nest, and if some prey species leave longer-lasting remains than others.

Having identified the important prey species, it is often necessary to measure their abundance and relate this to the raptor's numbers and breeding performance. Raptor biologists often find themselves learning to trap voles, count rabbits, census songbirds or survey carrion carcasses in an attempt to quantify the food supply of their chosen subject of study. This work may be less exciting than working directly with raptors, but it is no less important. Whenever food supply has been

measured, it has nearly always been shown to be the key to understanding the behavior and ecology of raptors.

Andy Rouse/Planet Earth Pictures

▲ By counting rabbits, scientists have determined that in some parts of Australia most Wedge-tailed Eagles (*Aquila audax*) breed only when the number of rabbits exceeds 16 per ten-kilometer transect.

◄ The analysis of prey remains and pellets has sometimes revealed prey species thought rare or absent in the area. Most often, however, it is the common species that feature in raptor diets. Wherever they occur, rabbits are captured by the larger raptors, here a Eurasian Buzzard (*Buteo buteo*). Partially eaten carcasses can usually be distinguished from those left by mammalian predators.

COUNTING CONDORS FROM MOLT PATTERNS

NOEL SNYDER

Noel Snyder

Francois Gohier/Jacana

Early studies of the California Condor were greatly hampered by difficulties in assessing the size of the wild population. Political constraints made marking of individuals impossible, while the birds' inconsistent flocking habits, their often unpredictable and long-range movements and the difficulties for researchers in traversing the species' mountainous range in southern California, all conspired to make census efforts more an art than a science. Even massive annual simultaneous counts from strategic lookouts spaced throughout the species' range were highly variable and bore an unknown relationship to actual population size.

Nevertheless, extensive efforts to photograph all individuals seen in flight throughout the species' range led ultimately in the early 1980s to accurate population counts based on individual identification of birds. The condor is fortunately large enough that photographs taken with powerful telephoto lenses can often reveal feather characteristics from great distances. Moreover, molt sequences, especially in the primary feathers, proved to be highly variable and individually distinctive for all birds older than recent fledglings. Because the interval from loss of a primary to its full replacement is close to four months, an individual needed only to be photographed about once a month to keep track of its molt pattern and individual identity. In addition, the frequent presence of broken or damaged feathers gave extra field marks to confirm individual identities.

Intensive photographic efforts from 1982 to 1985 yielded summer totals of 21, 19, 15, and 9 wild condors, respectively. It is unlikely that any birds in the population were missed. Almost all birds were photographed many times and in many locations.

The rapid drop in the wild population indicated a mortality rate far beyond compensation by reproduction. In 1985 a decision was finally made to bring the last few wild birds into captivity, with efforts towards re-establishing a viable wild population left for the future. Without the clear picture of the decline that the molt-census method provided, it is doubtful that such a decision would have been reached in time.

Kenneth W. Fink/Ardea London

▲ Attempts to monitor the wild population of California Condors included radio-tracking birds carrying a telemetric transmitter and following wing-tagged individuals (here a captive). Eventually, careful study of photographs of the wide-ranging, soaring birds allowed identification of individuals and provided convincing evidence that few survived.

CATCHING AND MARKING RAPTORS

A useful aspect of studying any animal population is the ability to tell individuals apart. This can show how they are distributed over the terrain, how often they breed or change territory, and how long they live. Raptors can be caught by a variety of methods, many of them based on the time-honored techniques of falconers. Prey decoys are sometimes used to lure the predators towards the trap, which may be a cage, a net or fine nooses that ensnare the feet. Unlike smaller birds, many raptors can be safely caught on the nest without the risk of causing desertion, and the technique is especially effective for incubating females.

Once caught, birds are given a unique mark which will allow them to be identified at a later date. Metal leg-bands are widely used, each having a unique number and a return address, in case the bird is recovered by a member of the public. Most countries administer their own banding scheme, and these have yielded important clues about the movements and life expectancies of raptors and other birds. The numbers on such bands are too small to be read on free-flying birds, so another mark may be used to reduce the necessity of having to re-trap the bird in later years. Colored plastic leg-bands or wing-tags are the usual method, and these may use numbers or color combinations to identify individuals. If nestlings are tagged, different colors may indicate year-classes, with numbers for individuals.

Wing-tags are attached by clips through the *patagium*, a thin flap of skin at the leading edge of the wing, and should stay in place indefinitely. They are a good way of marking conspicuous species, and have been used on many sorts of raptors from large eagles to small falcons. They are no use for secretive raptors such as accipiters, which are rarely seen for long enough to identify a tag. These species have to be banded and re-trapped if the fate of particular birds is to be followed over several years.

Although biologists usually identify individual raptors by artificial marks, they can sometimes use the distinctive markings of the birds themselves. In small populations of large raptors, notably the Californian Condor (*Gymnogyps californianus*), individuals can be recognized by their coloration, missing feathers or state of molt.

Shed feathers can also be used to identify individuals. In Eurasian Sparrowhawks, for example, the patterns of light and dark on the flight feathers are unique to individuals and persist from molt to molt. Female Sparrowhawks start to molt these flight feathers during incubation, and systematic collection and retention of shed feathers found around nesting territories can indicate changes of occupant from year to year.

All raptors, and indeed all animals, carry a unique biological marker that can be used for

identification: the DNA within the nucleus of their cells. DNA "finger-printing" is in its infancy, but it has already been employed to investigate the parentage of raptor nestlings. The DNA is extracted from small samples of blood, which can be taken from adults or nestlings without causing any harm. The DNA is chemically split and labeled, and the patterns of the separated DNA fragments are compared between individuals. This technique may have useful applications in measuring the frequency of cuckoldry in wild raptors, but a more practical use is in law enforcement. Biologists can now tell for certain if captive raptors were really bred from particular parents, or whether their owners stole young illegally from the wild.

▼▲ The matchstick thin leg of a Eurasian Sparrowhawk (above left) is fitted with a numbered band which identifies it if found later. Most raptors are banded as nestlings, but some are trapped as free-flying birds. Binoculars confirm the presence of a band, but to read its band number the immature Peregrine Falcon at right must be trapped.

▼ A young Bald Eagle, fitted with a lightweight harness to which a radio-transmitter is attached, will be tracked to determine its movements. Such birds have been followed by light plane across the United States.

RADIO-TRACKING RAPTORS

A technique that has revolutionized the study of raptors and other animals is radio-tracking, which allows even secretive and wide-ranging species to be followed day-by-day in the field. In raptors, it has been used to efficiently record dispersion, habitat selection, feeding behavior and movements during migration or when dispersing from the nest.

Radio-transmitters are small electronic packages that emit a signal of a particular frequency. This frequency can be varied slightly between transmitters, so several birds can be tracked simultaneously without confusion. The

PHOTOGRAPHING RAPTORS

PETER STEYN

Birds of prey are among the most fascinating of all photographic subjects. Not only are they noble in appearance and dashing in their habits, but at close quarters their behavior is of absorbing interest. Many of the leading exponents of raptor photography are also noted authorities on the biology of these magnificent birds. Long patient hours are required to achieve the best pictures, so it would be wasteful to make this considerable investment of time purely for the photographs. Much invaluable information has been gleaned during the course of photography, and one example will suffice. On Mt. Elgon in Uganda, an intrepid German photographer suspended his hide from a rope over a sheer cliff to take the first pictures of Taita Falcons (*Falco fasciinucha*) at their nest. In the course of his long watches he also made detailed notes which resulted in the most important information yet published on this rare and little-known species.

Photographic equipment is a matter for personal choice, but inevitably a range of lenses will be required, including a telephoto with a focal length of at least 400 millimeters (16 inches). Unless the subject is particularly confiding it pays dividends to photograph from a distance. A hide, or blind, is essential for photographing raptors at the nest. It should be introduced in careful stages or, in the case of raptors such as eagles that use their nests on a regular basis, it can be built prior to the breeding season. The photographer often needs considerable ingenuity—sometimes the hide can be concealed on a cliff overlooking the nest, or in the same tree, but inevitably certain species will require a pylon hide. A pylon can be improvised using local materials, but many raptor photographers use a lightweight scaffolding which can be transported on a vehicle and assembled at the site. It is vital to ensure that the hide is accepted every time it is added to or moved, and it is advisable to camouflage it with foliage.

A valuable research tool is a cinecamera concealed near a nest and set on a time-lapse mode. The resultant frames can be analyzed, and by using several cameras the researcher is able to monitor a number of nests at the same time. During a study of Verreaux's Eagles (*Aquila verreauxii*) in South Africa one camera revealed that a mongoose had killed and eaten an eaglet—its disappearance would otherwise have remained a mystery.

Many birds of prey can be lured down to bait, to achieve a striking portrait. Others can be photographed in flight with a telephoto lens on their migration routes, for example in Eilat in Israel, a favorite venue for raptorphiles.

W. Perry Conway/Tom Stack & Associates

▲ Among the most popular of all birds and also among the most difficult to photograph, raptors are perhaps most easily caught on film at the nest. Here a young Golden Eagle stands its ground.

While many raptors are confiding at the nest, others are notoriously suspicious. Some harriers and the Bateleur (*Terathopius ecaudatus*) of Africa are examples of extreme wariness and should not be photographed at the nest. In Britain a permit is required to photograph certain rare or sensitive species. The worst crime a photographer can commit is to cause the subject to desert, and this also brings the art of bird photography into disrepute. If there is any doubt about a subject's well-being then it should not be photographed.

Michael Freeman/Bruce Coleman Ltd

package consists of the transmitter itself, an antenna and a battery. Raptors can carry up to 4 percent of their body weight without discomfort. This sets an upper limit on the battery size and hence on the power and life of the transmitter. Large eagles can accommodate packages weighing 200 grams (7 ounces) with a range of over 20 kilometers (12 miles) and a life of about two years. Transmitters suitable for small accipiters or falcons have a maximum range of about 7 kilometers (4.5 miles) and rarely last more than four to six months.

Transmitters are attached either by a body harness or by sewing into the base of the central tail feathers. Harnesses are used mainly on large raptors, where the transmitter may outlive the life of the tail feathers and would otherwise be lost during molt. Most designs carry a "weak link" that eventually breaks and releases the harness when the battery is exhausted. Tail-mounts are preferred as they are less likely to interfere with flight, and the transmitter can sometimes be recovered when the tail is molted. The package is sewn into the quill of the tail feathers, which have no nerves and hold the transmitter firmly but painlessly.

Tracking is usually done with a portable receiver and a hand-held antenna. The signal is strongest when this receiving antenna is pointed directly at the transmitter, and this allows a tagged bird to be located by moving towards the source or by triangulation from two separate points. Radio-tracking requires some skill because the signal can bounce off hills, buildings or trees, making it difficult to distinguish the true signal from false echos. The signal is also severely attenuated by such obstacles, and the maximum receiving range is possible only if there is a direct

line of sight between the bird and the observer. Selecting high places from which to scan increases the likelihood of locating a signal, and the best (but most expensive) solution is to track a tagged bird from an aircraft or satellite.

STUDIES WITH CAPTIVE RAPTORS

People have long kept raptors for sport, and the scientists have used this accumulated knowledge to breed birds for study and release. Scientific interest in the captive rearing of raptors was largely fueled by the demise of some species and the need to have stock to reintroduce to the wild. Research was initially directed at techniques to increase the output of young, such as artificial insemination and multiple clutching. However, studies now cover a wide range of behavior, physiology as well as toxicology, often on less endangered species such as kestrels.

Another use for captive raptors is in studies of hunting behavior. Falconry-trained Goshawks (*Accipiter gentilis*) have been flown at flocks of pigeons in order to investigate the relationship of flock size to predation. Attacks by trained birds may not always mimic those in the wild, but they are easier to follow, and it would be difficult to study such behavior by other means.

CONCLUSIONS

Raptors offer an exciting but sometimes difficult challenge in trying to understand their behavior and ecology. With few exceptions, most raptors can be investigated without specialized equipment, and anyone willing to devote sufficient time and effort can make a significant contribution to knowledge of these birds.

▲ Licenced falconers now use the modern technology of telemetry to help them keep track of their valuable birds. Falconers' birds are often used to test types and weights of transmitters, and various means of attachment, during their development for use on wild raptors.

HABITATS AND POPULATIONS

IAN NEWTON

Raptors of one sort or another breed on every continent, except Antarctica, and in almost every kind of habitat, from forest to desert, farmland and cities. As in other birds, species numbers are greatest in the tropics, and decline with increasing latitude. Thus, while more than 100 raptor species breed in tropical forest in one part of the world or another, only four occur on the open tundra of the high Arctic.

▼ The particular environment preferred by each raptor, comprising the whole network of fauna, flora, soil and climate to which it is adapted, is known as its habitat. The Himalayan Griffon (*Gyps himalayensis*) is found only in spectacular alpine habitat, from the Himalayas to Mongolia.

Apart from some tropical forest species, most raptors occur in a range of habitats. Some, such as the Eurasian Buzzard (*Buteo buteo*), can thrive equally well in both forest and openland. For many such generalist species the quality of the habitat does not depend on particular vegetation or structural features (apart from a nest site), but rather on the availability of suitable prey. Even

species that are traditionally regarded as forest dwellers, such as the Northern Goshawk (*Accipiter gentilis*), can thrive in sparsely wooded landscapes, provided prey are abundant. Indeed in Europe this Goshawk reaches higher densities in cultivated landscapes with small woodlots, where rabbits, pheasants and other prey are plentiful, than in continuous forest, where prey are scarcer.

The world's 292 raptor species range from very common to very rare. Some of the most widespread species, whose ranges extend over more than one continent, are numbered in millions, whereas the rarest species, which occur only on small oceanic islands, have probably never exceeded more than a few hundred individuals. Other once-common species have become rare as a result of human activity, and now at least four species and two distinct subspecies have populations of less than 100 individuals. The rarest raptor in the world is probably the California Condor (*Gymnogyps californianus*) which, at the time of writing, numbers only 27 individuals, all of them in captivity.

No one has attempted to guess which is the most numerous raptor in the world, but it could well be the Old World Kestrel (*Falco tinnunculus*), which breeds over almost the whole of Eurasia and much of Africa, in any open terrain from hot desert to cold tundra. It accepts a wide variety of nest sites and is often the commonest local raptor. On recorded densities, there could well be 3–4 million pairs in the range as a whole. The more widespread a raptor species, the more difficult it is to count, so not surprisingly the most accurate population estimates refer to rare species, of restricted distribution.

While counts of particular populations are useful in conservation, it is more important to understand what determines the numbers of raptors: why some species are common while others are rare, and why some are common in one area but rare in another. For only if we know what determines the densities of raptors in particular landscapes can we take the steps necessary to conserve them and to increase their numbers, where this is deemed desirable. Almost all our current knowledge is based on studies in Europe, North America, South Africa and Australia, and we know very little about the populations of raptors in tropical regions.

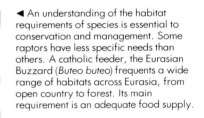

◄ An understanding of the habitat requirements of species is essential to conservation and management. Some raptors have less specific needs than others. A catholic feeder, the Eurasian Buzzard (*Buteo buteo*) frequents a wide range of habitats across Eurasia, from open country to forest. Its main requirement is an adequate food supply.

◄ Also important to conservation and management is a knowledge of density, or population size within a particular area—more particularly, what determines that density. Tolerant of a wide range of conditions, the Old World Kestrel occurs from Eurasia to Africa in semi-open country and woodland, even cities. Arguably, it is the most numerous raptor in the world. Other species have wider distribution, but are not found at such high densities.

W Perry Conway/Tom Stack & Associates

▲ Dry, open country of interior western North America, from southern Canada to western Texas, suits the Ferruginous Hawk (*Buteo regalis*). They breed in trees or on rock outcrops overlooking undisturbed plains, high deserts, sage grass and badlands. By winter, these chicks will have dispersed somewhat eastward, southward and westward to milder habitats. They will join the non-breeding segment of the population awaiting the maturity and opportunity necessary to move into the breeding population.

BREEDERS AND NON-BREEDERS

In the breeding season any raptor population consists of breeders and non-breeders. In most species, the breeders are paired and territorial, defending their nesting places against others of their kind. Once a number of breeding pairs have settled in an area, and occupied it to the full, their territorial behavior prevents additional birds from settling, and hence limits the local breeding density. Such breeding pairs may be present on their territories every year, but not all pairs necessarily nest every year.

The non-breeders consist of immatures, which are too young to breed, and adults unable to obtain breeding territories. Such non-breeders are unpaired; they live unobtrusively within the territories of breeders, or more usually in places not occupied by breeding pairs; in gaps beween breeding territories, in areas lacking nest sites, or

even in separate geographical regions from breeders. In many migrant species, the immatures may remain in the "wintering range" for a full year, while the adults move on to breeding areas.

As breeding pairs are tied to a fixed nest site for a large part of the year, they are easier to find and count than are the non-breeders. Indeed most population studies of raptors have been concerned only with the breeders, and have ignored the non-breeders. Thus, while we know a great deal about the breeding densities of raptors, and how they vary from place to place and from year to year, we know very little about the non-breeders. In some raptor species, which can breed in their first year of life, the non-breeders may form a small fraction of the total population, but in some larger species, which do not breed until they are several years old, the non-breeders may far outnumber the breeders.

NESTING PLACES

Within the habitats they occupy, the breeders in any raptor population require a nest site and a food supply. Most birds of prey choose for their nests special places, which offer some security from mammalian predators. Such places may be cliffs, isolated trees, groves of trees, or patches of forest or ground cover, depending on the species. Peregrines (*Falco peregrinus*) use cliffs, Northern Goshawks use woods, Marsh Harriers (*Circus aeruginosus*) use reedbeds, and so on. Such features are important because, in any landscape, they form the basis of distribution for any breeding population. The locations of other pairs are also important, because in solitary species the pairs tend to space themselves out, while in colonial ones they clump together. Raptor nesting places are often used over long periods of years. Particular cliffs are known to have been used by successive pairs of Golden Eagles (*Aquila chrysaetos*), or of White-tailed Eagles (*Aquila haliaeetus*), Peregrines or Gyrfalcons (*Falco rusticolus*) for periods of 100 years or more. Among 49 Peregrine cliffs recorded by British falconers between the sixteenth and nineteenth centuries, at least 42 are still in use today. Many cliffs may have had continued occupancy for centuries, long before there were ornithologists to record it. In trees, too, certain eagle nests have been used for longer than a man's lifetime and, added to year after year, have often reached enormous size. One historic Bald Eagle (*Haliaeetus leucocephalus*) nest in America spanned 8 square meters (86 square feet) on top and contained "two waggon-loads" of material, while another was 3 meters (9.8 feet) across and 5 meters (16.4 feet) high. Such nests sometimes become so heavy from the continued addition of material over the years that the supporting branch snaps and the birds are forced to start anew. Certain patches of forest (though not the same nest) have been used for long periods by other species, and even patches of ground cover were used by Hen Harriers (*Circus cyaneus*) for more than 50 years. In general, of course, sites on rock must be more permanent than those in trees, and sites in trees more permanent than those in ground cover.

Several authors have felt that the continued use of particular nesting places depended on each bird attracting a new partner to the same site, whenever it lost a mate. This may be so to some extent, but even where both occupants were shot every year, as in parts of Europe, places still remained in use. This may be explained by the superiority of such places over local alternatives, together with the need for any incoming birds to fit within a pre-existing territorial framework. The tendency of young birds to return to breed in the general area where they were born helps to ensure a continuing supply of new recruits to fill the gaps.

David A. Ponton

◀ The Northern Goshawk (*Accipiter gentilis*) nests in woodland and forest in North America and Eurasia. Certain patches of forest may be used by generations of Goshawks, not always building in the same tree, but preferring that local area because of desirable features, such as a particular forest structure, tree type or aspect.

Raptors fly varying distances from their nest to hunt, the area covered forming the "home range". They do not normally hunt all parts of their home range equally but concentrate where prey are most easily caught. In extreme cases, some pairs may hunt in several widely separated localities, using the intervening areas simply as travel corridors. The sizes of home ranges are thus determined by the overall availability of prey and by the distances between separate hunting areas. Some falcons have been recorded flying more than 20 kilometers (12.4 miles) from their nests for food, but such long-distance commuting is probably inefficient.

▼ Some nests sites are so favored and stable that the additions of a series of occupants over many years results in a massive structure. Osprey nests can be 1 meter (3 feet) or more across and 2 meters high; the sturdier the nest, the greater its ability to withstand storms. Throughout their almost cosmopolitan range, Ospreys always nest near water, and build in open situations, uncluttered for easy landing.

John Shaw/Tom Stack & Associates

Apart from the nesting place, the amount of ground that raptors defend against other pairs seems to depend on what is feasible. Where the birds can get all they need in a small area, they may defend it all, so that the home range becomes a "territory" with well-defined boundaries. But where birds have to range over wide areas to obtain their food, they cannot defend the whole area, and home ranges overlap widely between pairs. In addition, birds often forage even further afield to feed their growing young, so that home ranges may expand during the breeding season.

Mutually exclusive defended home ranges are common in various species of buzzards and eagles, whereas widely overlapping ranges are common in various kites and falcons. The differences are not clear-cut, however, and the same species may have small mutually exclusive home ranges in one area, and large overlapping ones in another, depending on how its food is distributed. Griffon Vultures (*Gyps fulvus*) and other colonial raptors have widely overlapping foraging ranges, but each pair defends a small area around its nest.

Most raptors defend territories only against others of their species, but some also exclude other species with similar ecology. Red-tailed and Red-shouldered Hawks (*Buteo jamaicensis* and *B. lineatus*) hold mutually exclusive feeding territories in North America, as do Common and Rough-legged Buzzards (*B. buteo* and *B. lagopus*) in northern Europe, and Golden and Bonelli's Eagles (*Aquila chrysaetos* and *Hieraaetus fasciatus*) in southern Europe. The species in each pair occupy mainly different regions or habitats, and overlap only in restricted places. Here they eat similar foods, so the advantage in mutually exclusive territories is clear, at least to the larger species which is dominant.

▼ Breeding densities are constrained by limited suitable habitat and also by social factors. Rough-legged Buzzards breed in the arctic tundra of North America and Eurasia and hunt small to medium-sized mammals. Pairs exclude not only other Rough-legs from their breeding territory, but also Common Buzzards, a species with similar ecology.

Ralph & Daphne Keller/Australasian Nature Transparencies

M. & A. Boël/Jacana

THE LIMITATION OF BREEDING DENSITY

Raptor breeding populations are normally regulated or limited in some way, and do not merely fluctuate at random. For many species, this conclusion is based on the following findings:

1. the stability of breeding populations, in both size and distribution, over periods of many years;

2. the existence of "surplus" adults, capable of breeding but attempting to do so only when a territory is made available through the death or removal of a previous occupant;

3. the re-establishment of populations, after their removal by humans, to about the same level as previously; and

4. in areas where nest sites are not restricted, a regular spacing of breeding pairs.

STABILITY OF BREEDING POPULATION

Certain raptors have some of the most stable breeding densities known among birds. This has been shown by long-term studies of Peregrines, Eurasian Sparrowhawks, Eurasian Buzzards, Golden Eagles, Black Eagles, and other observed

over periods of 10–40 years. In all these cases, breeding numbers remained either absolutely constant over the years, or fluctuated by less than 15 percent of the mean over the period concerned. Compared to findings on some other birds, and to what is theoretically possible, this represents a remarkable degree of stability. Other evidence involving shorter periods is available for many other species, and stability is evidently the norm in a wide range of raptors.

Stability of breeding density would be expected only in stable environments and not in habitats that were changing rapidly through vegetation succession or human action. Nor would it be expected in those populations recovering from some adverse human impact which depressed their numbers. Also, as observers tend to work in the better habitats, the stability in population recorded there might not be wholly typical of the same species in poorer habitats. Despite these caveats, however, there can be no doubt that the breeding densities of many raptor species remain remarkably stable compared with those of other birds.

Dennis Green/Bruce Coleman Ltd

▲ In southeast Asia Brahminy Kites (*Haliastur indus*) are commensal with people and are most numerous around cities and in rice fields, but in the Australian part of their range they prefer more undisturbed habitats, coastal forests and mangroves. Throughout their range from India to southern China and south to Australia, they are found near coasts or rivers.

◄ A secure nest site will last for centuries. Such sites allow stability of numbers in the breeding population. Golden Eagles and certain other raptors have breeding populations among the most unchanging of all birds. In four areas of Scotland, clumps of Golden Eagle pairs, numbering 16, 13, 12 and 8, varied by only one more or one less over ten years.

▲▶ Short wings and long tail enable the Eurasian Sparrowhawk to make short, agile dashes after small birds among the trees and shrubs of its country habitat. It breeds in cooler-climate woodlands across Eurasia, in northern Africa and the Middle East, and favors conifers for nests but also uses deciduous trees. In winter, some reach India and further into Africa.

SURPLUS BIRDS

In some populations, non-breeding, non-territorial adults were seen near nest sites, occasionally fighting with breeders, presumably in an attempt to take over the nest site. But the main evidence for the existence of surplus birds, which breed only when a place becomes available, is that lost mates are sometimes replaced in the same season by other birds, which then breed themselves. Scottish gamekeeper Dougal Macintyre (1960) wrote that, whenever a female Peregrine was shot from the eyrie, the male generally re-mated within 24 hours. He several times saw a bereaved male return with a new mate, and knew one male to acquire four adult mates in quick succession. Only once in many years of Peregrine shooting was the new female not in adult plumage. Macintyre suggested that this indicated the existence of a considerable reserve of non-breeding adults, as he found no indication that the new mates had moved in from neighboring eyries. Many other instances of swift replacement have been recorded in other Peregrine populations, in Europe, North America and Australia, and the phenomenon is also widespread in other raptors. In the ornithological literature there are records for more than 40 raptor species of lost mates being replaced the same season, from small falcons to large vultures. Both sexes are represented in these records, but most refer to females. This may be because females, which spend more time at the nest, are easier to shoot than males, or it may be because there are more surplus females than males available.

All these observations, incidentally, were made in former times when the shooting of raptors was commonplace. In recent years, however, anxious to learn more about this phenomenon, biologists have conducted properly controlled experiments, removing individual raptors from their territories and then checking to see what happens. In three species studied—the Old World Kestrel, the American Kestrel (*Falco sparverius*) and the Eurasian Sparrowhawk (*Accipiter nisus*)—replacement of removed individuals of both sexes occurred, sometimes within days. In each case, birds on neighboring territories were marked, so it could be shown that replacements had not simply moved from other sites nearby. The implication was that the areas concerned could support only a certain number of breeding pairs and that the territorial behavior of these established birds kept others out.

David Redfern/Planet Earth Pictures

Jack & Lindsay Cupper/Auscape International

▲◀ The Peregrine Falcon is found on all continents, except Antarctica, and many large islands. Approximately ten races, differing slightly in size and plumage, particularly the shape of the black helmet and the shade of body color, span the globe. The Australian Peregrine pictured has a full helmet typical of that subspecies. Australian Falcons are sedentary, but those from the far northern hemisphere are highly migratory, spending the non-breeding season in South America or Africa. With long, narrow wings and great speed it is well adapted to an expanse of open country and woodland, often near cliffs. One subspecies, the pale *Falco peregrinus tundrius*, breeds on cliffs in the treeless tundra of North America and Greenland, ranging far out over the tundra in search of Ptarmigan, shorebirds and songbirds. The Peregrine can be quite common, but has suffered local extinctions due mainly to pesticides.

RE-ESTABLISHMENT OF POPULATIONS

In Britain, instances are known of raptor populations over large areas being removed or depleted by human action, and then recovering to about the same level as previously, with pairs in the same places. On parts of the south coast of England, Peregrines were deliberately shot out during the 1939–45 war, because they attacked the pigeons used to carry military messages. After the war, the birds recolonized some areas to their former level within a few years, but in other areas the birds were still moving back when their numbers were again reduced by pesticide poisoning, as in the rest of Britain. Since then, the use of the offending chemicals has been reduced, and in at least five regions Peregrines have recovered to the same level as previously. Not only did the newcomers use the same nesting cliffs as their predecessors, but also in many cases the same nest ledges. Likewise, in many parts of Britain the Eurasian Sparrowhawk was also reduced by pesticide poisoning, but has since reoccupied former nesting places, so that the latest densities are about the same as those found 15–30 years earlier. Another striking example referred to the Merlins occupying two adjacent territories in

northern England. These birds were shot every year for 19 years, and produced not a single young, yet every year without fail two new pairs settled in the same places. On one place the birds used the same heather patch for all 19 years and in the other for the first 12 years until it was destroyed by fire. All this implies some constancy in the carrying capacity of the environment over the years, with consistent limitations on raptor breeding numbers. Again this would be expected only in landscapes that remained reasonably stable over the years, not in those altered by human action.

REGULAR SPACING OF TERRITORIAL PAIRS

In continuously suitable habitat, the nests of different pairs of a species are often separated from one another by roughly equal distances. This has been noted in many species, including various falcons, hawks, buzzards and eagles, and is evidently widespread among solitary nesting raptors. Such regular spacing is consistent with the idea of density limitation by territorial behavior. It would not, of course, be expected where nest sites were sparse and irregular in distribution, so restricting the location of breeding pairs.

Peter Steyn

▲▶ The medium-sized, slim-bodied African Hawk Eagle (*Hieraaetus spilogaster*) can be found scattered through woodland, acacia scrub, savanna, thornbush and forest habitats south of the Sahara. Flat-topped acacia dot the savanna, typical breeding habitat if there are some larger trees. Swift and powerful, the eagle takes medium-sized mammals and birds from the open ground between the trees, and can soar easily on broad wings in search of prey.

Nigel Dennis/NHPA

Taken together, these four arguments provide strong circumstantial evidence that breeding density is limited, that the limitation is through competition for breeding space (or territories), and that stability of breeding density is helped by the existence of surplus birds, encouraged to breed only when a territory becomes vacant but otherwise excluded by the birds in occupation. This does not necessarily mean that surplus birds are available at all times in all populations; nor does it imply that all non-breeders are capable of breeding that year if a place is available to them.

In many studies of fairly stable populations, a proportion of the territories remained vacant in any one year, despite the proven existence of surplus birds. In Britain the usual occupancy of Peregrine territories pre-1939 was about 85 percent and in some buzzard territories it was 77–83 percent. But territories vary in quality, in the opportunity they offer for survival and successful breeding, and possibly some poor territories are suitable for occupation only in certain years, or only by certain birds.

BREEDING DENSITY IN RELATION TO FOOD SUPPLIES

In the limitation of raptor breeding densities, within the habitats that are occupied, two resources seem of importance—food supply and nest sites. We can consider first the evidence for a link between breeding density and food supply in areas where nest sites are freely available.

BODY-SIZE AND BREEDING DENSITY

Comparing different species of raptors, there is a general correlation between body size, home range size and breeding density. In general, large species breed at lower density, with larger ranges, than do small species. The African Martial Eagle, one of the largest and most powerful raptors in the world, breeds at what must be some of the lowest natural densities for any bird: one pair per 125 square kilometers (48 square miles) in the Embu District of Kenya, one pair per 182 square kilometers (70 square miles) in Kruger Park in South Africa, and one pair per 300 square

Ardea London

A. J. Deane/Bruce Coleman Ltd

▲◄ The small, graceful form of a Black-shouldered Kite (*Elanus caeruleus*) can be seen hovering, or perched waiting, in most open savannas and grasslands of tropical and subtropical latitudes, from Spain to southern China, Indonesia to New Guinea. In Australia it is replaced by a very similar species, the Black-winged Kite (*Elanus notatus*), and a nocturnal species the Letter-winged Kite (*E. scriptus*). All prefer to hunt over long grass and are at times nomadic, moving to areas where their rodent food is seasonally abundant. In Africa (pictured), suitable habitat is plentiful.

kilometers (116 square miles) in Tsavo Park in Kenya. In other suitable areas, density is even lower, as nests may be separated by 30–40 kilometers (18–25 miles). This eagle lives mainly on game birds and mammals up to several kilograms in weight. Various other eagle species usually breed at densities of one pair per 30–200 square kilometers (11–77 square miles), various hawks at densities of one pair per 1–8 square kilometers (0.4–3 square miles), and small falcons and kites at one pair per 1–3 square kilometers (0.4–1.2 square miles). The overall trend presumably holds because larger raptors generally eat larger prey species, and large prey species live and breed less abundantly than small prey species. So, in each case, range size may be adjusted to food supply.

REGIONAL VARIATIONS IN BREEDING DENSITY

In some species regional variations in breeding density are associated with regional variations in prey supplies. In Eurasian Sparrowhawks, breeding densities in the woods of 12 different regions of Britain varied in relation to the local densities of prey birds, with an average of 0.6 kilometer (0.4 mile) between pairs in good prey areas and 2.2 kilometers (1.4 miles) between pairs in poor prey areas. Thus hawks nested closer together, at higher densities, in areas where their prey were most numerous. The woods in all these areas were of roughly similar structure, and the differences in prey densities were associated with variation in elevation and soil type. Similarly, the densities of kestrels in different areas and in different years were closely correlated with the densities of Field Voles (*Microtus agrestis*), which formed the main prey.

For other species, unlike the studies above, the prey have not been counted, but there is an obvious link between raptor density and prey abundance. Thus Eurasian Buzzard breeding densities in Britain are generally highest in areas where the main prey species, the Rabbit (*Oryctolagus cuniculus*), is most numerous. All the areas examined were fully occupied by territorial Buzzards, yet pair densities were up to 16 times greater in the best area than in the worst. Furthermore, in nine areas on the European continent, Buzzard densities were generally higher

Dennis Green/Bruce Coleman Ltd

John Shaw/Bruce Coleman Ltd

▲▶ Feeding its brood in a ground nest among the heather, the Northern Harrier (*Circus cyaneus*) occurs in similar habitats from the subarctic to California, Portugal and northern China. The population winters in kinder climates as far south as Central America, northern Africa and tropical Asia. Quite large, and low and slow flying, it can be seen quartering moorland, marsh and prairie. Low vegetation in open terrain suits the harrier well; it has little use for trees.

in deciduous woods on rich humus soil than in pinewoods on poor sandy soil, and higher in lowlands than in mountains. The differences were again correlated with the numbers of prey, which in these continental areas were mainly rodents.

Likewise in British Peregrines, density is broadly related to land productivity and food supply, with the highest breeding densities (2–3 kilometers or 1–2 miles between pairs) along coasts rich in seabirds, lower densities (5–6 kilometers or 3–4 miles between pairs) in hill areas of relatively high fertility or near to fertile valleys, and even lower densities (7–10 kilometers or 4–6 miles between pairs) in hill areas of low fertility or far from fertile valleys. Such variations in density would almost certainly correlate with prey abundance, though this has not been measured. Even higher Peregrine densities than in Britain were recorded on the Canadian Queen Charlotte Islands (1–2 kilometers or 0.6–1 mile between pairs), again linked with massive concentrations of seabirds, and even lower ones (11–15 kilometers or 7–9 miles between pairs) in parts of inland Alaska and elsewhere.

Unusually high densities of raptors are invariably associated with an unusual abundance of food. In natural situations, examples include the abundance of Peregrines around large seabird colonies and of Ospreys (*Pandion haliaetus*) around fisheries. But even greater concentrations of raptors occur in some African and Asian cities, where human activity provides the food. The city of Delhi, in India, covers 150 square kilometers (58 square miles), and in 1967 held an estimated 2,900 raptor pairs, a density of more than 19 pairs per square kilometer (0.4 square mile). These were mainly scavenging species, such as Black Kites (*Milvus migrans*) (15 pairs per square kilometer) and White-backed Vultures (*Gyps bengalensis*) (4 pairs per square kilometer), but also included some other species. This high density was associated primarily with a huge amount of food within the city (mainly garbage and animal carcasses), but also with an abundance of nesting sites, and an unusual tolerance by the human population.

In all these various raptors, breeding density was broadly related to food supply, and unusual concentrations were associated with unusual food abundances. Only in very few species, however, has both breeding density and food supply actually been measured in several different areas. The

▼ ◄ Open tundra above the treeline of undisturbed subarctic and arctic North America and Eurasia are the breeding grounds of the Rough-legged Hawk. During the non-breeding season, the entire population moves south to the

temperate farmlands of central USA and central Europe. It strongly prefers open country with low vegetation.

THE MERLINS OF SASKATOON

LYNN W. OLIPHANT

With ever-increasing urban habitat, it is not surprising that some raptors have adapted to this new niche. One of the most remarkable examples has occurred in the cities and towns of the Canadian prairies. The city of Saskatoon, Saskatchewan, with a human population of 185,000 had 25 nesting pairs of Merlins (*Falco columbarius*) in 1988. Merlins began breeding regularly in Saskatoon by the early 1970s and have rapidly expanded to form the densest breeding population of this species known in the world, with pairs sometimes nesting within a few hundred meters of one another. The ecological conditions that have allowed this invasion of the urban habitat appear to be simple. The planting of ornamental spruce trees early in the history of Saskatoon eventually resulted in trees large enough to attract nesting crows and magpies. These birds provided nest-sites for the Merlins, which like other falcons, do not build their own nests. The spruce trees chosen by the Merlins are in the older sections of town, in cemeteries, schoolyards and even next to people's homes. One year, four young Merlins fledged from a nest in Saskatoon's Exhibition Grounds during the annual carnival.

The other major requirement for the Merlins, besides a nest site, is an abundance of small birds to feed on. This prey base was established many years earlier with the introduction of the House Sparrow into North America. Approximately three-quarters of the diet of the Merlins in Saskatoon is made up of House Sparrows with an estimated 50,000 being eaten each year. Productivity of the Merlin population is excellent, averaging more than four young per successful pair. By late summer, after the young have fledged, there are 150 or more Merlins in the city. By fall, many of these birds have migrated, but over the past 20 years an increasing number of birds have remained for the winter. Many now regularly brave temperatures ranging below −40°C. Besides the House Sparrows, there are large flocks of Bohemian Waxwings that are attracted to the city in winter to feed on the crabapples and rowan berries, providing another source of prey for the Merlins. The urban environment— ornamental spruce and fruit trees, nesting crows and magpies and the sparrows—has provided an optimal habitat for the Merlin which is now rapidly colonizing other cities on the Canadian prairies.

implication from such natural variation is that raptors respond to the food situation, and that solitary species space themselves more widely, in larger territories, where food is sparse. It used to be argued whether raptor breeding densities were limited by food supply or by territorial behavior. In fact, both factors are involved, the food supply providing the underlying limiting factor, and territorialism being the behavioral mechanism that brings about the limitation, as the birds simply adjust their spacing to the resources available locally. So one line of evidence that breeding density is limited in relation to food supply comes from the long-term stability of populations, but at different densities in different regions.

It is probably not just the standing crop of prey that is important in influencing raptor numbers, but also its renewal rate. Any prey species that produces a succession of large broods through the year can support more predators than a prey species that lives at similar density but produces only one small brood each year. The crucial figure is the number of prey that can be repeatedly removed from an area without causing long-term depletion, and this figure is likely to be higher in more productive environments, and in small fast-breeding prey species than in large slow-breeding ones. It follows that, in comparing areas, one would not necessarily expect a linear relationship between prey numbers and raptor numbers.

ANNUAL VARIATIONS IN BREEDING DENSITY

For other species, the idea that breeding density is adjusted in relation to food supply comes, not from long-term stability in density, but from annual fluctuations in density, which parallel changes in food. Most such species in the regions concerned have restricted diets based on cyclic prey: creatures that fluctuate in abundance, with peaks and troughs at regular intervals. Two main cycles are recognized: (1) an approximately four-year cycle of small rodents on northern tundras and temperate grasslands; and (2) an

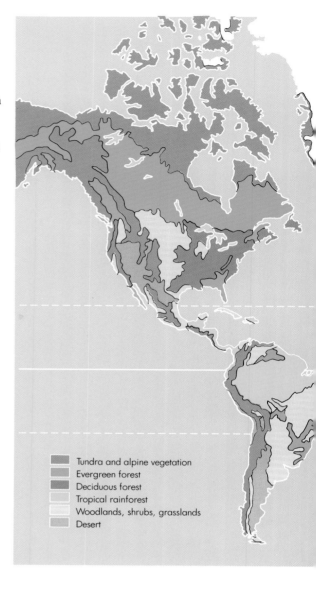

Tundra and alpine vegetation
Evergreen forest
Deciduous forest
Tropical rainforest
Woodlands, shrubs, grasslands
Desert

approximately 10-year cycle of Snowshoe Hares (*Lepus americanus*) in the boreal forests of North America. Some game birds are also cyclic, but whereas in Europe they follow the four-year rodent cycle, with peaks in the same years , in North America they follow the 10-year hare cycle. Black-tailed Jackrabbits (*Lepus californicus*) may also fluctuate on a 10-year pattern in the dry grasslands of the western United States, but the fluctuations are poorly documented. The populations of these various animals do not reach a peak simultaneously over their whole range, but the peak may be synchronized over tens or many thousands of square kilometers.

The main raptor species involved in these fluctuations are listed below; all have been found to nest at greater density, and most prolifically, in years when their food is most plentiful.

Rodent feeders: Old World Kestrel, Eurasian Buzzard, Rough-legged Buzzard and Northern Harrier in parts of Europe; Marsh Hawk and Rough-legged Buzzard in North America; Black-shouldered Kite in southern Africa.

▼ Smaller species of raptor tend to defend smaller nesting territories (inner oval) and forage over a more restricted area (outer oval) than do larger species. Hence, small raptors often occur at higher densities than do larger raptors. The illustrations are stylized. Territory shape, governed by the topography around the nest site, is doubtfully symmetrical, and the foraging range is probably even more variable and often not exclusive of that of the neighbours. In differents parts of their distribution, species may hold different-sized territories.

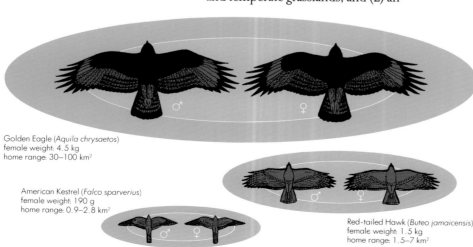

Golden Eagle (*Aquila chrysaetos*)
female weight: 4.5 kg
home range: 30–100 km²

American Kestrel (*Falco sparverius*)
female weight: 190 g
home range: 0.9–2.8 km²

Red-tailed Hawk (*Buteo jamaicensis*)
female weight: 1.5 kg
home range: 1.5–7 km²

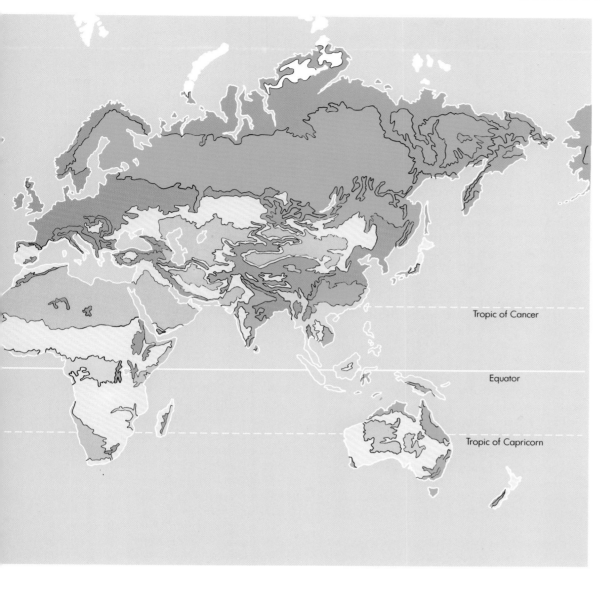

◄ The habitat requirements of raptors tend to be quite broad, and structural features of the habitat, rather than plant types, are usually most important. Thus raptor habitats can be categorized into a few, easily identified structural types of vegetation. In general, wherever a habitat type is found it supports a raptor community made up of similar species.

Hare or game-bird feeders: Ferruginous Hawk, Goshawk and Gyrfalcon.

The increase in the density of rodent eaters from one year to the next is often so great that it cannot be due merely to the high survival of adults and young from the previous year, but must be due partly to immigration. Later it is helped by good breeding, whereas decline is brought about by a combination of poor breeding, emigration and starvation. Through the worst conditions, birds may remain only in the best habitats, often at reduced density with enlarged home ranges, and vacate the poor habitats completely. Moreover, some species, such as the Goshawk, fluctuate in density where they feed on cyclic prey, but remain fairly stable in density where their food supply is more stable (often through being more varied). Such regional variation within a species provides further circumstantial evidence for a link between breeding density and food supply.

In general, three steps in the response of raptors to annual fluctuations in prey numbers can be recognized. Populations that are subject to the most marked prey cycles show big local fluctuations in both densities and breeding success (e.g. Northern Goshawks in boreal regions); those subject to less marked prey cycles show fairly stable densities but big fluctuations in breeding success (e.g. Eurasian Buzzards in temperate regions); while those with stable prey supply show stable densities and fairly stable breeding success (e.g. Peregrines in temperate regions). Much depends on how broad the diet is, and whether alternative prey are available when favored prey are scarce. The more varied the diet, the less the chance of all food species being scarce at the same time.

Prey abundance is not always a good measure of food supply, when other factors influence availability. In some small raptors, such as the Old World Kestrel, year-to-year changes in resident breeding populations have been linked with winter weather, which influences the availability of mice and voles. Marked decline in Kestrel numbers, associated with heavy mortality, occurs in years with prolonged snow cover, when rodents remain hidden for long periods. Larger raptors, which can withstand longer periods on reduced rations, seem to be much less affected by hard winters.

LONG-TERM CHANGES

Long-term changes in raptor densities are often associated with human activities. The development of natural or semi-natural areas for stock-raising or agriculture almost always leads to a drop in the numbers of prey and in turn in the numbers of raptors. The truth of this view is evident from the case histories of particular areas, and also from a comparison of natural areas with cultivated ones, a difference readily apparent, but seldom documented.

Conversely, the artificial inflation of food supplies sometimes leads to high raptor breeding densities, as in the city scavengers discussed above, for it is inconceivable that these birds existed in such numbers in the original habitat.

To take specific instances of change, in parts of Britain Buzzard breeding densities dropped in one or two years, following the sudden and almost total elimination of rabbits (the main prey) by the viral disease, myxomatosis. In one area the territorial Buzzards dropped from 21 to 14 pairs between one breeding season and the next, and to 12 pairs by the following season. Twenty years later, neither rabbits nor Buzzards had recovered to their former numbers. Similarly, the Peregrine population of Langara Island off western Canada dropped from about 20 to six pairs, following a crash in the seabird prey.

Other species have occasionally colonized or increased in areas where extra food was provided by humans. Lake Naivasha, in Kenya, originally contained no fish suitable for Fish Eagles (*Haliaeetus vocifer*), but the lake was stocked artificially, and by 1968 it held more than 56 breeding eagle pairs. The Fish Eagle has also greatly increased its range and numbers in southern Africa, following the widespread construction of dams and the resulting expansion of fish populations. All these various instances may seem unsurprising, yet together they form a strong body of evidence for the dependence of raptor breeding density on prey populations.

BREEDING DENSITY IN RELATION TO NEST SITES

Raptors are among the few groups of birds whose numbers and nest success are in some regions clearly limited by the availability of nesting places. To pick an obvious example, most specialist cliff-nesters are restricted geographically to breeding in areas with cliffs. Within such areas their breeding density may be limited by the number of cliffs with suitable nest ledges, and their breeding success by the accessibility of those ledges to predators. Other raptors may be limited in open landscapes by

shortage of trees, and even in woodlands, nest sites may be fewer than they at first appear. In a large area of mature forest in Finland, less than one in a thousand trees was judged by a biologist to be suitable for nests of White-tailed Eagles, while in younger forests, suitable open-crowned trees were lacking altogether. The fact that most raptors are territorial, defending a large area around their nests, accentuates the shortage, because it normally means that any other suitable sites nearby are banned to other pairs. Thus a cliff with many suitable ledges will hold no more than one pair of Peregrines, while a clump of trees will support no more eagle pairs than a single tree.

In some districts, therefore, raptor breeding densities are held below the level that food supply would support by a shortage of appropriately spaced nest sites. The evidence is of two kinds: (1) breeding raptors are scarce or absent in areas where nesting sites are scarce or absent, but which otherwise appear suitable (non-breeders may live in such areas); and (2) the provision of artificial nest sites is sometimes followed by an increase in breeding density. Kestrel numbers increased in one year from a few pairs to more than 100 pairs when nesting boxes were provided in a Dutch polder area with few natural sites. Similar results were obtained with other populations of Old World Kestrels, and also with American Kestrels. An increase in Prairie Falcon (*Falco mexicanus*) pairs from seven to 11 followed the digging of suitable holes in riverine earth banks, and increases in Osprey pairs in several areas followed the erection of nest platforms. Likewise, nesting on buildings and quarries has allowed Peregrines and others to occupy areas devoid of natural cliffs.

Sometimes the provision of nest sites has facilitated an extension of breeding range, as exemplified by the Mississippi Kite (*Ictinia mississippiensis*) and other species, which nest in tree plantations on North American grasslands. Likewise in South Africa, Greater Kestrels (*F. rupicoloides*) and Lanner Falcons (*F. biarmicus*) have spread by using pylons, as have Black Sparrowhawks (*Accipiter melanoleucus*) by using exotic eucalypt or poplar plantations. In none of these species is it likely that prey populations increased, and the spread could be attributed entirely to the provison of nesting places. Conversely, the destruction of nesting sites has sometimes led to reductions in breeding density: in Peregrines when cliffs were destroyed by quarrying; and in certain eagles when large free-standing trees were felled.

Where nesting trees or cliffs are scarce, the presence of one species may influence the numbers and distribution of another. Golden Eagles take precedence over Peregrines at cliffs and Peregrines over Kestrels. When four eagle pairs occupied an area, two Peregrine pairs immediately moved to alternative crags, and two other pairs

▶ In some areas, a scarcity of nest sites, rather than food, prevents a greater number of pairs from breeding. When extra nests are provided they are quickly occupied and the density of the breeding population increased. Quality as well as quantity is important; prime nest sites can be used in all weathers and endure for centuries. The build-up of white excreta shows that Australian Kestrels have used this cliff site in a Northern Territory gorge for years.

Lee Lyon/Bruce Coleman Ltd

▲ An adult African Fish Eagle (*Haliaeetus vocifer*) attacks a younger bird. Breeding pairs of most raptor species exclude other adults and immature birds from their breeding territory. The unpaired birds tend to stay where they are not in competition with breeders and, because they are not tied to a nest site, may move to temporary abundances of food. While breeding pairs are relatively easily counted and studied, a detailed knowledge of the non-breeding section of a population remains elusive.

disappeared altogether. When Peregrines were further reduced by pesticides, Kestrels took over many of their nesting cliffs, only to be displaced when Peregrines returned.

On certain grasslands in western Northern America, nest sites were provided mainly by the trees around abandoned farmsteads. At any one farmstead, only one raptor species was usually found, and the large, early-nesting Great-horned Owl (*Bubo virginianus*) had precedence, followed in order by the Red-tailed Hawk, Swainson's Hawk (*Buteo swainsoni*) and Kestrel. Competition for limited sites thus affected the species to varying extents, but the owls could occupy a site only until the nest collapsed. The site then reverted to one of the two large hawk species, because only they could build a new nest.

In conclusion, to judge from available evidence, the carrying capacity of any habitat for breeding raptors is set by two main resources, food supply and nest sites, and whichever is most restricted can limit breeding density. However, research has given little inkling of how many populations may be up against these limits at any one time. This is because biologists have tended to study fairly dense populations and to avoid sparse or sporadic ones that provide less information. Studied populations tended to be in good habitats and may therefore have been more stable, with greater occupancy of territories, than many unstudied ones. Some such populations are clearly held below the carrying capacity of the habitat by persecution or pesticide use, but others could be

kept down by natural factors, not necessarily acting in the breeding areas. Thus some migrant raptors might be limited in numbers while in winter quarters, so that they could never occupy their breeding habitat fully. To my knowledge, this has not been shown for any raptor (except where pesticides were involved), but is well known for other kinds of birds. Finally, it is worth reiterating that most of our information refers to temperate-zone species, and that we know very little about tropical raptors.

Considering the abundance of various birds and other kinds of animals in many modern cities, and the presence of tall trees and buildings for nest sites, it is not surprising that raptors now breed in cities around the world. The habit seems to have increased in recent decades, perhaps partly because of an increasing acceptance by the human population.

NON-BREEDERS

Unpaired non-breeders live away from nesting territories, and may include some birds too young to breed and others old enough to breed but unable to get a breeding territory. Practically nothing is known of how the numbers of such unpaired birds are limited, or even what proportion of a population they form. In general, they live wherever they can avoid competition and harassment from breeders, and have been found: (1) unobtrusively within the home ranges of established pairs, at least for short periods, as in Golden Eagle; (2) in spaces between the territories of breeding pairs, as in Buzzard, Red-tailed Hawk and Black Eagle; (3) in those areas in the same region that are unsuitable for breeding (often through lack of nest sites), as in Red-shouldered Hawk, Golden Eagle and certain vultures; or (4) mainly in different geographical areas (e.g. "winter quarters") from breeding birds, as in Osprey and Montagu's Harrier (*Circus pygargus*). Moreover, more than one system has been found in the same population.

It depends on food supply whether such non-breeding raptors live solitarily or gregariously. Their numbers have been found to vary between areas and years, and to fluctuate considerably while breeding density remained unchanged. On Lake Naivasha in Kenya, adult Fish Eagles increased by 40 percent and immatures by 11 percent between 1968 and 1971, but breeding numbers remained constant at 56 pairs. Because they are not tied to a nest, non-breeders have greater freedom of movement than breeders, and more often exploit temporary abundances of food, as is especially true of various kites and eagles. Where not restricted by food or habitat, their numbers are presumably set at the balance between inputs to the non-breeding sector (mainly through breeding) and losses (mainly mortality and recruitment to the breeding sector).

WINTER DENSITIES

Some raptors stay on their breeding sites all year, but others spread over a wider area after breeding, or migrate to a completely different area. These different strategies seem to represent progressive adjustments to decreasing availability of prey in winter. Outside the breeding season, nest sites are less important, so in theory the birds have greater freedom to move around, and can exploit temporary food sources in a way not possible while breeding. Some northern raptors, which winter in Africa, may spend the whole period between breeding seasons on the move, following rain belts, and exploiting temporary abundances of termites, locusts and other prey. At this season, therefore, food can take over as the all-important limiting factor.

Few studies have been made of raptors which remain in the same area all winter but these imply that food supply has a major influence on density. For example, in one detailed study, the raptor population in an area of Michigan was compared in two different years, one with a high mouse population and the other with a low one. In the good mouse year, 96 raptors of seven species were present in the area, but in the poor year only 27 individuals of five species were counted. In the first year the raptors had smaller home ranges than in the second year, and the wintering population contained more juveniles.

Other studies, in which particular species were counted over longer periods, came to similar conclusions, with the local density of birds varying from winter to winter, in tune with the prey supply. Such findings were apparent in Prairie Falcons, which fed on larks on the American grasslands, and in European and American Kestrels, which fed mainly on small rodents. Moreover, in a study of Golden Eagles over nine years in Norway, more birds stayed in the study area, and for longer periods, in years when carcasses of domestic animals were provided as food, than in years when no extra food was given.

Similar relationships have been found in tropical regions. In one study, spanning a wide range of areas, the numbers of insectivorous raptors (of 11 species) in particular areas correlated with the numbers of grasshoppers, the main prey. In another study, in Tsavo National Park in Kenya, 12 raptor species were resident through the year, nine others were migrants from elsewhere in Africa, and 11 were migrants from Europe and Asia. The resident species were of similar abundance in both years, but most of the migrants reached much the greatest numbers in the year of heaviest rainfall, when all kinds of prey were more plentiful. The totals reached about 106 migrants per 100 kilometers (60 miles) of transect in the wet year compared with about 51 in the dry, the difference being marked among Bateleurs (*Terathopius ecaudatus*), Wahlberg's Eagles (*Hieraaetus wahlbergi*) and Steppe Eagles (*Aquila rapax*). Hence, the main findings of these tropical studies were similar to those of the temperate zone, with annual differences in raptor numbers in particular localities associated with annual differences in food supply. From the evidence available, therefore, it seems that, within the habitats that particular raptors occupy, food supply is a major factor influencing their densities at all times of year. This contrasts with the situation in some other animals, in which predation or disease may limit their numbers.

▼ Food availability appears to govern winter densities and choice of habitat. Many species from the far northern hemisphere desert their breeding grounds when prey becomes seasonally scarce, and migrate to where food is abundant. In the wintering grounds they join the resident species to increase the total raptor population. Some populations of Old World Kestrel are migratory, others only partially so. Winter counts of Kestrels in Britain were found to be directly related to small mammal numbers. Fewer voles meant fewer Kestrels.

Michael Leach/Oxford Scientific Films

TROPICAL FOREST RAPTORS

JEAN-MARC THIOLLAY

The rainforest is the dominant type of forest among the tropical forests, which also include montane, cloud, swamp, mangrove, monsoon or semi-deciduous types. Primary rainforests are typically tall (over 40 meters (130 feet) high), evergreen, with a closed canopy but a more open understory, a heavy rainfall (over 2 meters(6.5 feet) annually), a short dry season, a high structural complexity and species richness. They originally covered about 11 million square kilometers (over 4 million square miles) of which 19 percent were in Africa, 27 percent in Southeast Asia and Australasia and 54 percent in tropical America. They disappear at such an alarming rate that probably less than 10 percent of this area is still intact. Shifting cultivation, large plantations and logging are mainly responsible for this ecological disaster. Lowland rainforests are threatened everywhere—they are the most species-rich forest type and the richest terrestrial ecosystem. One hundred and eleven species of raptors—39 percent of the world's total—live in the rainforests which may now cover only 1 percent of the land surface of our planet. Forty of them are found in continental America, 12 in Africa, 28 in Southeast Asia and 22 in New Guinea (from the Moluccas to the Solomons and northeastern Australia). The species richness is higher in the New World than in the Old World and in both regions increases towards the equator. The Amazonian forest is by far the richest, with up to 27 (French Guiana) and 34 (Peru) breeding species in the same forest area. After colonizing forested oceanic islands, species belonging to genera living in open habitats became highly adapted to life in dense forests (falcons and harriers in the Indian Ocean, buzzards in the Antilles).

The ecology and even the basic biology of most species are very little known. For instance, the nest or eggs of 75 species have never been found or have been described only once or twice. Statements on their diet often rely on a few analyses of stomach content. Such species are usually very secretive, though not shy, and difficult to see in their natural habitat. They are more easily detected in clearings, along forest roads or when they are calling or soaring above the canopy. Radio-tracking, although time-consuming, remains a promising method by which to study them.

Tropical forest raptors are usually sedentary, and long-distance seasonal movements are known only in some populations from the outerparts of the tropics. Individual territory sizes seem to be of the same magnitude as those of similar temperate species, but the distribution of many tropical species appears more patchy at both local and regional scales. Understorey species may exhibit strong morphological and behavioral adaptations: long tail, short rounded wings, large eyes, reluctance to soar above the forest, loud calls or song-like vocalizations, notably at dawn (forest falcons). A surprising proportion of New World species have a very contrasted plumage pattern with much white. There is no satisfactory explanation for this conspicuousness, which is not found in the Old World species where only young birds tend to be lighter than adults. Following a general trend in tropical species, they have a low fecundity, and fledged young have long periods of dependency. At least in equatorial, wet primary forests, many species have clutch sizes of one or two eggs, and large eagles rear at most one young every second year. Some species have evolved unusual diet specializations, such as wasp grubs in the foliage (*Daptrius*), arboreal snails (*Chondrohierax*), caterpillars (*Aviceda*), flying insects (*Ictinia, Elanoides*), and palm fruits (*Gypohierax*). The New World vultures (notably *Cathartes*) have an extraordinary sense of smell enabling them to find carcasses invisible under a 40 meter-high (130 feet) dense forest.

The Red Data Book of the International Council for Bird Preservation lists 64 species of diurnal raptors as threatened, 41 of which are rainforest species. Island forms are the most endangered. The single main threat to their survival is the large-scale deforestation that occurs throughout the tropical world. Few forest species survive when the forest is drastically opened, logged or fragmented. They are usually species associated with edges or natural gaps, and hence rare, in the former primary forest. But then most understorey species suffer heavily or quickly disappear. Because of the low density and patchy distribution of many of them, such species can only be preserved within very large forest reserves where disturbance and habitat degradation are kept at a minimum.

Forests managed for sylviculture, traditional agriculture or bioforestry are often a poor substitute to natural forests and usually harbor a small subset of the original avifauna. The human hunting pressure (direct persecution of raptors and reduction of prey species) always increases with forest opening and is an additional and particularly widespread threat, often serious for large species.

▼ The Palmnut Vulture (*Gypohierax angolensis*) is found in the forests, mangroves and wetter savannas south of the Sahara. Within the primary rainforest, it frequents natural openings, especially near water. It is almost always found near oil palms — their husk is a favorite food.

Gordon Langsbury/Bruce Coleman Ltd

BUSH CAPITAL: CANBERRA, CITY OF RAPTORS

PENNY AND JERRY OLSEN

Early this century an essentially treeless grassland, broken by rolling hills, was chosen as the site for Australia's seat of government. A few years later, in 1912, an American, Walter Burley Griffin, won an international competition for a city design. His plan was truly original and farsighted. It made maximum use of natural features, blending topography, grand buildings, and suburbs, linked by a formal, strongly geometric network of roads. Tree planting was a necessity of the design and began in ernest. While Burley Griffin's plan has never been completed, his concept of orderly, environmentally conscious, development remains. Later town planners overcame the problem of housing Canberra's expanding population, now well over a quarter of a million, with a number of interconnected semi-independent towns, made up of garden suburbs, nestled in valleys and separated by tree-covered hills. Trees dominate the landscape and give the city its cohesiveness; drawing the surrounding bush down the grand avenues that are the mainstay of Burley Griffin's design, through pocket parks and open spaces, along wide street verges, to the open, uncluttered, foreshores of a central lake. The trees are alive with birds, some resident, others seasonal visitors from the surrounding bushland.

Raptors flourish in Canberra. Eight species regularly breed within the city limits, and another eight pass through occasionally. Canberra's wooded hills, embracing the suburbs, are favored places for nesting. Brown Goshawks (*Accipiter fasciatus*) build their stick nests in tall eucalypts rising from hillside gullies. These hawks hunt starlings, rosellas and other small birds that live and feed around the shopping centers and green spaces. Overlooking the lake and Government House, Little Eagles (*Hieraaetus morphnoides*) raise their single youngster on rabbits and starlings gleaned from the foothills. A few Whistling Kites (*Haliastur sphenurus*) scavenge along the river where it widens into Lake Burley Griffin. Collared Sparrowhawks (*Accipiter cirrhocephalus*) nest on the hills and in the introduced pines gracing small city parks; they slip quietly through backyards, unnoticed except by the small, local birds which chitter their "hawk-abroad" warning to others.

The well-watered suburbs are a refuge from the summer dry and winter cold, both for the city's residents and for birds arriving from the surrounding countryside during harsh periods. Some of the raptors leave before the crisp winter, when snow caps the ranges abutting the city, and travel to warmer parts of Australia. Some Australian Hobbies (*Falco longipennis*) leave in about March with the departing passerines, and return the following spring. Winter is left to the Australian Black-shouldered Kites (*Elanus notatus*). They arrive in autumn to breed in open land adjacent to industrial areas, the University and the Australian Institute of Sport.

When the Hobbies return in spring they must wait for the nest-building ravens to finish breeding; freshly refurbished raven's nests on power pylons are favored nest sites. The Hobbies zig-zag swiftly above parks and gardens in pursuit of birds and, in the evening, hawk moths attracted by the lights of the city. They have also nested, largely unnoticed, in front of the Old Parliament House, above the parliamentry rosebeds. Australian Kestrels (*Falco cenchroides*) have chosen an even more sensitive area as two or more pairs have nested on the office blocks housing the Department of Defence. Watched by office workers in adjacent blocks, they come and go with impunity from an area out of bounds to most people.

Canberra is a gem, no other capital can rival its extraordinary blend of nature and urban and administrative need. Every city should have space for raptors.

Raptor species seen in Canberra include the following: Australian Black-shouldered Kite (*Elanus notatus*)*, Black Kite (*Milvus migrans*), Whistling Kite (*Haliastur sphenurus*), Brown Goshawk (*Accipiter fasciatus*)*, Collared Sparrowhawk (*Accipiter cirrhocephalus*)*, Variable Goshawk (*Accipiter novaehollandiae*), White-bellied Sea Eagle (*Haliaeetus leucogaster*), Wedge-tailed Eagle (*Aquila audax*), Little Eagle (*Hieraaetus morphnoides*)*, Swamp Harrier (*Circus approximans*), Spotted Harrier (*Circus assimilis*), Black Falcon (*Falco subniger*), Peregrine Falcon (*Falco peregrinus*)*, Australian Hobby (*Falco longipennis*)*, Brown Falcon (*Falco berigora*)*, Australian Kestrel (*Falco cenchroides*)*.

* Regular breeders

▼ On a hillside above Canberra, the capital of Australia, a Brown Goshawk prepares to cross an opening in the woodland, Retention of the major natural features of the landscape, and tree planting, have made the city a haven for raptors—eight species breed within the city limits, and another eight are occasional visitors. All are species usually associated with wild places. Canberra is truly a city designed for an environmentally conscious future.

P. & J. Olsen

THE WORLD'S RAREST RAPTORS

IAN NEWTON

The seven raptor species described here are some of the rarest in the world. Some are island forms, so would never have been numerous, but others were once widespread. Human activities, of one form or another, have reduced the numbers of all these species, so that all are in danger of imminent extinction.

The California Condor (*Gymnogyps californianus*) is the largest of all raptors, and the largest flying bird, with a weight up to 14 kilograms (30 pounds) and a wingspan of 3 meters (9.8 feet). It was once fairly widespread in western North America, feeding on the large carcasses of bison or deer in inland areas, and on seals and other animals on the coast. With the coming of Europeans, the destruction of wild game and the introduction of cattle and sheep, the Condor changed to feeding largely on the carcasses of domestic animals. At the same time it began to decline, eventually being restricted to a part of California, where its numbers fell to about 150 individuals in 1950, 50–60 in 1968, 21 in 1982 and nine in 1985. At that time the last few birds were taken and added to existing birds in captivity, in the hope of forming a breeding stock for eventual return to the wild. The birds were divided between the San Diego and Los Angeles zoos. In 1988 the total population stood at 27 individuals, the lowest level in the history of the species, but that same year a chick was also raised from an egg laid in captivity. Persecution was probably one of the main reasons for the decline, especially in the early stages. Latterly lead poisoning may have been important, as Condors obtain lead fragments from eating bullets that are in the carcasses of game animals which are shot but not recovered by hunters.

The Madagascar Fish Eagle (*Haliaeetus vociferoides*) is endemic to the island of Madagascar, feeding on fish from the sea and freshwaters. It is somewhat similar to the African Fish Eagle (*H. vocifer*), from which it probably evolved. It is now restricted to a 600 kilometer (373 mile) stretch of coast on the west side of the island, north of Morondava. During 1982–86, 48 occupied sites were found comprising 40 pairs and other isolated birds, giving 96 individuals in total. Large protected areas are urgently needed to secure this species.

The Madagascar Serpent Eagle (*Eutriorchis astur*), a medium-sized raptor, is a rare inhabitant of primary rainforest in Madagascar. It is known only from eleven museum specimens and, apart from unconfirmed reports of its continuing presence in the Maroansetra area, it has not been seen alive since 1932, despite searches. Possibly the species is already extinct, but as suitable habitat still remains, further survey is needed. Nothing significant is known of its habits.

The Great Philippine Eagle (*Pithecophaga jefferyi*) is one of the largest and most striking forest eagles in the world. In a distinct genus, this eagle is endemic to the Philippine Islands of Luzon, Leyte, Samar and Mindanao. It builds a huge stick nest in an emergent forest tree, and hunts various large birds and mammals, including monkeys. It has greatly declined, because of extensive deforestation. Recent estimates suggest a population of less than 200 individuals. The forests of the Sierra Madre mountains on Luzon represent the largest single stronghold for the species, but if deforestation continues at the present rate, it could soon become extinct there. The island of Samar is still well forested and could hold appreciable numbers.

The Spanish Imperial Eagle (*Aquila adelbertii*) is a large, mainly brownish, raptor, which formerly occupied much of Iberia and parts of North Africa, but is now restricted to a few areas in Spain, where suitable habitat remains. The species is found in open woodland, mostly in low gentle foothills, and feeds on medium-sized birds and mammals. The population has been estimated at around 105 pairs, plus non-breeders.

This eagle was formerly classed, not as a distinct species, but as a subspecies of *Aquila heliaca*, which has a much wider distribution, from southeast Europe, across Asia into China. Even this species is rare and declining, however, and in total could possibly number less than 1000 pairs.

The Javan Hawk Eagle (*Spizaetus bartelsi*) is endemic to the forests of Java, occurring in both lowland and montane areas. Because of extensive deforestation, the species is now confined to a few areas of remaining habitat. During a survey in 1986, it was found in three areas, which together could have held 30–36 pairs. It may also occur in mountain forests in eastern Java, but still the total population is likely to number less than 60 pairs. To preserve the species, large forest reserves are needed.

The Mauritius Kestrel (*Falco punctatus*) is a small forest-dwelling falcon, endemic to the island of Mauritius in the Indian Ocean. It is an aberrant falcon, with short rounded wings in adaptation to forest life, and no plumage differences between male and female, which is unusual for a kestrel. It feeds mainly on finger-length, arboreal, bright green *Phelsuma* geckos, and nests in holes in cliffs or trees. The species once occurred over the whole island, in several vegetation types, but declined from loss of habitat, persecution and finally pesticide use. It survived in one small area of native forest, in the Black River Gorges, the only part of Mauritius where DDT was not used. By 1973-83 only one to three breeding pairs were known. With the help of a captive breeding and release program, the population grew to ten pairs in 1988, some of which were in new areas. The island could probably still support more than 30 pairs.

In addition to these species, several other raptors are of unknown status, but are probably very rare. They include the Black Honey Buzzard (*Henicopernis infuscata*) of New Britain island, the Solomons (or Sandford's) Sea Eagle (*Haliaeetus sanfordi*) of the Solomon Islands, the Kinabalu Serpent Eagle (*Spilornis kinabaluensis*) of Sarawak, the Dark Serpent Eagle (*Spilornis elgini*) of the Andaman Islands, the New Britain Sparrowhawk (*Accipiter brachyurus*) of New Britain island, the New Caledonia Sparrowhawk (*Accipiter haplochrous*) of New Caledonia island and Gundlach's Hawk (*Accipiter gundlachi*) of Cuba.

Maurice Tibbles/Survival Anglia Ltd

▼ California Condor ▲ Great Philippine Eagle ▼ Spanish Imperial Eagle

Jeff Foot/Bruce Coleman Ltd

Dr Bernd-U. Meyburg

FEEDING HABITS

R.E. KENWARD

The aerial prowess of birds of prey often evokes awe and inspiration—their feeding habits equally often cause revulsion, resentment, and even fear. Close-ups of vultures pulling entrails from a carcass, especially from a Parsee funeral tower, may not enthrall everyone. Perhaps eagles seldom have the chance to seize babies nowadays, but as some large eagles feed regularly on monkeys, it would be foolish to maintain that human infants could never have been attacked by such large birds.

Although exceptions to the normal raptor diet often attract public attention, it is the routine diet that is of most interest to the biologist, because this is what sustains populations. The variations in this food supply, which occur across country, through the seasons and through the years, help to determine where raptors hunt and how many can survive and breed at any one place and time. Food supplies may also influence survival and breeding by providing sources of pollutants, such as heavy metals and organochlorines. To conserve raptors, we need an accurate assessment of their diet through the year. We may also need an understanding of raptor feeding habits in order to reduce their impact on prey of particular value to humans.

▼ Tales and illustrations such as this, on the cover of the September 1906 issue of *Le Petit Journal*, cannot simply be dismissed as folklore. They recur in many cultures and parts of the world, from the French countryside to the jungles of New Guinea. Although often exaggerated, many probably have a basis in fact. A large eagle is perfectly capable of carrying off a small unguarded infant.

Mary Evans Picture Library

RAPTOR DIETS

Raptors are predominantly meat eaters. They all have hooked beaks to help them tear meat from a carcass, and many species also possess powerful feet that help subdue their prey and maintain balance while they feed. Some raptors eat large meals at irregular intervals, storing food in a large crop before they digest it. Since meat is easier to digest than much vegetable material, which may require extensive grinding to break down cellulose cell walls, raptor digestive tracts are generally shorter and less muscular than those of herbivores, so that raptors are relatively light in weight and thus agile on the wing.

A long-standing tenet of zoology, Gause's theory, maintains that two species cannot have an identical feeding "niche" because the resulting competition would eliminate one of them. Meat eating is a comparatively narrow feeding niche, so there are generally fewer species of raptors than of herbivorous birds in an area. Nevertheless, the available meat is packaged in many different-sized species, which can be captured in a variety of different ways—or eaten as carrion. Each raptor species tends to be adapted to eat prey of a particular type and size range, and for a particular hunting style or habitat.

For example, some species that feed mainly on birds, bats and flying insects, tend to have long legs with slender toes for seizing agile but relatively fragile prey. Examples include the true hawks (*Accipiter*) and falcons (*Falco*), together with the forest falcons (*Micrastur*), falconets (*Microhierax, Spiziapteryx*), the African Pigmy Falcon (*Polihierax semitorquatus*), and the Swallow-tailed Kite (*Elanoides forficatus*). Among these raptors there is an emphasis on aerial agility, with food frequently seized after a dashing stoop, or a helter-skelter chase through woodland. Such agility is at a premium for the Bat Hawk (*Machaerhamphus alcinus*), and the unrelated Bat Falcon (*Falco rufigularis*), swooping to snatch bats, swifts and swallows near the entrances to the caves were they roost or nest.

Other hawks and falcons, together with many buzzards (*Buteo, Parabuteo*), some kites (*Elanus*) and most of the eagle genera (*Aquila, Geranoaetus, Hieraaetus, Ictinaetus, Spizastur, Spizaetus, Terathopius*) frequently kill mammals on the ground, though many of these raptors are also opportunistic predators on birds and reptiles. Compact legs with relatively short toes and large claws are useful for handling mammals, whose four feet and powerful jaws can offer serious resistance to an attacker. Three large forest eagles—the Crowned Eagle (*Spizaetus coronatus*), Harpy Eagle (*Harpia harpyja*) and Great Philippine Eagle (*Pithecophaga jefferyi*)—have particularly massive tarsi and toes, suitable for rapidly subduing monkeys and other large mammals

seized in the trees. Members of the smaller eagle genus (*Circaetus*), the serpent eagles (*Spilornis, Dryotriorchis, Eutriorchis*), the more buzzard-like (*Leucopternis*) and the Lizard Buzzard (*Kaupifalco monogrammicus*) favor reptiles as prey, though some of them also take insects and other ground-dwelling animals. Kites of the genera *Leptodon, Harpagus* and *Ictinia*, together with the bazas (*Aviceda*) and buzzard eagles (*Butastur*) generally confine themselves to smaller reptiles or insects. Black hawks, of the genus *Buteogallus*, often live near lakes or coastal regions and add amphibia and even fish to their diet; the Rufous Crab Hawk (*Buteogallus aequinoctialis*) has become a specialist on crabs.

Wetlands and coasts are also the haunts of raptors that specialize on fish, including the almost cosmopolitan Osprey (*Pandion haliaetus*) which hunts mainly in flight, and the Fishing Buzzard (*Busarellus nigricollis*) which, together with the fishing eagles (*Ichthyophaga*), dives mainly from perches. The latter eagles are closely related to larger species of the genus *Haliaeetus*, which

◄ Although a capable hunter, the Bateleur (*Terathopius ecaudatus*) often scavenges. The tail of this reasonably sized crocodile may well be the remains of another's meal.

▲ Agility and long, slender legs and toes make the Collared Sparrowhawk (*Accipiter cirrhocephalus*) an effective hunter of the small birds it snatches from vegetation or snares in the air.

▼ Largest of the African eagles, the impressive Martial Eagle (*Hieraaetus bellicosus*) can catch mammals as large as a young gazelle. Nevertheless, it seems to prefer bustard, guineafowl and other large terrestrial birds.

supplement a diet of fish with mammals and birds. The White-bellied Sea Eagle (*Haliaeetus leucogaster*) also consumes large numbers of sea-snakes. This genus contains the largest of the truly raptorial (i.e. non-carrion eating) birds of prey, the awesome Steller's Sea Eagle (*Haliaeetus pelagicus*) of the west Pacific basin, which is known to kill birds as large as cock Capercaillie (*Tetrao urogallus*) weighing up to 6 kilograms (13 pounds), as well as foxes and young seals.

Much smaller prey suit the insectivorous Western Honey Buzzard (*Pernis apivorus*) and the American Red-throated Caracara (*Daptrius americanus*), which specialize in robbing the nests of wasps and other colonial Hymenoptera. Other invertebrate specialists include the Hook-billed Kite (*Chondrohierax uncinatus*), and the related Everglades Kite (*Rostrhamus sociabilis*), two tropical American species feeding almost exclusively on snails, with beaks shaped for crushing the shells or teasing the molluscs from within. Soft-bodied invertebrates, such as caterpillars, are taken occasionally by many other raptors, while earthworms are often taken from temperate pastures by kites, buzzards and kestrels.

Some groups of raptors have very catholic tastes, being opportunist hunters of birds, mammals, reptiles, amphibia and invertebrates, whichever are most available. Harriers (*Circus*) and their allies (*Polyboroides, Geranospiza*), together with the Square-tailed Kite (*Lophoictinia isura*), frequently hunt such prey from the air, whereas the Savanna Hawk (*Heterospizias meridionalis*) is more terrestrial in habits, and the Secretary Bird (*Sagittarius serpentarius*) spends most of its day stalking these prey in grasslands and cereal fields. Many of the caracaras (*Daptrius, Milvago, Phalcoboenus, Polyborus*) are also seen mainly on the ground, where they are generalist predators and scavengers. Striated Caracara (*Phalcoboenus australis*), also called the Johnny Rook, is an inveterate scrounger around penguin colonies of the treeless Falkland Islands and Tierra del Fuego, feeding on moribund chicks and invertebrates. A combination of aerial scavenging

▼ Typically a scavenger and hunter of scraps, frogs, crabs, and small snakes on the ground, the Brahminy Kite (*Haliastur indus*) also occasionally glides down from a perch to scoop a small fish from the water.

Frans Lanting/Minden Pictures

Dieter & Mary Plage/Survival Anglia

with a generally catholic diet make kites of the genera *Milvus* and *Haliastur* a common sight at garbage dumps in the warmer parts of the world.

Other birds of prey specialize in eating carrion. These include the cathartid vultures (*Cathartes, Corogyps, Sarcorhampus*) and condors (*Gymnogyps, Vultur*) of the New World, and the Old World vultures (*Aegypius, Gypaetus, Gyps, Necrosyrtes, Neophron*). All have a relatively large wing area for soaring while they search over wide areas for food, and species that occur together are often adapted—in terms of size, beak structure and degree of feather loss from their heads—for feeding on different parts of a carcass. The Bearded Vulture (*Gypaetus barbatus*) is unusual in retaining

the feathers on its head, but is less likely than the others to become soiled by body fluids. It reduces competition with the other vultures by feeding last from the carcass, taking the bare bones to drop and break them so that it can extract the marrow. The Bearded Vulture also takes some live prey, including tortoises which are opened in the same way as bones.

Some species supplement a diet of carrion with live animals. The Turkey Vulture (*Cathartes aura*) and the Black Vulture (*Coragyps atratus*) vary their menu in this way, and the Egyptian Vulture (*Neophron percnopterus*) can subdue part-grown rabbits. These three species also eat young birds, and even the largest raptor, the

▲ Life can be harsh on the bleak Falkland Islands, where the Striated Caracara digs for insects with its blunt, strong claws and scavenges along the shoreline. When the seabirds return each year to breed, the Caracara scrounges around penguin and albatross colonies for chicks and scraps.

Andean Condor (*Vultur gryphus*), takes eggs from seabird colonies. The Egyptian Vulture is famous as an avian tool-user, because it throws stones to break the thick shells of Ostrich eggs; and there are claims that the Black-breasted Buzzard Kite (*Hamirostra melanosternon*) may drive Emus (*Dromaius novaehollandiae*) from their nests so it can attack the eggs in this way.

Many of the more predatory raptors take carrion if they have the opportunity. Most eagles come into this category, especially from the genus *Haliaeetus*. The so-called Bald Eagle (*Haliaeetus leucocephalus*), the United States' avian emblem whose head is in fact covered with white feathers,

is a frequent scavenger of salmon kelts along the Pacific Coast and of shot waterfowl in inland areas. Even the Northern Goshawk (*Accipiter gentilis*), a killing machine *par excellence*, takes carrion if it is readily available.

Perhaps the most atypical raptor diet is that of the Palm Nut Vulture (*Gypohierax angolensis*), an African species commonly seen eating the nut husks from oil or Raphia palms. These fruits are also eaten by generalist raptors, including Black Kites (*Milvus milvus*) and African Harrier Hawks (*Polyboroides typus*). A number of other species, especially the Black and Turkey Vultures, sometimes eat vegetable matter.

FOREST VULTURES DEPEND ON SMELL

DAVID C. HOUSTON

It may come as a surprise to discover that the most important scavenging animals in the rainforests of South America are vultures. They are among the most abundant of all birds of prey in this habitat, and in undisturbed forests will locate almost every large carcass that comes available. The birds fly above the tree canopy, and yet they locate carcasses far below on the dimly lit forest floor. The members of the *Cathartes* genus, such as the Turkey Vulture (*C. aura*) do this almost entirely by using their keen sense of smell.

Whether these vultures could smell at all has been a controversial subject. The first scientific paper published by the American artist and naturalist Audubon in 1826 was on his experiments to test if Turkey Vultures could smell, and he concluded that they could not. It was not until Kenneth Stager carried out some detailed experiments in 1964 that it was conclusively shown that the Turkey Vulture is one of the few

birds to show a highly developed sense of smell. The reason for this disagreement is probably that the early experimenters used extremely rotten meat for their trials, and assumed that the more foul-smelling the food the more likely the vultures were to find it. In fact vultures will often choose not to eat badly decomposed meat even if they can smell it.

These vultures cannot detect animals that have only recently died, but within one day a carcass will be smelling sufficiently to enable birds to locate it. There are other vulture species which also congregate at any carcass, such as Black Vulture (*Coragyps atratus*) and King Vulture (*Sarcoramphus papa*), but these species do not seem to be able to smell. They find food by flying higher over the forest, and watching the movements of the *Cathartes* species below them. Whenever they see these vultures circling over the forest they follow them down and are led to the food.

▲ One of the few birds for which the sense of smell has been found to be of special importance, the Turkey Vulture can locate food, a rotting carcass, out of sight below the tree canopy, even ignoring bodies too decayed. With its less exceptional sense of smell, the King Vulture (above right) sometimes makes use of the Turkey Vulture's keen sense and follows it to food. A more powerful beak allows the King Vulture to open tough beasts, making access easier for the weaker Turkey Vulture. This interaction may thus be mutually beneficial.

HUNTING TECHNIQUES AND PREY SELECTION

Birds of prey can be divided roughly into those that forage mainly in flight, from perches, or on the ground. Many of the vultures have a low wing-loading and live in areas where they can use thermals or other air currents to soar with little effort while they scan for food. Other species use flight to hunt for active prey in areas with no convenient perches. Peregrine Falcons (*Falco peregrinus*) hunt over flat moorland areas in this way, sometimes circling at great height in any available upcurrents, and then ambushing prey flying below by stooping at speeds that may reach 320 kilometers (200 miles) per hour.

Flying high helps to survey a wide area, but many birds and mammals have acute eyesight to help spot distant predators. When a raptor flies low, it can remain hidden by vegetation until almost on top of the prey, which then has little time for escape. Thus harriers can be seen quartering low over ground vegetation, flying slowly so that they can check rapidly and dive on any small birds or mammals they may surprise. Accipiters skim the ground in faster flight, using hedges and other tall vegetation as cover for approaching flocks of birds feeding in the open. One may well wonder at the degree of foresight behind such attacks. Does the raptor perceive that the reedbed will hide its approach, or does it simply fly as low as possible, and thus remain below the reed tops? When a hawk flies along one side of a hedge, and then suddenly slips over the top straight into a flock of sparrows on the other side, was the attack really planned in advance, or was the hawk simply unaware of the prey until it caught a glimpse or a twitter through the hedge? Perhaps the predator had remembered that a

Thomas Kitchin/Tom Stack & Associates

▲ When the salmon are running, America's national bird, the Bald Eagle, has little need for its predatory skills and, for a time, has an abundance of easy prey.

◄ These colonial Griffon Vultures (*Gyps fulvus*) fly off from their roost in one direction, then fan out to search for food. Many pairs of eyes are better than one; together they can prospect a wide area, each bird searching within sight of its neighbor. Once a carcass is found, large numbers may descend to feed.

François Gohier/Ardea London

Frans Lanting/Minden Pictures

▲ Panic and confusion overcome this flock of shorebirds as a Merlin (*Falco columbarius*) hurtles past in a surprise attack. Such hunting tactics often enable the falcon to spot a vulnerable bird in the mêlée, and it gets above the flock ready to launch a dive attack.

change of course had led to a kill once before, and therefore repeated the maneuver in speculation.

Many raptors spend a large part of their time hunting from perches. Sometimes a particular perch tree, crag, or pole is used to survey the surrounding country for hours at a time, and the bird is said to be "still-hunting." At other times, however, the raptor may keep flying from perch to perch, stopping for no more than a few minutes at each, and thereby scanning a much wider area for prey. Goshawks and sparrowhawks hunt mainly in this way, using relatively inconspicuous perches within the tree canopy. When they fly between trees, they drop down steeply to ground level, thus converting height into flying speed before skimming inconspicuously to the next tree, where they swoop steeply up to a suitable branch, converting speed back into height. In each flight the hawk is visible as a silhouette for only a second or so, moving almost vertically without a tell-tale wing beat, and prey have little chance to realize that a predator is now watching for their next

movement. This "short-stay perch hunting" uses much less energy than continuous flight, but is more costly than still-hunting.

When raptors have a choice of hunting techniques, they seem to use the method that costs least energy to meet their food requirements. Thus Old World Kestrels (*Falco tinnunculus*), which are well-known for their hovering behavior, tend to hunt from perches such as telegraph poles if they have only themselves to feed. If they are seeking food for their young, however, they often favor the more expensive but more profitable method of hovering on the wing.

When raptors sit relaxed on a favorite perch after a meal, they can swoop on unwary prey as they become hungry again. Such still-hunting is to some extent a chance occurrence in species which normally hunt from perch to perch or in continuous flight. Those birds may, however, revert to a still-hunting strategy once their energy reserves have reached a very low level. Sitting with feathers fluffed out for maximum insulation, they

Richard & Julia Kemp/Survival Anglia

◀▼ Wings outstretched, presenting the snake with a large target to strike at harmlessly, this young Short-toed Eagle (*Circaetus gallicus*) tackles one of its favorite prey. The eagle's rough, short toes are well adapted for clamping onto the writhing reptile. Head secured, the eagle kills the snake with twisting bites to its skull and backbone, then may swallow it whole.

are ready to descend with cramp-like grip on any creature coming near enough.

Once a hunting raptor has detected living prey, it does not always launch an attack. If the raptor is not particularly hungry, lack of an attack can indicate that the prey is a species with which the raptor has had little success, or perhaps is in a location where many previous attacks have failed. Raptors, like many other predators, are able to learn from their experience and to recognize and direct their attacks at individuals that are especially vulnerable, perhaps as a result of weakness or disease. On one occasion, when Woodpigeons (*Columba palumbus*) were flying to join a flock feeding in a field, a radio-tagged goshawk sat watching them from about 150 meters (160 yards) away. The hawk had relaxed plumage, with one foot tucked up, and little apparent interest in making an attack in a place where it had seldom made a kill. Suddenly, however, a single pigeon appeared over the hedge, flying with obvious difficulty to join the flock. The hawk immediately became alert, took off and caught the pigeon almost before it had landed. The emaciated pigeon had a recent shot wound in its breast.

On other occasions, the radio-tagged hawk had apparently made no choice of target before attacking a flock of feeding pigeons, and selection of weak prey occurred only if such individuals dropped behind as the hawk chased the departing flock. Healthy Woodpigeons could outfly the hawk if they spotted the attack in time. If they did not, however, and were struck before take-off, there was no selection for weak individuals. Pheasants are less able to outfly a goshawk, and normally feed close to cover when there are hawks about. They can then reach shelter easily, giving little opportunity for a chase by the hawk, and captured pheasants tend not to be in especially poor condition. However, during autumn and

Richard & Julia Kemp/Survival Anglia

winter, goshawks tend to kill hen pheasants more often than cocks, probably attacking the smaller birds to reduce the risk of being injured.

The selection process is therefore partly a matter of predator choice, and partly a product of attack and escape behavior. Selection of defective prey is to be expected during prolonged chases, and is less likely during surprise attacks unless the raptor can pick out a disadvantaged individual at the last moment. When flying birds flock tightly together and turn in unison, they are not only providing a multitude of similar targets to confuse an attacking falcon, but are also making any defective prey conspicuous among them—a Jonah strategy, whereby the predator can easily select a victim, and the others have wasted minimal time and energy in defending themselves. Unfortunately, this may mean that the stooping falcon is particularly likely to take the most

▼ The large Northern Goshawk (*Accipiter gentilis*) hunts through woodland. It moves short distances from perch to perch in search of prey and is capable of a tremendous final burst of speed to snap up a victim. The Goshawk catches small female pheasants more often than larger males, probably to reduce the risk of injury.

Andy Rouse/Planet Earth Pictures

BEHAVIOR OF VULTURES AT A CARCASS

PETER MUNDY

Vultures demolishing a carcass make an exciting spectacle. They gather in their dozens and possibly hundreds at the same food source, and fight vigorously over who gets the meat first—unique features among birds of prey. In a matter of minutes a strong bird can swallow enough food to sustain it for the next three days. For example, a White-backed Vulture (*Gyps africanus*) can eat one kilogram (2.2 pounds) in two minutes; it may, of course, need to go hungry for the next two weeks. Feast and famine are part of most vultures' lifestyle, as is strong physical exertion in getting food at all from a carcass.

There are 22 species of vulture, 15 in the Old World and seven in the Americas, but six is the maximum ever seen at a carcass, and this only in parts of East Africa such as the Serengeti National Park. In other parts of Africa, in parts of India, and in northern South America, five species may gather together, along perhaps with kites, eagles, Marabou Storks, and even jackals, hyenas and lions.

In whatever area, each species gathers in numbers typical for it—some such as griffons and American Black Vultures (*Coragyps atratus*) in hordes, others such as White-headed Vultures (*Aegypius occipitalis*) and King Vultures (*Sarcoramphus papa* and *S. calvus*) (American and Indian) in half-dozens at most. Those in the first group actually depend on the carcass for food, as they have few if any alternatives; those in the second group do not and seem to gather instead for social reasons rather than to gorge themselves.

Presented with an intact carcass the size of an antelope, or larger, most vultures are unable to break the skin, and have to enter at mouth, anus and occasionally groin. Now the antics begin, because only two birds can start the feeding (one at each end) but dozens of hungry vultures may have gathered. Fights, lunges, pecks, cackles are freely offered, the air is blue, and the birds get covered in dust. Soon, through sheer force of numbers, they will have effected several entrances to the meat and offal of the carcass. When this happens the food disappears down vultures' throats at a phenomenal speed: given enough birds, an impala can be stripped in 30 minutes, and a cow (with its tougher skin) in three hours. Generally, adults are dominant over immatures, and those with full crops move away to loaf, yawn, and preen. Probably smeared with blood, these successful birds will soon need to bathe.

In Africa, during this mêlée, the Lappet-faced Vulture (*Aegypius tracheliotus*) occasionally makes a dramatic entrance by leaping on the carcass and literally scattering 20 griffons by powerful lunges and wing beats. As likely as not, though, it will wander away without feeding; it does not depend on large carcasses for food.

Soon the food is gone, and the successful (replete) birds depart, but the action continues—by immatures, and those birds that arrived for socializing rather than to feed. Competition for food at a carcass is in fact largely within a species, and not between species. The different vultures have different lifestyles so that competition is mostly avoided; nevertheless each is also something of an opportunist, and will avail itself if possible of the choicest and easiest cuts.

▼ Up to 150 Rüppell's Griffon Vulture (*Gyps rueppellii*) have been seen gathered around carrion. More often, smaller groups arrive to socialize and feed accordingly to a strict hierarchy, white-headed adults before brown-headed immatures. Their long, sparsely feathered necks allow them to rummage deep inside a carcass.

Eric & David Hosking

polluted prey, either by active choice of the bird with slightly unusual behavior or because this is the one which lags in the chase. The diving Osprey or fish-eagle is thus perhaps most likely to secure the fish that contamination has brought close to the surface. On the other hand, one would expect no marked selection when the Harrier Hawk uses its long, double-jointed tarsi to reach deep into a tree cavity and plunder the nestlings therein.

Just as selection within a species leads to relatively more weak, diseased, small or odd-colored prey being taken than are present on average in the environment, the same process applies to selection between species. Differences in the success of attacks on different species, augmented by instinctive and learned behavior, lead to some species being eaten more frequently than one would expect from their local abundance. This process reaches its extreme in those raptors which feed almost exclusively on one prey species, but specialists also occur within species that normally have a broad diet. Specialists are most obvious when they have learned to kill prey that is difficult to find or catch, so that other raptors of the same species seldom attack it. Thus a pair of cliff-nesting Peregrine Falcons can specialize in ambushing flocks of racing pigeons, whereas neighboring pairs take a broad spectrum of resident coastal prey. Other Peregrines on the same coast may bring inland prey to their eyries, rather than coastal species, but this is more a case of favoring different hunting habitats than specialization in a particular prey species.

The success of an attack will depend on the degree of surprise, the presence or absence of disadvantaged individuals, the proximity of cover and many other factors. As a result, attack success varies greatly between raptor species, from 5 percent for attacks on birds by wintering raptors to some 90 percent for Ospreys diving for fish. In general, attack success in winter, varying from 5 percent to 15 percent for attacks on birds and mammals, is lower than the success rates of 11 percent to 84 percent recorded for similar raptors and prey in summer. The summer attacks may be more successful because raptors are then hunting harder to feed their young, because the hunting is then being done mainly by experienced adults which choose not even to launch fruitless attacks, or because the summer is a time when prey populations contain many young and inexperienced individuals. However, records of attack success should be treated with caution unless individual raptors have been watched continuously. Otherwise one may well observe the least successful attacks, because those most noticeable to human observers are probably also most noticeable to the prey, and therefore most easily avoided.

When the attack is successful, prey may be killed in a variety of ways. Small prey may simply

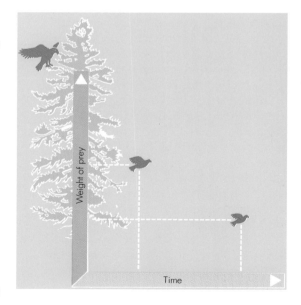

▲ Systematically quartering a patch of ground with its buoyant, low flight, a Montagu's Harrier (*Circus pygargus*) scans the ground below for prey. Its long legs enable it to reach into long grass and reeds. Here the Harrier drops onto a vole, caught while attempting to cross a bare area and therefore vulnerable.

◄ Hawks and Doves: A surprise attack allows the Northern Goshawk to capture a pigeon of average weight. However, if its attack results in a chase the Goshawk will probably catch only a low-weight, presumably less vigorous pigeon.

be crushed in the beak and swallowed whole. Larger prey are in many cases killed by pressure from the feet, driving talons into vital organs until any struggling ceases. Unlike other raptors, falcons tend to kill with a bite, using a notch in the side of the beak to break the neck of their victims. The blow from a swooping falcon is sometimes enough to kill a bird in mid-air, and there used to be argument about whether the impact was delivered by the falcon's breast or feet. We now know that the feet are used, typically with the front toes curled up and the rear one extended. Some mammals tend to die rapidly from shock when seized by a bird of prey. However, if an animal ceases to struggle without being killed, raptors have no scruples about eating the hapless creature alive. The aim of the raptor is only to immobilize its prey for eating, and this need not always entail killing it first.

FOOD THROUGH THE YEAR

Since changes in prey vulnerability influence attack success, they can lead to changes in raptor diet from season to season. Young rabbits are frequently found at the nests of many raptors that are not strong enough to take healthy adult rabbits in winter, and young corvids are killed frequently in summer by raptors that seldom manage to catch the wily adults in winter. Young birds are so important a food source for Eurasian Sparrowhawks (*Accipiter nisus*) that the eggs tend to be laid when the first small passerines fledge.

Changes in diet may also depend on the presence or absence of migratory prey. In Sweden, the main summer food of Northern Goshawks is young passerines, and pigeons are also killed quite frequently, but in winter the pigeons have moved south, and the passerines that remain are hard to catch. The hawks then feed mainly on mammals and game birds.

Apart from seasonal changes in diet, there are several other reasons why prey items seen at raptor nests may give a poor picture of diet through the year. Kestrels and kites, which take many insects and other invertebrates away from the nest, seldom bring these small items to their young, probably in part because it is not worth returning with this food to the nest. Remains found at nests can give an even more misleading impression of overall diet if, instead of being based on observations from hides or with automatic camera systems, they rely on collections of pellets and other food remains: remains of large prey are more likely to survive uneaten or undigested than are the fragile bones and other traces of smaller animals in the diet.

Similar problems affect diet assessments based on chance observation of kills, or prey remains found away from the nest. In a German study, unaided observers found most of the pigeon kills made by radio-tagged hawks, but only one in three Common Pheasants (*Phasianus colchicus*) and one in five rabbits, because the pale pigeon feathers showed up much better than the darker feathers of pheasants, and were less easily washed down into the grass than the rabbit fur. Even when a raptor is

▶ Sharp, curved talons and spines on the soles of its feet help the White-bellied Sea Eagle (*Haliaeetus leucogaster*) to grasp its slippery prey of fish, eels and sea-snakes. Great opportunists, they also pirate food from other raptors, scavenge, and hunt rabbits in open woodland.

▼ The composition of a raptor's diet varies according to the availability of suitably prey. Northern Goshawks in Boreal Sweden live on birds in the summer but switch to squirrels when the birds migrate. In Southern Sweden, rabbits are common, and Goshawks eat more of them than they do squirrels.

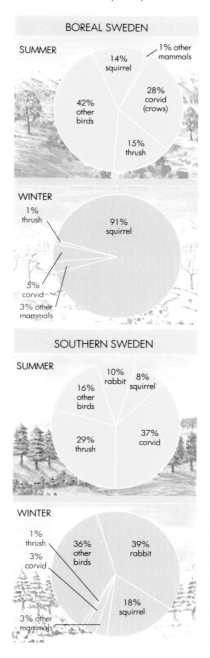

BOREAL SWEDEN

SUMMER
1% other mammals
14% squirrel
28% corvid (crows)
42% other birds
15% thrush

WINTER
1% thrush
91% squirrel
5% corvid
3% other mammals

SOUTHERN SWEDEN

SUMMER
10% rabbit
8% squirrel
16% other birds
29% thrush
37% corvid

WINTER
1% thrush
3% corvid
36% other birds
39% rabbit
18% squirrel
3% other mammals

ROLE OF VULTURES IN THE SERENGETI

DAVID C. HOUSTON

Most people have a mental image of the way African vultures feed, picturing them sitting in a forlorn ring around a pride of lions, waiting to snatch any scraps that the predators leave behind. This is quite wrong. Studies from the Serengeti region of Tanzania show that vultures get very little food from predator kills. The reason is quite simply that the predators are usually too short of food themselves to allow vultures to steal significant amounts. Vultures feed by finding animals that have died some other way—by disease, an accident, heavy parasite infestation, malnutrition or quite simply old age. In the Serengeti most of the ungulates (wildebeest and zebra, for example) die from such causes.

The total number of animals that die each year in the Serengeti can be calculated from the various studies made on the large grazing mammals there. This comes to about 40 million kilograms (88 million pounds) a year, representing the total weight of carcasses available for all the meat-eating animals: predators and scavengers.

From studies such as Dr. George Schaller's work on lions and Dr. Hans Kruuk's on hyenas, the total food intake of these animals has been estimated, and the results suggest that the large carnivores are responsible for only about a quarter of ungulate deaths and consume only about one-third of the available meat per year.

The Serengeti ecosystem is dominated by migratory ungulates, for the three species that undertake extensive migrations—the wildebeest, zebra and Thomsons Gazelle—account for over 70 percent of all the ungulates. The major predators, however, are unable to follow these herds, and their numbers are probably determined by the far smaller numbers of resident ungulates. As a result, most of the migratory ungulates that die each year are not killed by predators, but die from other causes, and this is where the vultures find their role.

Vultures are far more efficient than any of the mammalian scavengers at locating carcasses and consuming them quickly. Because they can fly high they can spot food over a great area, travel fast to reach it, collecting many other birds on the way, and do all this while using extremely little energy. For these reasons vultures are the major scavenging animals in African savanna systems, and may even consume more meat than all the mammalian carnivores combined.

▼ In the rush of their annual migration, wildebeest and zebra are sometimes killed or injured in the crush. Vultures (waiting in the trees) and other scavengers are quick to dispose of the casualties.

Keith Scholey/Seaphot Ltd/Planet Earth Pictures

seen to kill, it may have been noticed because the hunt was for prey that live in open places, or because there was a prolonged chase for a species that is difficult to kill and therefore relatively seldom taken.

Another problem with records of prey remains is that they provide little information on selection of poor-quality individuals. This information is important for assessing the impact of raptors on prey populations. For instance, if the prey are selected because they were starving and on the point of death, the raptor is having no real impact on their population because food shortage is the ultimate cause of the reduction in prey numbers. This is no trivial point when examining raptor predation on game and livestock. Lambs are not infrequently found at eagle nests in sheep country, but only an examination of the remains while still fresh can show whether the lamb was killed by the eagle or taken as carrion: scavenged lambs show no bruising around punctures made by the claws. In such cases the farmers have no cause for complaint, because without eagle scavenging the dead lambs might have attracted other predators to sheep flocks. But eagles are not always blameless; in parts of the United States, Golden Eagles are quite commonly seen killing kids and lambs.

Despite the sources of bias which affect collections of pellets and prey remains, these records can be useful for studying variation in diet between areas and years, because the bias should be similar for each collection. Moreover, some studies have found ways of correcting for bias, for instance by feeding combinations of the different prey species to captive birds to determine differences in digestibility. Diet records can then be combined with estimates of food consumption and wastage, and average prey weights, to estimate numbers taken through the breeding season.

Food consumption varies considerably with raptor size, so that small hawks and falcons need to eat flesh weighing 25–30 percent of their bodyweight each day in captivity, whereas eagles and vultures require less than 5 percent. So if a vulture packs its crop with food weighing 20 percent of its bodyweight, it can go several days between meals, whereas a small raptor needs a similar meal each day.

Nevertheless, data from nest observations and radio-tracking show how careful one must be about using food consumption data to estimate numbers of prey taken. While young were in the nest, some sparrowhawks and their broods in Britain ate prey totalling no more than 5–6 kilograms (11–13 pounds), but broods that received larger prey accounted for more than 13 kilograms (28 pounds), apparently "over-eating" to some extent. The meat consumed by radio-tagged wild goshawks in Sweden was equivalent to 15–16 percent of their bodyweight in mid-winter

(15–20 percent more than captive birds), but there was great variation in the proportion of each kill that was wasted. Hawks normally ate a squirrel completely in one meal, but required two to three days to finish eating a pheasant, and longer for a hare. Since foxes frequently scavenged these large kills, about 55 percent was unavailable to the hawks.

IMPACTS ON WILD AND DOMESTIC PREY

Evidence that raptors could reduce prey numbers, at least locally, came initially from studies of prey near raptor nests. Thus sparrowhawks in Britain substantially reduce the numbers of Great Tits (*Parus major*) and Blue Tits (*P. caeruleus*) within 200 meters (218 yards) of the hawk nest, and goshawks in North America can eliminate drumming Ruffed Grouse (*Bonasa umbellus*) near their nests. In contrast, Woodpigeon breeding is enhanced near goshawk nests in Germany, apparently because the hawks reduce Carrion Crow (*Corvus corone*) and Magpie (*Pica pica*) numbers and thereby reduce nest predation on the pigeons. Predation impact of breeding raptors is not always confined to the nest area: in Scotland, Hen Harriers can reduce the numbers of young Red Grouse (*Lagopus lagopus scoticus*) over wide areas by 15–30 percent during the course of the breeding season.

It tends to be winter, however, when raptor predation has most impact on a prey population. At that time the impact is estimated most accurately by radio-tagging, an approach used mainly to study goshawk predation on game. When hawks are radio-tracked, kill rates can be measured directly, without the need to estimate food consumption and wastage, and fresh kills can

▼ Prey are not always defenseless against raptors. The speed and agility of this hare has probably saved it from the power of the eagle.

Silvestris/Australasian Nature Transparencies

▲ With its back turned, this Martial Eagle does not daunt a mother gazelle as she gamely but hopelessly attempts to save her calf. But the sight of the eagle as it lunges around, with wings raised to full height and yellow eyes blazing, startles her. The calves, although often hidden in grass or under logs, are easy prey once found.

be examined to see if victims are in poor condition. Although some small kills are not found, a comparison with prey in the stomachs of shot Swedish hawks suggested that only 8 percent of the biomass was missed. Radio tags were also used to estimate raptor density, by noting the proportion of tagged hawks among those seen at random: the total number in the study area was the number of radio-tagged birds divided by this proportion. This raptor density, which included adult, juvenile and other non-breeding birds, combined with the average kill rate to give the overall predation rate, expressed as a percentage of total prey numbers. In one area, goshawks killed

56 percent of the hen pheasants over winter. Since the total over-winter loss (64 percent) was higher than could be replaced by breeding, pheasant numbers were declining. The hawks killed pheasants in average condition, without marked selection for those about to die of disease or food shortage.

In another area, pheasants as well as hawks were radio-tagged to provide an independent estimate of hawk predation. Tagging of prey provides information on the proportion of prey killed, without the need to estimate hawk and prey densities, but it is sometimes difficult to be sure which predator made a kill, or indeed whether the

predator killed the prey or scavenged it after death. Moreover, radio-tagged prey are seldom recovered quickly enough for a thorough autopsy to study their condition before capture.

Findings from various areas showed that pheasants were a preferred prey even when they were at low density. So when goshawks gathered in an area where rabbits were abundant, there was particularly heavy predation on the local pheasants too. An abundance of alternative prey, such as rabbits, probably serves only to "buffer" predation on game if the alternative prey is preferred. Sometimes human activities, such as introductions of prey species or changes in land-use,

substantially improve feeding prospects for the raptors, and thus change their relationship with minor prey. For example, the introduction of rabbits to Australia improved food supplies for Whistling Hawks (*Haliastur sphenurus*), Little Eagles (*Hieraaetus morphnoides*) and Wedge-tailed Eagles (*Aquila audax*).

Since Northern Goshawks are not territorial in winter, they tend to gather where food is abundant. The resulting predation appears to depress grouse numbers in North America when goshawks irrupt during the low phase of the cycle of the Snowshoe Hare (*Lepus americanus*) further north, and in Sweden the wintering hawks

▲ Tool users, Egyptian Vultures (*Neophron percnopterus*) use stones to open ostrich eggs, then eat the contents. Standing, the vulture holds a stone in its mouth, raises its head and hurls the stone down in the general direction of the egg. After several attempts the bird usually succeeds. (Australian Black-breasted Buzzards also use this technique, as well as cracking the eggs themselves against a stone.)

BONE DROPPING BY BEARDED VULTURES

C. J. BROWN

Wind direction ▶

The Bearded Vulture (*Gypaetus barbatus*) is a large (about 5.7 kilograms; 12.5 pounds), solitary, cliff-nesting raptor that inhabits mountainous regions in Eurasia and Africa. It feeds on carrion, ranging in size from small rodents to the carcasses of large ungulates, such as cattle and eland. Bearded Vultures will feed on meat and soft tissue when this is available, but they prefer bones and marrow. Also, they are unable to compete for meat with the gregarious and larger griffon *Gyps* vultures, which usually dominate at a carcass. Bearded Vultures normally wait to one side until the other vulture species have cleaned a carcass of most soft material. They then remove the bones from the carcass, either singly or in sections, depending on the size of the dead animal. Limb bones are selected first, followed by ribs, vertebrae and skull. The overall diet of the Bearded Vulture normally comprises about 70 percent bone and marrow, 25 percent meat and 5 percent skin.

The Bearded Vulture has a large gape (about 70 millimeters; 3 inches) and is able to swallow whole bones or parts of bones up to at least 250 millimeters (10 inches) long and 35 millimeters (1.4 inches) in diameter; sharp, splintered ends seem to cause no discomfort. Bones that are larger than this are also utilized but are first dropped by the birds onto rocks, which breaks them into smaller pieces and allows access to the marrow. Once a bone has been removed from the food source, it is carried to a bone-dropping site, or ossuary. The bone is held in both feet, lengthways and tucked up against the body. Bone dropping is a deliberate and precise activity which has developed as a regular and important part of food preparation. Adult birds spend an average of 15 minutes per day dropping bones.

Each pair of Bearded Vultures has a number of ossuaries (mean = 2.4; range 1–4) within a few kilometers of its nest. An ossuary usually consists of a smooth slab of exposed rock on a gentle slope (10–20°) facing into the prevailing winds. If no such site is available birds occasionally make use of an area with a high concentration of loose boulders. Ossuaries range in size from 50 to 1500 square meters (60–1800 square yards) and are mainly found on the summit of a hill, ridge or escarpment from where the bird has a clear all-round view.

The Bearded Vulture glides down-wind towards the dropping zone in a shallow dive at about 60–80 kilometers (37–50 miles) per hour. A few seconds before dropping the bone, the angle of the dive is made a little steeper, the legs are lowered and the bone is clasped with only one foot while the other one steadies it. At the point of release the bird checks its flight by lowering its tail a little and fanning its wings slightly upwards. The bone may either be dropped or pushed forcefully away from the body. Variations include the execution of a sharp

turn at the point of release, which gives the impression that the bone is being flung at the ossuary, and a sharp braking, even hovering for a wingbeat or two, just before the bone is released. This last method is used mainly by inexperienced young birds.

Bones are dropped from a height of about 60 meters (197 feet) with great accuracy. In over 400 observed bone drops over rock slabs none missed the target, while the success rate over concentrations of boulders was about 60 percent.

Immediately the bone is released, the Bearded Vulture turns sharply into the wind and descends almost vertically with fanning wings to land beside the bone or fragments. The descent is fast to forestall other birds which might steal the food. Bones rarely break on the first drop, and the same bone may be dropped 20 or more times. On average, however, a bone needs to be dropped about six times to reduce it to pieces small enough to be swallowed. Most bones which are dropped are limb bones of medium to large ungulates. Bones of smaller animals are swallowed whole, and bones such as ribs do not achieve sufficient velocity when dropped to break apart.

The bird then retrieves the bone and feeds on any pieces small enough to swallow. When it has fed it takes off into the wind with the remainder of the bone clasped in one foot, while the other is used to push off. The bird rises up on slope lift, then glides back over the ossuary for another drop, and the whole process is repeated until the bone has been consumed.

The Bearded Vulture is specialized both physically and behaviorally to feed on a remarkable diet of mainly bones. It has no serious avian competitor for this food over most of its range and, in addition, the energy content of its diet is about 15 percent higher than that of an equivalent mass of meat.

David Hollands

reached a density close to one per square kilometer (0.4 square mile) on an estate where pheasants were released. Under these circumstances, the goshawks were a real problem for game managers. However, almost 80 percent of these hawks were dispersing juveniles, and licenses could be obtained to trap and remove them. Goshawks could also be killed legally at farmyards where there were poultry at risk. In one study area, the radio-tagging of 350 hawks showed that 36 percent were subsequently killed in this way, but without reducing the breeding population to the level at which first-year hawks could breed.

For many people, such destruction of raptors is unacceptable. When raptor numbers were low, partly as a result of organochlorine pesticide use, research suggested that their predation could have little impact on game. More recent findings, from larger raptor populations, indicate that raptors can not only compete severely with human hunters for the post-breeding yield from game stocks, but can also sometimes reduce the numbers of breeding

prey. Occasionally the heavy predation results from changes in land-use which to some extent can be reversed: for example, by improving game cover in intensely agricultural areas. In other cases the removal of raptors is the only effective way to conserve game, or to preserve rare non-game species, and therein lies a dilemma. If it became illegal to protect pheasants from goshawks in Sweden, most pheasant management would cease and pheasant numbers would fall. But goshawks numbers would probably fall too, because wild pheasants, in areas where they are managed for shooting, can provide 40 percent of the winter food for male hawks. If raptor predation makes it impractical to manage heather moorland for Red Grouse in Scotland, should one allow predator control and thus help to prevent the game management being replaced by some alternative form of land-use less favorable to wildlife? If one accepts management of livestock and game, why not limited management of raptors too where this is necessary? These are often difficult problems for the conservationist to resolve.

▲ Brown Falcons (*Falco berigora*) and other raptors have taken advantage of the introduction of rabbits to Australia. The falcons often prey on young, inexperienced kittens, but seldom tackle larger rabbits, perhaps fearing failure and even injury.

▼ The Honey Buzzard sometimes brings the combs of wasps, hornets and bees back to its nest, eating them and any larvae, pupae or adults they contain. Its stiff, snug plumage probably protects it from the insects' angry stings.

Guy Robbrecht/Bruce Coleman Ltd

SOCIAL BEHAVIOR

PENNY OLSEN

Aloof, solitary and aggressive, this is the popular view of a raptor—social is not a word that springs to mind. Yet vast wheeling flocks of Black Kites returning to roost side by side for the night, or crowds of vultures bluffing and bickering over a carcass, are obvious and well-known examples of raptor sociality. Indeed all raptors are social while breeding, and many species are gregarious for at least part of their lives. Nor are raptors more aggressive towards each other than are the individuals of many other bird groups. Certainly raptors are heavily armed and therefore potentially dangerous but, through social behavior, close combat is usually avoided and aggression has become largely ritualized. A series of escalating threats or social signals, beginning with calling and direct, sustained eye contact and threatening posture, or powerful flying displays, usually establishes the superiority of one of the contestants well before they lock talons, and the loser retreats.

▼ In the rosy light of sunset, Black Kites (*Milvus migrans*) gather at a communal roost to settle for the night. As many as 100 birds may arrive nightly at favored roost trees, some of which are used all winter for several years. Such sociability contrasts strongly with the popular image of a raptor as a fierce, independent loner.

Y. Eshbol/Israel Raptor Information Center

Social behavior can be defined as any kind of behavioral interaction between individuals. Like other aspects of animal nature, it has evolved because it benefits the individual. Just as we may make economic decisions with the aim of maximizing monetary profit, raptors make evolutionary decisions with the aim of maximizing the number of successfully reproducing offspring they have over their lifetime. However, they don't weigh up the costs, benefits and uncertainties to make a conscious decision—natural selection makes it for them. Individuals that make the best decisions survive to breed successfully, in the process passing on their genes to future generations, whereas individuals that make the wrong decisions fail to reproduce. In any social situation, individuals that behave inappropriately have reduced chances of survival and reproduction, while those that give and respond to signals in acceptable ways are successful in attracting a mate, acquiring a meal, or holding a territory.

Even solitary raptors must possess social skills, not only to form pair bonds for reproduction, but also to avoid unnecessary conflict in encounters with others over food, territory, mates or roosts. Many raptors that live solitarily, or as mated pairs during much of their lives, form loose flocks during their first few years, where food is abundant, or during migration (see the chapter on migration). Where locusts swarm, or where grass fires burn, a variety of species may gather, each observing certain rules that maintain individual distance (the exclusive space around an individual), preventing collisions and keeping aggression to a minimum so that feeding can proceed unhindered. Such gatherings are social rather than sociable. At the other end of the spectrum to the loner are raptors that roost and

▼ Each member of a pair of Secretarybirds (*Sagittarius serpentarius*), engrossed in the ritual head bowing of courtship, must send and react to behavioral signals. If either behaves inappropriately, they may fail to breed.

Francois Gohier/Jacana

▲ Even disputes over food are social. A tug-of-war between Striated Caracaras (*Phalcoboenus australis*) over a scrap of food appears harmless, but it would not have gone ahead if the relationship between the two and their behavior towards each other had not been appropriate. Recklessness is risky.

► Wings hitched and half open, and head lowered, an Egyptian Vulture (*Neophron percnopterus*) takes exaggerated footsteps as it approaches a rival (out of picture) with food. Aggressive towards its own kind, the vulture usually defers to other species.

◄ Social behavior is also important in dealing with other species. In a dispute over a carcass, a Tawny Eagle (*Aquila rapax*), approached by a menacing Lappet-faced Vulture (*Aegypius tracheliotos*), rises to maximum height and spreads its wings wide.

▼ Visual signals are particularly important to diurnal birds of prey. Some species have adornments used to signal status or intent. The floppy crest feathers of the Long-crested Eagle (*Spizaetus occipitalis*) can be raised to communicate aggression or readiness to attack.

Angelo Gandolfi

Stan Osolinski/Oxford Scientific Films

Stan Osolinski/Oxford Scientific Films

breed in colonies and hunt together. In these raptor societies there is usually a hierarchy or peck order, the most dominant individuals taking precedence over nest sites and food supplies.

SIGNALS

Sociality implies communication. Raptors, like other animals, use signals to communicate information that elicits a response or influences another in some way. Sometimes the signals are directly functional—the begging of a chick signals hunger and the parent responds by feeding it. In other situations, signals have become ritualized, particularly during courtship, for example, when the female begs for food from the male, by whining and assuming a low, submissive posture. While she may be hungry, and the male may feed her, the interaction is an integral part of a stereotyped behavior (ritual) that typically culminates in copulation.

Signals convey not only intention but also information about the signaler. Status, age, size, strength and species can often be ascertained at a glance. Size is a powerful signal, and many raptors make themselves appear larger when threatened by fluffing out their feathers, spreading their wings and tail, and standing tall. Mantling over food to retain it and bluffing an intruder in a close encounter are situations where large size is advantageous. The Great Philippine Eagle (*Pithecophaga jefferyi*), crested eagles, bazas and some other raptors have crests that they raise when threatened, presumably adding to the illusion of great size and ferocity. Conversely, small size can be less threatening, and crouching is an effective submissive posture used by the female during courtship or by a loser in a conflict attempting to appease the winner.

Visual signals are particularly important to raptors, but vocalization, an auditory signal, is also widely used. Many raptors call excitedly and determinedly during aggressive encounters, perhaps hoping to deter the opponent by the strength and persistence of the cacophony. Courtship involves softer, often nestling-like, vocalizations and also sharper, more excited calls as sexual excitement builds up, all part of a reciprocal ritual that bonds the pair together and culminates in reproduction.

Signals need not be actively sent. The color and pattern of many species identify their age group or sex. Australian Kestrels (*Falco cenchroides*) of both sexes have chestnut heads and tails and tend to be heavily marked with black in their first year; adult females are similar but more lightly marked, while adult males have gray heads and tails which they use to advantage in displays. Some species, for example goshawks and Peregrines, are vertically streaked in their first year and horizontally barred in later years. Eye color may also change with age. Variable Goshawks

(*Accipiter novaehollandiae*) begin life with gray eyes which soon change to the yellow of the first-year bird, and then, with increasing age, to orange and finally a fierce deep red. A few raptors have sexual accessories that signal sex and status. Mature male Andean Condors (*Vultur gryphus*) have colorful wattles and combs that may attract females and deter other males. The bloom or richness of the plumage or comb may also advertise the health and status of the individual.

Birds with a more threatening, mature appearance may be less likely to be attacked by congeners than those with immature characters. Young hawks are often driven from place to place in their first few years, until they have the strength and experience to hold their own territory. Their plumage signals their inexperience, and they are unlikely to put up much opposition to a mature territory holder. Mature birds, on the other hand, may be serious challengers and are not likely to be tackled until they have been assessed, through a series of rituals escalating in aggression, and the odds weighed up. The encounter may begin with a territory owner perching prominently, displaying his mature plumage. If the intruder approaches, direct eye contact is maintained and the intruder visually followed and an aggressive, ready-to-attack stance taken. Then there is an aerial chase with much calling and stooping, and finally physical contact. Either bird may flee before contact if the signals coming from its opponent indicate that it is outclassed and unlikely to win. Such aggressive encounters occur when a raptor attempts to obtain or keep resources for survival or successful reproduction (food, nests, nestlings and mates). Owners seem most often to be the victors; and challengers, having judged the size, strength, status and intention of the defender, often appease or flee to avoid the potential cost of injury or death.

Some signals may be the result of conflicting responses. Perched American Kestrels (*Falco sparverius*) and Black-shouldered Kites (*Elanus caeruleus*) quite often repeatedly flick their tail up in a jerky, annoyed manner, when faced with a potential intruder. This may be the result of a conflict between the desire for both fight and flight, but probably conveys a warning to the intruder. Other signals seem less ambiguous. During the breeding season bachelors, and mated males, of some species are often noisy and excited and carry prey around dangling conspicuously from their feet, clearly an invitation to females. The vigor of the display of male Northern Harriers (*Circus cyaneus*) reflects body condition, so it is an honest advertisement of health and skill. Once a mate has been found, the appropriate rituals must be observed by both partners to establish and maintain the pair bond. Falcon pairs perform a mutual bowing display. Such exchanges may help synchronize the hormonal cycle of the pair so that they are ready to breed at the same time.

Annie Price/Survival Anglia

◄ While visual signals are important, auditory communication is a notable part of many encounters. In an attempt to upstage an aggressive intruder, a Striated Caracara throws back its head and repeatedly broadcasts a high-pitched screech.

Dieter & Mary Plage/Bruce Coleman Ltd

◄ Fighting is usually avoided through an exchange of various less-aggressive behaviors during which the birds gauge each other's status and strength and the inferior bird defers or flees. Here a young Sea Eagle (*Haliaeetus leucogaster*) has not avoided attack by an adult. Inexperienced, it may have blundered into the adult's territory or ignored its warning signals. The pair lock talons in a spectacular but risky aerial battle, which the adult, in the superior position above, will almost certainly win.

▼ Soft gray plumage contrasting with deep orange to red legs and facial skin, and red-brown eye, immediately distinguish this adult Pale Chanting Goshawk from the brown-plumaged, pale-eyed immature. These passive signals not only denote a bird's age—the richness of the colors may be a sign of health or vigor used to attract breeding partners or deter rivals.

Peter Steyn/Ardea London

FIRST SOCIAL INTERACTIONS

Even before raptor chicks begin the laborious process of opening the shell, they may call from within the egg and their parent may answer. Soon after hatching, one of the chick's first experiences is likely to involve social behavior, peeping for warmth if cold or for food if hungry. The mother will respond to these signals by brooding the youngster or giving it tiny slivers of meat. Later, the chick must deal with nest mates. Young siblings may huddle together for warmth and when older will nibble and play with each other. When the

mother returns with food, the chicks respond by crowding towards her wailing to be fed, and take the pieces she offers, usually in an orderly fashion. Feeding time may bring out some boisterous rivalry, especially among older nestlings, but most of the aggression is bluff and grab, and peace soon returns. In a few large raptors, however, nest life is short for the weaker or smaller chicks as they are killed by their siblings, usually in the first few days. Crowned Eagles (*Spizaetus coronatus*), Verreaux's Eagles (*Aquila verreauxii*) and Lesser Spotted Eagles (*Aquila pomarina*) usually have two eggs but only one nestling survives. The first hatched

▶ The first social interactions in any raptor's life occur in the nest. Soft but insistent peeping by Bald Eagle (*Haliaeetus leucocephalus*) chicks stimulate the female parent to feed them. She gently proffers small slices of meat, turning her head slightly so that they can reach up and take the food from between her upper and lower beak. The whole sequence is instinctive but runs more smoothly as both parent and chicks gain experience.

Lori Lauber/Oxford Scientific Films

chick always relentlessly attacks its sibling until it dies or falls from the nest. Nestling harriers and those of some other species only kill the weakest chick when food is scarce.

During nestling life another important social process, *imprinting*, begins. The chick imprints on whatever feeds it, be it parent species or some substitute, and forms an early attachment. In later life it may react sexually to that species. If it has been raised by humans, especially if contact has been maintained, the raptor may court and mate with particular individual humans and aggressively scorn others. Raptors socialized (imprinted) in this way have been used in captive breeding programs to facilitate artificial insemination. In nature, imprinting may help to maintain the discreteness of species.

Raptors do not seem to recognize their individual offspring. Osprey (*Pandion haliaetus*), sparrowhawk and kestrel fledglings may join a neighboring brood, particularly a younger one where they are at an advantage in competition for food, and are tolerated and fed by the adults. Nevertheless, after leaving the nest most fledglings remain with their parents for a time. Some, for example, Ospreys and Snail Kites (*Rostrhamus sociabilis*) follow their parents to hunting areas. Not only do they gradually learn to hunt but their relationship with their parents changes. When first leaving the nest they are usually given food by their parents and pursue them vigorously whenever their parents return with food. Later the parent reacts aggressively to these demands for food, and some males (for example, Peregrines) may even eventually drive their fledgings from the territory. Depending upon the species and circumstances, the fledglings may then disperse from their natal territory. Occasionally, siblings remain together or join a loose group of fledglings and unattached adults (for example, Australian Kestrels and several other falcon species). Others remain with their parents in a family group, and some of these may help their parents during the next breeding season (examples are Harris' Hawks (*Parabuteo unicinctus*), Galapagos Hawks (*Buteo galapagoensis*), and perhaps occasionally Peregrine Falcons (*Falco peregrinus*)). Still others may eventually take their, usually junior, place among the colony (Eleonora's Falcon (*Falco eleonorae*), Griffon Vultures (*Gyps coprotheres*)).

RELATIONSHIP BETWEEN THE SEXES

Breeding is the most important social event in a raptor's life, for it is the only way to pass genes on to future generations. Successful breeding in raptors necessitates a cooperative effort by both parents, and in most raptors the division of duties according to sex is marked. The female does most of the incubating and caring for the nestlings; the male hunts for the female and, later, the nestlings, from the courtship period well into the nestling

Francois Gohier/Ardea London

period when the female may also begin to hunt. Vultures, with their special feeding habits, show no division of parental duties according to sex.

As well as holding a territory, a male raptor must be a skilled salesman, for females are discriminating buyers. Pair formation entails a series of activities, particularly courtship feeding, during which the male must give food to the female and often displays his vigor in skillful flying displays. His diligence at keeping her supplied with food is necessary for egg formation and is thought to be an important indicator to the female that he is a high-quality male, likely to be able to sustain the breeding attempt. If he cannot keep her well fed, the female may move on. Female Hen Harriers (*Circus cyaneus*) sometimes join the harem of an experienced male (on a good territory) rather than pair with an inexperienced bachelor.

DIMORPHISM

Over 200 years ago, Darwin suggested that in species where the sexes share a lifestyle but differ, say in size or color, the difference can be attributed to the struggle between the members of one sex for possession of the other. The unsuccessful competitors do not necessarily die but usually have few or no offspring.

In most birds males are the larger sex. In most raptor species, however, females are bigger than males; in some species females are as much as twice the male's weight. Females are often not just scaled-up versions of the male but, pro rata, may be more heavily armed. It has been argued that dimorphism has evolved through sexual selection; large body size in females is favored because it increases the chances of success when competing for males—that is, it increases the likelihood of successful breeding.

▲ Unlike most other raptors, vultures show no division of parental duties. Both sexes incubate, brood, bring food to the nest and regurgitate scavenged food for their chicks. Once fledged, this Eurasian Griffon (*Gyps fulvus*) nestling will join a colony.

▼ Nestlings quickly learn to respond to the distinctive head and facial pattern of their parent. The process is known as imprinting and in later life helps with species recognition. A puppet surrogate is used to deliver food to these captive-bred Peregrine Falcons.

Frans Lanting/Bruce Coleman Ltd

David A. Ponton

▲ The male of most raptor species is smaller than the female. Because this is unusual among other birds, where if one sex is bigger it is most often the male, the difference between the sexes is known as reversed size dimorphism (RSD). The male Cooper's Hawk (at right) might weigh 380 grams (13 ounces) and is dwarfed by the 560 gram (19 ounce) female.

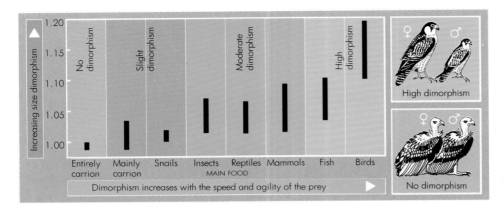

▲ A relationship between the degree of difference in size of the sexes (dimorphism) and diet is evident. In general, in species that need the greatest speed and agility to capture prey, the female is much larger than the male (highly dimorphic). At the other end of the spectrum are species that feed on slow-moving, easily caught prey or carrion; they show little or no dimorphism in size (weakly dimorphic or monomorphic). Bars show the range of dimorphism found among species in each dietary group.

▼ Squabbling around a carcass, male and female Eurasian Griffons (*Gyps fulvus*) are indistinguishable in size. Aspects of their social system give clues to why the females of some other species are so much larger than the male, a question that has fascinated scientists for decades. One possible explanation is that most male vultures are adequate foragers so that there is little competition among females for breeding partners. The males of highly dimorphic bird hunters must be very skilled to be able to catch enough birds to support a breeding attempt; hence competition between females for those relatively scarce, skilled males is fierce, and bigger females are the most successful competitors.

There have been many other theories as to why female raptors are larger and why in some species there is a bigger difference between the sexes than in others. The second question has proved easier to answer than the first. Raptors that feed on carrion show little or no difference in size between the sexes, insect-eaters are slightly more dimorphic, then reptile-eaters, mammal-eaters, fish-eaters and, the most dimorphic of all, bird-eaters. In general this explanation involving a link with diet holds, although exceptions to the rule show that it is oversimplified. The bird- and mammal-eating harriers are among the most dimorphic of raptors, the gecko-eating Mauritius Kestrel (*Falco punctatus*) is more dimorphic than the mammal-eating Old World Kestrel (*Falco tinnunculus*), while the bird-eating Eleonora's Falcon and Square-tailed Kite (*Lophoictinia isura*) are only moderately and weakly dimorphic, respectively. A more comprehensive explanation seems to be that in species which typically depend on either food or nests that are hard to acquire, then dimorphism is greatest. The Mauritius Kestrel, for example, hunts in a forest, while the Common Kestrel hunts in the open, Eleonora's

Falcon catches tired migrant birds, and the Square-tailed Kite lives on nestling birds.

The hunters of difficult prey are the most dimorphic. Prey may be difficult because it is fast and agile, large, or hard to catch for other reasons. In these raptors it is more difficult to be a high-quality male than it is in species living on food that is easier to collect, when it is relatively easy to be a male capable of supporting breeding. Similarly, in harriers, it may be more difficult for a male to hold a breeding territory (and again, to be a high-quality male) than it is in species where territories are numerous and widely scattered. Competition for these high-quality males is probably fierce. Big females may be more able to deter other females and breed, so that sexual selection favors bigger females. Herein lies the most likely explanation for the reason why females are larger than males. In dimorphic species, males have remained about the same size while intrasexual competition has selected for big females (*intrasexual selection*). Females compete among themselves for a scarce resource (a good male with a territory); the scarcer the resource the bigger the female.

Color dimorphism is also likely to have evolved and be maintained by sexual selection. It is not particularly common or obvious in raptors but, as in most birds, the adult male of color-dimorphic raptors is the more vibrantly plumaged, while the adult female tends to remain similar to the juvenile. Perhaps the most striking males are those of the polygynous harriers which must compete intensely with other males to attract and retain a harem. Their attention-drawing plumage may advertise that they are better than the next male (*intrasexual competition*), and females may choose to stay with the more attractively hued males rather than their plainer competitors (*intersexual selection*).

BREEDING SYSTEMS

Breeding in raptors requires a great deal of cooperation between the sexes, achieved for the most part through social interaction. This cooperative effort is referred to as the mating system, and each species has a particular system adhered to by most individuals. Because bi-parental care is mandatory in raptors, at least for part of the breeding cycle, the options are limited and most species are *monogamous*.

Brown Falcons (*Falco berigora*), Peregrines in Australia, Lesser Kestrels (*F. naumanni*), Black Eagles and several other raptors typically remain with the same partner year round for several seasons. Peregrines in the tundra, Australian Kestrels, Tawny Eagles (*Aquila rapax*) and other non-resident raptors may winter apart but return to the same breeding territory and often re-unite with the same partner. Fidelity seems to be a feature of species even when, because of conditions in some regions, the sexes spend the non-breeding season apart. However, some raptors are monogamous only for the duration of a single breeding attempt, taking a new mate the following year. Yet others are monogamous for most of the breeding attempt and may then move on to another partner (*successive polygamy*). Snail Kites of either sex may leave their partner to finish raising the nestlings and, presumably, move on to another. Female Black-shouldered Kites leave their fledglings in the care of their mate and may pair again with a different male.

Sometimes it may be difficult to distinguish a polygamous (polygynous or polyandrous) breeding attempt from *cooperative breeding*. About 10 percent of a breeding population of Peregrines in France had an extra bird, usually an immature female, which helped with feeding and defense, and increased the breeding success of the

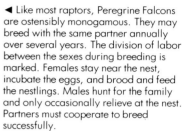

◀ Like most raptors, Peregrine Falcons are ostensibly monogamous. They may breed with the same partner annually over several years. The division of labor between the sexes during breeding is marked. Females stay near the nest, incubate the eggs, and brood and feed the nestlings. Males hunt for the family and only occasionally relieve at the nest. Partners must cooperate to breed successfully.

pair, but did not breed. Helpers usually do help by increasing the chances of successfully fledging chicks. At one Red-tailed Hawk (*Buteo jamaicensis*) nest with a helper, the chicks were brooded much longer than at a nest with a pair. This was especially important during a severe rainstorm. For Harris' Hawks the benefit of having helpers is not an increase in the number of chicks at a single nesting, but biannual nesting by the group rather than the annual nesting of pairs.

Harris' Hawks frequently breed in groups focused on the breeding pair which are assisted by some of their, usually male, offspring from previous years. They were once thought to have a *polyandrous* breeding system, but it is now considered that, in most cases, only the dominant male mates with the female. Two males have been seen attending the same female at the nest of the Black-breasted Buzzard (*Hamirostra melano-sternon*) and Galapagos Hawk. In the latter species

◀ Galapagos Hawks (*Buteo galapagoensis*) often breed in trios of one female and two, sometimes more, males. If the female mates with both males, as is thought to be the case, then they are polyandrous. In habitats where prey is scarce or difficult to catch, two males may be needed to provide enough food to the female and their offspring. These adults have captured a marine iguana.

females are thought to mate with more than one male (true polyandry) and breeding associations of up to two females and five males have been found, although two or three males with one female is more usual.

Another alternative to monogamy is *polygyny*, which among raptors, is only frequent in harriers. Certain male harriers are able to monopolize several females, who nest within their territory. Older, more experienced males tend to have more wives than young males. Male Hen Harriers occasionally have six females at a time, but up to three is more usual. Within the harem there tends to be a hierarchy; one female receives more food than the others and is an earlier and more successful breeder. Not all male harriers have more than one mate, however.

Other species are polygynous on occasion, seemingly when the territory, season or male is good enough to support the breeding attempt of more than one female. Common Buzzards, several kestrel species, Red-tailed Hawks, sparrowhawks and Ospreys are just some of the raptors that are normally monogamous but in which occasional males have been found supporting two breeding females laying in the same or separate nests.

When most species are regularly monogamous and all have at least some pairs breeding monogamously, why do some choose other systems? When just a few individuals breed polygamously it is probably in response to exceptional local conditions. When polygamy becomes characteristic of a species, it has presumably evolved to fit the species to its environment and ecology. The polygyny of harriers appears to suit them to a rich but patchy habitat. A small swamp may offer an abundance of food and nest sites and can be monopolized by one or a few males. At least the more experienced of those males may be able to feed several females. Polyandry, on the other hand, may have arisen in species occupying areas where food is scarce or difficult to catch; where two males (or more) are more likely to be able to provide more consistent support to a breeding attempt than one, particularly if they hunt cooperatively.

HYBRIDS IN NATURE AND IN CAPTIVITY

PENNY AND JERRY OLSEN

Hybrids are an exception to a rule. They challenge the most widely accepted characteristic used to define a species, that it does not hybridize with other species. Various isolating mechanisms—geographic, climatic, behavioral or mechanical—generally ensure that mates are chosen from among the same species. Where barriers are broken down, hybridization may occur, most commonly where two previously spatially separate populations are brought together, or near the borders of a species range where mate choice for one species may be limited. At a cliff typically frequented by Prairie Falcons (*Falco mexicanus*), a male Peregrine Falcon (*F. peregrinus*) drove off a male Prairie Falcon and bred with the female. Hybrids also occur where both species are rare; for example, Black Kites (*Milvus migrans*) and Red Kites (*M. milvus*) have hybridized in Germany and Sweden.

Nevertheless, hybrids are extremely rare in nature, especially in raptors where a prolonged courtship, involving many exchanges of visual and auditory signals, makes mistaken identity unlikely. Moreover, some cases of apparently natural hybridization may involve escaped captives, whose history may have led them to make inappropriate choices of mates.

In captivity, many of the natural barriers are removed and isolation and confinement can lead to hybridization. The more closely related the species, the more likely they will pair (although hybridization is not necessarily proof of relatedness). Congeners, the Whistling Kite (*Haliastur sphenurus*) and Brahminy Kite (*H. indus*) find each other suitable substitutes for partners of their own kind when caged together, producing

▲ Nesting in a remnant of what was once typical Variable Goshawk habitat, now extensively cleared, a pair of hybridizing goshawks have bred successfully for several years. The combination of male Variable Goshawk (white form) (*Accipiter novaehollandiae*) and female Brown Goshawk (*A. fasciatus*) is akin to a leopard-lion or zebra-horse cross.

offspring with characteristics of both parents. Manipulation too can increase the chance of interbreeding. Young raptors placed in the nest of a different species imprint on their foster parents and are likely candidates for future hybridization. Artificial insemination bypasses most of the obstacles to hybridization. Curiosity and the quest for a super-bird for falconry have led to some unlikely combinations; hybrids have been produced artificially from a cross between a 200 gram (7 ounce) Merlin (*Falco columbarius*) and a Gyrfalcon (*F. rusticolus*) up to ten times as heavy.

For polygamy to evolve it must offer greater benefits to the participants than monogamy. In a population of Harris' Hawks, trios raised an average of two young per year compared with just over one for pairs, so that each individual benefited from nesting in a trio. A study of Hen Harriers showed that males with four wives had 74 percent, and males with two wives 30 percent, more young than those with one. The benefits for females were less clear as each harem member produced, on average, fewer young than did a female in a monogamous relationship. Nevertheless polygamy offered them a chance to breed which they might not otherwise have had, and possibly enhanced their survival.

Another means of breeding is worth mentioning, although it is not yet well documented in raptors. Extra-pair copulation or *cuckoldry* can increase the number of offspring a male fathers, with little cost to him as he does not contribute to their care. If a female mates with an intruder, her male may be fooled into raising some nestlings that are not his own. A female is not able to increase the number of her offspring through cuckoldry but may gain from whatever beneficial genes the cuckolding male may successfully pass on to her offspring.

SPACING SYSTEMS

Breeding territories: As Aristotle observed "one does not find two pairs of eagles in the same wood," implying that a pair of eagles excludes others. They may not only exclude others of their kind but also similar raptors. They are defending a resource necessary for breeding, and the resource must be limiting otherwise it would not be worth defending from competitors. Scarce (limiting) resources include food, breeding sites and mates. However, many raptors appear to hold breeding territories not merely to monopolize the food they contain. Rather, they hunt over a wider area often overlapping in home range with their neighbors and appear to hold territories mainly to monopolize nest or mates. Nevertheless, food requisition is also involved because raptors space themselves more widely where food is scarce than where it is abundant. For a given raptor species, spacing between pairs tends to be regular, which suggests not only defense of a resource but also a spacing system.

Male raptors appear to need a territory before they can attract a female. They may either find a vacated territory and advertise for a female or drive off another male and usurp his territory and mate. Territories are a common source of conflict for both sexes which are largely concerned with intruders of the same sex. A consequence of territoriality is that some birds cannot breed. These non-territorial birds are called floaters. Usually a floater moves in almost immediately a territory-holding bird is removed or dies. Territory quality

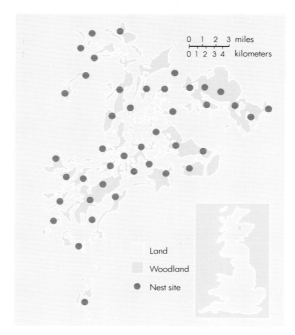

Land

Woodland

● Nest site

◄ Although somewhat constrained by the patchiness of woodlands (shown here in green), nesting pairs of Eurasian Sparrowhawk space themselves regularly. Dots mark the place where the pair builds its nest. Regular spacing is indicative of a spacing system, territoriality. For such a system to be necessary, the territory must contain a defensible resource—food, nest or mate, or all three.

is important and may be an additional reason for conflict. Female Eurasian Sparrowhawks (*Accipiter nisus*) on poor territories often move to a better territory the subsequent breeding season, never to a poorer one.

Most raptors nest as *solitary* pairs. This is thought to be because, in general, sites for nests and food are fairly evenly distributed and predictable. Raptors that depend on clumped or unpredictable prey tend to be *colonial* nesters. Less than 15 percent of raptor species nest in colonies, a similar percentage to that for all birds. Occasionally, individual pairs of most of these colonially breeding raptors will nest solitarily. There is a continuum from solitary nesting species with pairs spaced several kilometers apart through to species whose pairs nest a few meters apart in tight colonies. For our convenience, colonial breeders can be divided into two types: those that nest at traditional colonies year after year and those that tend to be nomadic and usually breed where prey is temporarily and sporadically abundant.

Many kites nest in temporary groups; sometimes several pairs may nest in the same tree, even sharing a nest at the same time (Letter-winged Kites (*Elanus scriptus*)) but, more often, if enough nest sites are available, are spaced more widely. Letter-winged Kites have been found nesting in groups of up to 50 pairs within 300 to 1000 meters (327–1090 yards) of woodland, with other colonies about 5 kilometers (3 miles) away. After dusk, when the Kites and their principal prey, the Long-haired Rat, become active, the colony is a busy, noisy center with nests at every stage from newly refurbished but empty, to those full of hungry nestlings. The colonies wax and wane in size, and as the rats become less common some nestlings are left to starve when the colony moves on or disbands.

Black Kites (*Milvus migrans*) and Red Kites (*M. milvus*) may nest in mixed colonies, numbering as many as 54 pairs (49 pairs of Black Kites and 5 of Red Kites), although less than 10 pairs is more typical. The colony members usually hunt independently, but may use the same area. In mixed colonies social signals of the two species must be sufficiently similar for them to live together successfully, although one species may be dominant in disputes over nests or food.

Those colonial species that use traditional sites are usually found where food is clumped and predictable and usually at least seasonally abundant. In some parts of the world Ospreys nest in groups and each pair defends an area around their nest of only 50 meters (164 feet). Eleonora's Falcons nest in falcon apartment blocks, on highly weathered cliffs and islands, and are aggressive to

neighbors breaching their territory of about 20 meters (65.6 feet) centered on their nest. The territory is little more than a place to breed, with a few nooks and crannies in which to cache prey. A hierarchy is often evident in these traditional colonies. The dominant birds hold the highest, perhaps largest nest areas, and are unchallenged by other colony members. Bachelors, if they have an area, may be towards the foot of the cliff near the seaspray zone and continually challenge the pairs of middle-ranking status. The Falcons hunt independently but form falcon walls that block the passage of the thousands of migrant birds that pour past the colony. There is also a good deal of piracy among the colony members. Griffon Vultures breed as well as feed gregariously in large numbers. Their food is unpredictable in space and they must cooperate to search a wide area.

▶ A solitarily nesting Australian Osprey (*Pandion haliaetus*) lands on its huge nest high on a rock pinnacle. Elsewhere, Ospreys sometimes nest in colonies and share information on the whereabouts of schooling fish. In such colonies the arrival of a male with a school fish is noisy and obvious. Neighboring males quickly respond by leaving in the direction from which he arrived. They have much greater success and catch fish more quickly than do uninformed males. Sharing benefits the colony members.

COLONIAL NESTING IN ELEONORA'S AND SOOTY FALCONS

H. S. WALTER

Eleonora's Falcon is a sociable species breeding in small groups and large colonies of over 100 pairs on rocky cliffs and islets in the Mediterranean Sea and eastern Atlantic. The largest colonies occur where three conditions are met: (1) minimum human disturbance, (2) plenty of prey, and (3) rocky surfaces with hundreds of cavities, pot-holes and protected ledges for nesting. The abundance of prey is provided by migrant birds which form a continual stream past the nesting areas of the falcons.

In a large Moroccan colony, the average spacing between nests was 10 meters (33 feet). A pot-hole covered islet with at least 48 pairs of Eleonora's Falcon (*Falco eleonorae*) had an average density of one breeding pair for every 69 square meters (745 square feet) of horizontal and vertical space. In this particular case, incubating falcons were sitting in deep pot-holes less than 2 meters (6.5 feet) away from each other. As a general rule, more complex and irregular rock surfaces were associated with higher breeding densities of these falcons.

These colonial falcons show nearly all behavior known from solitary Peregrines (*Falco peregrinus*). They establish exclusive personal space for nesting, perching, feeding and roosting. All activities (except hunting) occur on a tiny cliff area; sometimes a ledge is so small that feeding, preening, resting, roosting, displaying, prey caching and sunning occur within 1–3 meters (3–9 feet) around the nest. Young falcons often sit on a thick cushion of prey feathers because their parents carry the prey directly to the nest. In order to avoid disturbing the neighbors, each falcon learns to use specific flight corridors when arriving and departing. Aggressive incidents rarely occur because of the efficacy of threat displays shown by territorial neighbors. The falcon colony maintains a dynamic balance of power on the ground; in the air, falcons will collectively defend their colony area against potential predators.

Richard Vaughan/Ardea London

▲ A dramatic example of a colonially breeding raptor, pairs of Eleonora's Falcon nest in falcon apartment blocks. Rocky islets and cliffs hold large numbers, with as little as 2 meters between nesting pairs. Observance of certain social behaviors helps keep the peace.

The Sooty Falcon (*Falco concolor*), of Africa and Arabia, is less colonial than its Mediterranean relative. In Oman, a breeding cliff was 500 × 250 × 66 meters (1640 × 820 × 216 feet). Some 47 nesting territories were located there. Again, each pair "possessed" part of the cliff surface containing sunny and shady perch sites, prey-caching sites, and one or more potential nesting sites. Other falcons and gulls flying repeatedly at low height (5 meters or 16 feet) over a territory violated the territorial integrity and were quickly pursued for a short distance. Where nesting sites and prey are limited, Sooty Falcons breed in low densities, approximating the nesting patterns of solitary breeders like Peregrines and Lanners (*F. biarmicus*).

▲ Two Marsh Harriers (*Circus aeruginosus*) squabble over winter carrion. Typically, raptors do not like to share food. Even mated pairs will quarrel, and one may have to wait its turn while the other eats. They have cause for worry—piracy is common, and the larger, hungrier raptor is most often the victor.

Non-breeding territories: In the non-breeding season, some raptors remain near their breeding territory and defend an area. Others form loose, seemingly non-territorial flocks. Eleonora's Falcons continue to associate with each other after breeding, during migration and while wintering in Madagascar. Many species, highly territorial during breeding, become quite tolerant of others and migrate together en masse. In northern Australia, Brown Falcons (*Falco berigora*) and Black Falcons (*F. subniger*) congregate in mixed groups ahead of the regular winter, dry-season fires. Still other raptors have a winter area, distinct from the place where they breed, from which they exclude all conspecifics. Sometimes the sexes winter in different habitats; female American Kestrels and Eurasian Sparrowhawks have territories in more open country than do their respective males. Hen Harriers not only escort conspecific intruders from their winter territory but attack other raptors and drive them away to prevent piracy of their fresh and cached prey.

FLOCKING

Some species are more gregarious than others when not breeding. Many are solitary or remain as lone pairs. Some Peregrine and Brown Falcon pairs in Australia stay in loose contact near their breeding territory all year. Other solitary breeders form loose aggregations during migration or, often, in areas where food is abundant. Colonial breeders, Eleonora's Falcon, Letter-winged Kites and Griffon Vultures, for example, tend to stay in

flocks after breeding. Young raptors are more likely to flock than adults; perhaps it affords them some protection (from starvation and predators) while they learn and gain experience before finding their own territory. The benefits of flocking are hotly debated, but may include protection from predators, increased foraging efficiency (many pairs of eyes are better than one; more chance of getting a meal) and increased opportunities for learning from others. Lesser Kestrels and some of the other small, insect-eating falcons spend their lives in flocks. They feed on gregarious insects, such as grasshoppers. Presumably another advantage of flocking is that their numbers tend to stir up insect swarms, making them easier to catch.

Raptor groups can be fleeting and fortuitous. Several small raptors may band together to drive off a larger one. The combined stoops of kestrels and goshawks are an effective deterrent to eagles intruding into their air space. Other mixed groups are less temporary. Turkey Vultures (*Cathartes aura*) and Black Vultures (*Coragyps atratus*), and Red and Black Kites may nest, roost and hunt together in areas where prey is abundant and preferred nests are clumped. The most social of raptors breed, feed and roost together year round, occasionally numbering thousands. Flock members may perch in the same tree by day and roost close together at night. Some species tolerate closer contact than others and perch with bodies touching; but usually they are more widely spaced. Before settling for the night, raptors may fly or soar

▶ Eurasian Griffons (*Gyps fulvus*), gathered on a clifftop in the Pyrenees, are among the most gregarious of raptors—they roost, feed and breed in flocks. When foraging, one of the benefits of group living becomes obvious: many eyes are better than one. Dotted over the sky the group can scan a vast area. Once a carcass is found, the sight of a descending bird signals the others, and they all converge.

together over the communal roost, the group gradually growing in size as more birds join from the surrounding countryside. In the morning they either disperse to hunt individually (Swamp Harrier) or leave to forage together (Lesser Kestrel).

The *Information Center Hypothesis* offers an explanation why raptors, which unlike many birds have little need for protection from predators, gather at communal roosts. It proposes that these roosts have a social function—they are places where unsuccessful hunters can meet, gain information from and follow successful hunters to food. A bird may be a successful hunter (a leader) one day and unsuccessful (a follower) the next, so that in the long run all birds benefit. Unsuccessful hunters may simply follow successful foragers because they leave the roost in a direct, vigorous or determined manner (passive exchange of information). Male Ospreys, however, returning to their partner and nestlings with a school fish (e.g. alewife, smelt, pollock) sometimes advertise their success noisily and with an undulating display flight, and, apparently in response, a number of other males leave the colony in the direction from which the successful hunter returned. Foraging time for these informed males is dramatically reduced. They may find fish quickly, and the attacks of several male Ospreys may disrupt the school and make individual fish easier to catch. Conversely, the possessors of non-schooling fish (e.g. flounder) arrive more discreetly and elicit no response from the other colony members. Sharing information about fish schools is mutually beneficial in the long run. At another Osprey breeding colony, located further from their foraging area (15 kilometers vs 2 kilometers), such information wasn't exchanged; presumably it was not useful at that distance from the feeding ground because fish schools would have moved on by the time informed Ospreys arrived.

Current thinking is that where food is patchy, ephemeral and locally plentiful there is little point in an individual or pair defending it, and some point in having several eyes looking for pockets of prey abundance and pooling their knowledge. In the long run all parties benefit by the reduction in periods spent without food. Scavengers such as cathartid vultures, that rely on ephemeral, non-evasive prey, are highly gregarious, and, while many find food by observing others congregating around a carcass (local enhancement), there is evidence that some information about the location of carcasses is exchanged at their night-time roost. Black Vultures were held in captivity without food then returned to their roost at nightfall. The next day they were among the last to depart the roost and accompanied other vultures to chicken carcasses put out during their confinement.

FORAGING

Most raptors hunt alone, but even among solitary breeders it is not uncommon for a pair to hunt together, with one bird flying ahead to stir up the prey and the other usually lower and behind to snatch up a startled, distracted victim (*cooperative*

Mike Gillam/Auscape

▲ Engaged in vicious battle over a bloody livestock carcass, these Wedge-tailed Eagles (*Aquila audax*) could have stepped out of a farmer's nightmare. Seemingly a free-for-all, even here certain "rules" of behavior are observed. Adults are dominant to immatures, and hungry birds usually prevail over sated birds. A challenger weights up the odds and probably attacks only those most likely to retreat.

▼ Tenderly preening the neck of her mate, a female Bateleur (*Terathopius ecaudatus*) lays to rest the popular notion that all raptors are solitary and aggressive.

hunting). Some of the more social raptors regularly hunt together. A flock of Sooty Falcons feeding on insects could be regarded as engaging in cooperative hunting.

For Harris' Hawks the advantage of group hunting is a key aspect of their social system. By hunting together they can depend on large, quite dangerous prey (jackrabbits) for their survival. In groups of about average size each individual gets more than it would if hunting solitarily, and eats more regularly. Other raptors also hunt together when prey is difficult. Wedge-tailed Eagles will band together in pairs or bigger groups to hunt

large Kangaroos and Dingos. The group members take turns swooping and harassing the prey until it tires. Later they normally share the kill, but not without conflict.

Eleonora's Falcons form a wall to block migrating passerines passing over the sea. They space themselves 100–200 meters (328–656 feet) apart and chase birds individually. The migrant would regard this as a joint effort, as it must flee from as many as 150 hunting male falcons with no place to take cover. Sooty Falcons also take advantage of the vulnerability of migrants stranded over water, and two or more falcons may make group chases over the sea. Tunisian Peregrines hunting in cooperative pairs caught their prey during 38 percent of attacks, lone hunters were successful only about 20 percent of the time; if they shared meals, individuals that hunted in pairs were more successful than those that hunted individually.

Vultures commonly forage cooperatively and have a visual communication network. When carrion is scarce they spread out high and wide; when it is more abundant they soar lower and closer together. In East Africa, White-headed Vultures (*Aegypius occipitalis*) and Lappet-faced Vultures (*Aegypius tracheliotos*) usually arrive at a carcass first, followed by Rüppell's Griffons (*Gyps rueppellii*). There is a clear hierarchy in feeding order that is functional as well as social. Lappet-faced Vultures feed first and are the most aggressive; they mantle over the carcass and rush and strike at the other birds. They also have the size and strength to open the beast. The other vultures eat later. Each species has different feeding habits so that the carcass is shared, with something for everyone.

Many species have been seen either stealing food from a conspecific or from another species (*kleptoparasitism*). This usually involves an attack to upset the successful hunter and make it drop its prey, but may be the pirating of cached food. Usually the larger bird prevails; in fact, pirating from a larger bird is often not attempted. Whistling Kites have been photographed in pairs harrying a Heron until it dropped its fish.

In conclusion, contrary to popular opinion, not all raptors are solitary and aggressive. If social behavior is defined as any interaction between individuals then all raptors must be social in order to breed. Indeed, the social behavior of raptors is directly related to reproduction and survival. Examples can be found among raptors of most of the social behaviors and social systems found in other bird groups. Variations in this sociality can be explained by general ecology, particularly feeding habits and the spatial distribution of food. How and why the various social systems and behaviors work are some of the most interesting, challenging and relatively unstudied aspects of raptor biology.

Jonathan Scott

SOCIAL HUNTING IN HARRIS' HAWKS

JAMES C. BEDNARZ

Why are some raptors social? This question embodies one of the most interesting paradoxes confronting today's raptor scientists. Most raptors, especially predators of warm-blooded prey, by their very nature are competitive and aggressive. This is evident in the ferocity with which the typical hawk expels intruders from its territory. Hence, most of us harbor the image of the hawk as a lone hunter.

Contrary to this stereotypic portrait of a solitary hunter, the Harris' Hawk (*Parabuteo unicinctus*), is extremely social, and has been classified as a "cooperatively breeding species," in which groups of more than two birds commonly contribute to the rearing of young at a given nest. Research on Harris' Hawks in the deserts of New Mexico has attempted to answer the seemingly enigmatic question: Why are Harris' Hawks social? During the course of this research, several hypotheses that had been advanced to account for social living in this species were refuted. One of the remaining possibilities was that these hawks need to hunt in teams. The primary question that had to be answered was: Are hawks hunting in tandem substantially more successful in capturing and obtaining prey than solitary Harris' Hawks?

Fifteen hawks that were members of eight different social groups, of two to six members, were caught and fitted with small radio-transmitters. These hawks were followed on their hunting forays and their behavior observed. They almost never hunted solitarily, and seldom in pairs, but usually formed "hunting parties" involving four to six individuals. At dawn, the hawks of a particular family group, consisting of a male and female and their offspring up to 36 months of age, would often assemble on one tree. The party would then break up into small subunits (typically of two or three hawks) and alternately make short "leap frog" flights from tree to tree in one general direction. During these team searches, hawks of individual subunits continually monitored the activities and location of other group members. When prey was sighted, the entire hunting party immediately converged on the area, and implemented a variety of apparently coordinated hunting tactics in an effort to dispatch the prey, often a rabbit. Three tactics were effectively employed in variable sequence during the course of a chase.

1. The "surprise pounce" involved several hawks quickly converging on a rabbit that was isolated from cover.

2. If a rabbit reached cover, it was flushed out of its refuge by one or more hawks, while the others waited nearby in ambush: the "flush-and-ambush" technique.

3. Occasionally hunting parties participated in long-drawn-out chases in which individual hawks, by stooping at the appropriate moments, herded or deflected the prey into the pursuit field of their fellow hunters, thereby continually "passing" the role of lead pursuer from one hawk to another; this tactic was dubbed the "relay attack."

In all techniques the rabbits eventually became confused or exhausted, so that one hawk could dispatch the prey with minimal risk of injury to itself. The hazards of taking large prey

▲ Co-operative hunting by a group may allow capture of prey too large or elusive for a lone individual to tackle. Harris' Hawk families combine forces to ambush jackrabbits. At 7.34 am, perched on a powerline, this group detected prey. By 7.35 one bird had flushed the rabbit from its temporary refuge into the open, directly under the other three hawks waiting, alert in ambush.

may be a critical element favoring team hunting in this species because adult black-tailed jackrabbits weigh roughly three times as much as male Harris' Hawks and twice as much as females. After the quarry was secured all members of the hunting party guarded and shared the food.

A significant discovery was that the number of successful captures of rabbits increased per unit time as the size of the hunting party increased from two to six hawks. Hunting groups consisting of five or six members were estimated to have the greatest amount of food available for consumption by individual party members. These larger party sizes were most commonly observed during the non-breeding period, suggesting that the hawks "adjusted" their group to the size which provided the maximum food benefits to each individual hawk. These results support the hypothesis that successful cooperative hunts by Harris' Hawks are a key factor contributing to the development and maintenance of sociality in this species.

REPRODUCTION

ANDREW VILLAGE

Breeding in raptors is similar to that in other nidicolous birds (those that rear their young in nests): a courtship of variable duration culminates in the laying of eggs, which are incubated for a fairly fixed period before the young hatch. The chicks are fed by their parents and remain in the nest until they are ready to fly. After leaving the nest the young depend at first on their parents, but eventually they learn to feed themselves and wander away from the natal territory. In order to breed successfully, a raptor needs a mate, a suitable nest site, and a food supply sufficient for the whole breeding season.

The division of labor between the sexes sets raptors apart from some other birds. Raptors eat prey items that can be carried long distances to the nest, so the male is able to bring food to the female, rather than simply relieve her at the nest while she feeds herself. Most female raptors rely entirely on their mates for food from late courtship until the chicks are old enough to be left alone. The exceptions are species such as the larger vultures that eat food which cannot easily be transported. Males of these species share equally in incubating the eggs and brooding the chicks. This division of labor has profound effects on the behavior and ecology of raptors, and may be one reason why females are usually larger than males.

▼ Breeding is the most important event in a raptor's life. To produce this Wedge-tailed Eagle (*Aquila audax*) chick, the parents must have survived to breeding age, then found a suitable mate, nest and food supply for breeding. Barring accidents they should raise the chick to independence, no mean feat since only a minority of eagles contribute offspring to the next generation.

Jean-Paul Ferrero/Auscape

NESTS AND NESTING TERRITORIES

Raptors vary greatly in where and how they make their nests. Some eagles build huge nests that are added to each year and may eventually contain thousands of sticks. At the other extreme are species that do not build a nest, but merely scrape a depression in a soft substrate, into which they lay their eggs.

Whatever the nest, many raptors can be found breeding in the same locations from year to year. In some species this is because they re-use the same nest site, such as a particular cliff, hole in a tree or stick-nest. But even species that build a new nest each year often do so in the same restricted localities called *nesting territories*. Territories may be used by the same individuals for several successive years, and the habit of breeding at particular locations may persist for many generations.

Within a nesting territory, pairs may nest in a slightly different place each year. This is most noticeable where a new nest is built at each attempt, but pairs of most species will usually have more than one site in their territory where they could breed. Eagles often have several stick-nests in their territory, and they may add material to each one every year. Peregrines can scrape several nesting ledges before they finally choose one, and some pairs have alternative nesting cliffs that are several kilometers apart.

In general, large raptors have large nests that are often re-used, while small species build flimsier structures that are used for only one breeding attempt. There are exceptions to this rule, such as Snake Eagles (*Circaetus* spp.), which build relatively small, short-lived nests for their size, and Ferruginous Hawks (*Buteo regalis*) which build larger nests than closely related species of a similar size.

Of the 80 or so genera of Falconiformes, about 85 percent consist of nest-building species, nearly all of which build stick-nests in trees. Some tree-nesting species will also build on cliffs or on the ground if no suitable trees are present, but only one group, the *Circus* harriers, are largely confined to building nests on the ground. Raptors that do not build nests include the New World vultures and the falcons. They must find a ledge on a cliff or building, a suitable hole in a tree, the stick-nest of another bird species or a protected site on the ground.

The main requirements of a nest are that it gives some protection from predators, is able to hold the eggs and chicks safely and, if possible, gives shelter from extreme heat, cold or rain. Locating the nest high in a tree, or on a steep cliff, gives protection from most mammalian predators, and small accipters also build under the canopy, which gives additional protection from avian predators and rain.

Dave Watts/Australasian Nature Transparencies

Shortage of suitable sites for nests can prevent raptors from breeding in some areas, and this can be a particular problem for large species that require big trees or tall cliffs. However, many species will occasionally nest on the ground in open areas if there is some chance of escaping predators. Bald Eagles (*Haliaeetus leucocephalus*) nest on the ground in the Aleutian Islands, where there are no Arctic Foxes, and European Kestrels (*Falco tinnunculus*) nest among dense heather in the Orkney Islands, where there is no threat of mammalian predators.

▲ None of the falcons are known to build a nest. By scraping with its feet and shuffling its body in the debris on the floor of a high cliff ledge, this Peregrine Falcon shaped a depression to hold its eggs. Prime nest sites are often used year after year by successive generations.

▼ Generations of Ospreys (*Pandion haliaetus*) may have contributed to this huge, sturdy structure which now simply needs refurbishing to prepare it each year for nesting. Both birds bring sticks to weave the body of the nest, finally lining it with moss and other soft material.

Keith Scholey/Planet Earth Pictures

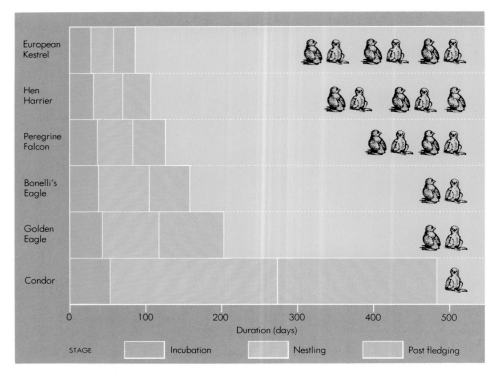

STAGE

Incubation   Nestling   Post fledging

▲ Duration of the breeding cycle. To breed successfully a raptor must complete a sequence of events known as the breeding cycle, from pair formation, through the various stages of nesting, to the independence of young. In general, larger raptors (bottom) take longer to breed than do smaller (top). Species characteristically either invest relatively little time in raising many young, or spend an extended time rearing one chick.

BREEDING SEASONS

Most raptors raise only a single brood each year. The time taken to do this depends mainly on the size of the species. Small falcons and accipiters incubate for about 28 days, and the young are in the nest for a further 26 days or so. Small raptors can thus complete the whole breeding cycle, from pair formation to independence of the young, in less than 100 days. Larger species take longer at each stage, and the extremes are the condors and some large eagles, which take over a year to breed and cannot raise more than one chick every other year or two chicks in three years.

Within a species, there may be some variation in the duration of the breeding cycle. Pairs may curtail courtship, so that eggs are laid soon after the pair is formed, or they may reduce the time spent feeding young that have left the nest. Species that breed at high latitudes, where springs are late, produce eggs soon after migrating to their breeding territories. Individuals of the same species breeding at lower latitudes spend much longer in courtship before laying. Late breeding European Kestrels may further curtail their cycle by abandoning their fledged young sooner than do early nesters.

THE TIMING OF BREEDING

Breeding imposes an extra strain on birds, and in raptors this falls largely on the male. Critical times are during courtship, when the male must provide sufficient food to bring the female into breeding condition, and during the early nestling stage, when he alone feeds the whole family. Breeding therefore takes place at the time of year when prey is abundant, though laying normally begins before food supply reaches its seasonal peak so that the breeding cycle is completed before food becomes scarce again.

Size again plays an important role in determining when laying starts. In general, large species, with long breeding cycles, start earlier in the year than small species to ensure their young are independent before the next winter arrives. The type of food eaten modifies this trend, however, because different prey species become abundant at different times of year. Raptors that eat birds or mammals usually breed earlier than those of a similar size that eat fish or insects. Thus, in central Europe, rodent-feeding Kestrels begin laying between mid-April and early June, but the similar-sized Hobby (*F. subbuteo*), which feeds partly on flying insects, begins between late May and early July.

In extreme cases, raptors adapted to particular food sources breed at totally different times of the year from other species in the same region. Good examples are the Eleonora's Falcon (*F. eleonorae*) and the Sooty Falcon (*F. concolor*), which breed on offshore islands and feed on migrating songbirds. They do not lay until midsummer, so their young are reared during the peak fall migration of passerines between Eurasia and Africa.

In temperate regions, most raptors time their egg-laying so that the young hatch when food is abundant. This requires a mechanism that will start breeding in spring, when food is scarce but increasing, rather than in fall, when it is plentiful but likely soon to decline. As in most birds, temperate raptors rely partly on daylength to time their breeding seasons. Daylength affects the hormonal system and prevents raptors from breeding at inappropriate times of year. The long days of midsummer repress the reproductive system, which is not "reset" until individuals experience short days in winter. Once this has happened, the lengthening days of spring

► Adapted to the vagaries of their prey, Australia's Letter-winged Kite may not breed in many years, but good rains and the resulting abundance of Long-haired Rats signal a period of frenzied breeding activity. The kites seemingly materialize out of the arid inland to congregate and breed in colonies. They raise several broods in quick succession, sometimes abandoning the last brood when rat numbers decline, then disappear as suddenly as they arrived.

N N Birks

stimulate the production of hormones that cause growth of the gonads.

Once the reproductive organs are developed in spring, the precise date of laying depends mainly on a pair's ability to obtain food. In any area, laying is earlier, on average, in good food years than in poor ones, though there is often a spread of several weeks between the first and last pairs to start laying. In rodent feeders, such as kestrels or buzzards, laying is earlier when voles are abundant than when they are scarce. Similarly, European Sparrowhawks (*Accipiter nisus*) begin laying early in mild springs because young songbirds, their main prey, fledge earlier than in cold, wet springs.

Raptors in the tropics also breed in relation to peaks in food abundance, but these may not be as obvious as in more seasonal climes. In Africa, some raptors breed mainly after the rains, when prey species are most numerous. However, laying is less synchronized between pairs than it is in

temperate zones, and, in some species, different pairs in the same area can be found nesting in every month of the year.

Some raptors in arid regions have adapted to the unpredictable peaks of prey abundance that follow periodic heavy rain. In Australia, Letter-winged Kites (*Elanus scriptus*) are long-lived and highly nomadic. They may have to wait some years to breed, but arrive rapidly in great numbers to exploit plagues of rodents that sometimes follow rainfall. Pairs form soon after arrival, and may rear several large broods in quick succession before moving elsewhere. Similar behavior occurs in Black-shouldered Kites (*E. caeruleus*) in southern Africa, and some females are able to breed up to three times a year during rodent plagues. They abandon their mates when the young leave the nest and quickly find another mate because there are surplus males in the population. Their original partner is left to rear the young single-handed to full independence.

▲ When food is plentiful, Wedge-tailed Eagles may breed early and raise more chicks than their usual single young. The fledglings remain dependent for some time; their parents bring them food while they learn to hunt prey such as this raven. Starvation claims many in their first few years, and for those that survive, it takes five or more years to gain sufficient hunting prowess to support a breeding attempt.

BREEDING RATES

The number of young raised by an individual during its lifetime depends on the age at which it starts to breed, the number of times it breeds and the number of young raised at each attempt. These factors are highly variable among raptors, both between and within species.

Much of the variation between species is again related to size. In general, large raptors are longer-lived, start breeding at a greater age, have more breeding attempts and produce fewer young per attempt than do small species. A typical small falcon, for example, can breed when a year old, rarely breeds more than five times, but can fledge up to six young in a single year. Compare this with a large eagle or vulture that does not begin to breed until it is four or five years old, hardly ever fledges more than one chick at a time, but where the longest-lived individuals may breed for 20 years or more.

Both types of lifestyle can adapt to annual fluctuations in the food supply, but in different ways. Short-lived species may well die before they reach another breeding season, so they must fully exploit every opportunity to breed by fledging as many young as possible. Parents will not easily abandon a breeding attempt, and some pairs will lay a second clutch if their first attempt of the year fails. Most young will not live to breeding age, so the parents invest in the quantity of young, rather than in the quality of post-fledging care.

Large raptors, however, are unlikely to die between breeding seasons, so they can afford to wait for another year if conditions are not wholly suitable. Long-lived species are more prone to stop their breeding attempt if they are disturbed, and more often forgo breeding altogether in some years than do short-lived species. When they do breed, large raptors fledge one or two young at most, and these stay with their parents for months after leaving the nest.

AGE OF FIRST BREEDING

Raptors do not usually start to breed while in subadult plumage, and it has been suggested that this is because they are not sexually mature. However, this seems unlikely because yearlings or subadults of many species can breed successfully under some circumstances.

The main reason why young raptors rarely breed is probably because they cannot compete successfully with adults for nesting territories or mates. If adults are removed from breeding territories in spring they are often replaced by yearlings or subadults which will then breed, sometimes successfully. When immature raptors breed in natural circumstances, it is usually because there are ample resources but few adults to exploit them. In species with a fluctuating food supply, such as European Kestrels, yearlings breed mainly in good food years, especially if the population is expanding. Populations that are increasing for reasons other than improved food supplies can also have a high proportion of subadults breeding. This happened in the European Sparrowhawk when populations were recovering after pesticide poisoning.

In many species, the age of first breeding differs between the sexes. Usually females start breeding earlier in life than do males. This could be because females suffer a higher mortality than do males, so there are more vacant breeding places for young females. Alternatively, the difference may relate to the roles of the sexes during breeding, and the need for males to provide all the food. Young females could therefore breed by mating with older males, but the reverse would not be true because young, inexperienced males may be unable to obtain enough food.

▼ Brimming with an unusually large brood of five, probably the result of high food availability, the compact nest of the Black Kite (*Milvus migrans*) more often holds only two nestlings. Because eggs are laid at two-day intervals and incubation doesn't always begin immediately, there is likely to be about a week's difference in age between the oldest chick (right, at rear) and youngest (left). As can be seen, kites like to add plastic and other rubbish to their nests.

Jozef Mihok/Survival Anglia

◀ Perhaps 66-75 percent of Gray Falcons (*Falco hypoleucos*) die before they reach breeding age. At the end of her first year this immature female will molt into adult plummage, but she may not breed for another year or two unless she can find an experienced mate. Her male siblings will have to wait even longer, until they are proficient hunters with a territory of their own.

EGGS, CLUTCH SIZE AND LAYING INTERVAL

The number of eggs laid in a given species depends largely on size and diet. Large vultures and condors may never lay more than a single egg at each breeding attempt, while small falcons and accipiters can lay six or more. Raptors that feed on rodents usually lay more eggs than those of a similar size that feed mainly on birds or insects. This is probably because rodent feeders can experience the best feeding conditions during plague years, and therefore need the potential of rearing large numbers of young to exploit such an abundance of prey.

The majority of raptors lay their eggs on alternate days, though the interval can be three or four days in some larger species. Individuals laying six eggs will thus take about 10 days or more to complete the clutch. Incubation develops gradually during laying, so the eggs are not properly incubated until the clutch is completed. This means that hatching takes less time than laying in most raptors, and is partly synchronized.

In single-brooded species, some pairs that fail in their breeding attempt will lay a second clutch later in the season. Repeats may be in the same nest or at a new site, and are most likely in pairs that fail early in the breeding season. In species that experience annual fluctuations in food supply, failed pairs are more likely to try again in good food years than in poor ones.

VARIATION IN BREEDING RATES WITHIN SPECIES

The productivity of individuals within a species varies enormously. The extreme longevity of some raptors gives scope for considerable variation in the lifetime breeding output of individuals. There is little information for large raptors, but in the European Sparrowhawk, a small accipiter, 70 percent of fledged young die before they reach breeding age. Of those that do breed, 15 percent produce about half of the young fledged in the next generation.

Many factors will affect the outcome of a particular breeding attempt, but in most species older birds are more productive than young ones. Young pairs are less likely to lay eggs than older ones, and, if they do, will have smaller clutches and be more prone to nesting failure. The difference is most obvious between adults and those breeding as immatures, but in European Sparrowhawks improvements in clutch size were evident until the third or fourth year of life, well after adult plumage was attained.

Even individuals of the same age show considerable variation in breeding output. In most cases this is probably related ultimately to food availability, either because pairs have territories with different levels of food, or because individuals differ in their ability to find food. Separating these two factors is difficult because superior hunters may also be better at competing for territories, so individual quality is closely related to territory quality.

As in many other birds, the most productive pairs in a given area are usually those that start to breed earliest in the season. Early pairs generally lay larger clutches, and are less prone to total breeding failure, than late pairs, so they usually fledge more young. Seasonal declines in productivity are widespread among raptors, and have been found in small species, such as European Kestrels and Sparrowhawks, as well as larger species such as Common Buzzards (*Buteo buteo*) and Bald Eagles.

The cause of this seasonal decline in clutch size has puzzled ornithologists, because later pairs are laying in better food conditions than early pairs and ought, therefore, to produce more eggs, not fewer. Possibly, however, late pairs are inferior breeders and cannot produce as many eggs as early pairs, even though the food supply is improving.

RAPTOR EGGS: THE RANGE OF VARIATION

PENNY OLSEN

In 1928 two men stood proudly on a clifftop to be photographed. At their feet lay coils of climbing rope and a pyramid of blown Peregrine eggs. The stack of eggs, said to number 64, was the year's harvest from Dorset. Other parts of Britain were similarly plundered. At the time, egg collecting was popular, particularly among naturalists and ornithologists. Raptor eggs were prized for their beauty and variability, made more attractive by their relative rarity and the physical challenge of scaling a high tree or dangling from a cliff. Proof of this often obsessive pastime now fills countless museum drawers. The pillaging was not always in vain, for many collectors and their data cards continue to contribute to our ornithological knowledge and are an invaluable historical record that helped establish the connection between DDT, thin-shelled eggs and disappearing raptor populations.

As the collectors noticed, raptors have strikingly colored eggs that show great variation in pattern and hue both within and between clutches, far more interesting than a drawer full of uniformly colored eggs. At laying, the eggs are more matt than glossy, although they may acquire a sheen after being incubated for a while. White or white with red-brown blotches, streaks, spots or smears in the Accipitridae (hawks, eagles, etc.), they are similar in the Falconidae but usually more finely and thoroughly speckled. When the eggs are held to the light a diagnostic difference between the two families is apparent. The eggs of hawks and their allies have a greenish translucence, those of falcons appear red-yellow. In shape, raptor eggs are not so variable—most are broad oval, occasionally some are more pointed at the small end (pyriform) than others or more spherical. Some vultures (*Gyps*) have long oval eggs.

The eggs are pigmented as they pass down the oviduct. If they are moving when pigment is applied, they may be streaked or smeared; if still they are blotched or speckled. Many are more heavily pigmented towards one end, and often the last eggs in a clutch are less heavily pigmented than first eggs. No two are patterned exactly alike. The markings are thought to camouflage the eggs by breaking up their outline. Why some raptors have white, unmarked eggs is not clear as they are not all large, highly predatory species with little need for secrecy, nor do they nest in dark places, both of which are explanations evoked to explain the unmarked eggs of some other birds.

For their size, raptors lay slightly larger eggs than most birds. A 100 gram (3.5 ounce) falcon lays a 15 gram (0.5 ounce) egg, whereas the egg of a dove of the same body weight is only about 6 grams (0.2 ounce). One of the reasons for this difference is that raptors grow quickly and leave the nest almost full-sized; a bigger egg allows room for a bigger, more advanced chick with a headstart in life. Dove chicks, on the other hand, hatch at an earlier stage of development and leave the nest and feed themselves before they reach full size. Within the raptors, larger species tend to have smaller eggs for their size than do small species. Large eagles and vultures lay an average clutch of one or two, with each egg weighing less than three percent of the female's body weight. At the other extreme, the diminutive female American Kestrel (*Falco sparverius*) lays about five eggs, each 11 percent of her weight, a total effort equivalent to well over half her own weight. This means that large species are able to produce eggs by using body reserves while smaller species rely heavily on food eaten around the time of laying.

Generally, eggs within a clutch vary little in size or weight: the exceptions are some of the eagles in which the second egg is often noticeably smaller than the first. The chick from this second egg is also small and may not survive unless the first egg fails to hatch or the first chick dies.

▲ Rounded-oval, buff, blotched and smeared with purplish-brown, no two exactly alike, the eggs of a Black-shouldered Kite (*Elanus notatus*) nestle in a neat, eucalypt-lined nest. Measuring 40 x 31 mm (1.6 x 1.2 inches) each weighs about 5 percent of the female's body weight.

▲ The bulky, rubbish-lined nest of the Egyptian Vulture (*Neophron percnopterus*) holds its single, oval egg. Chalky white and heavily pigmented with brown, the 60 x 50 mm (2.4 x 2 inches) egg weighs less than 5 percent of the female's weight.

BREEDING FAILURES AND LOSSES

Total breeding failure may occur even before the eggs are laid, or after laying, during the incubation or nestling period. Some pairs lose only part of their clutch or brood so that breeding success is reduced. Total or partial failures can usually be traced to food shortage, predation, human interference, pesticides or accidents. The relative importance of these factors varies between species, and between populations within a species, depending on the prevailing circumstances. In some populations, a high proportion of pairs will fledge young, and partial losses are slight; in others the production of young is insufficient to maintain the population, and few pairs ever succeed. Such populations either decline, or are maintained by immigration of birds from areas where breeding success is better.

Food supply has a major influence on raptor breeding success at all stages of the breeding cycle, causing failure to lay, desertion of the clutch, or the loss of unattended chicks when both parents are away hunting. In raptors that have fluctuating food supplies, fewer pairs lay, and more abandon their eggs, in poor food conditions than in good ones.

Predation of eggs or chicks can occur even among well-fed pairs, but it rarely destroys more than a few percent of nests. Larger raptors are less vulnerable to predators than are small ones but, in all species, the safety of the brood is dependent largely on the location of the nest and the attendance of the parents.

Humans may deliberately kill or remove raptor eggs, chicks or adults, or accidentally disturb nests by activities such as lumbering, farming or recreation. Raptors that nest in areas where game is reared may be heavily persecuted, with many nests being destroyed each year, whereas those in remote areas may go completely unmolested. In general, larger raptors are more sensitive to disturbance than smaller species, and all species are less likely to be driven away once they have chicks.

Pesticides are mainly responsible for losses of eggs through breakage or embryo deaths, and cause significant total failures in heavily contaminated populations. Failures due to accidents include the collapse or flooding of the nest, or loss of fragile eggs and chicks that fall from the nest.

R. T. Smith/Ardea London

▲ Crushed into tiny pieces, this thin-shelled Peregrine Falcon egg, with its nearly full-term chick, was unable to withstand the normal rigors of incubation. Interestingly, such eggs can often survive to hatch in an incubator. DDT, ingested in contaminated prey, causes female raptors to lay abnormally thin-shelled eggs, and has resulted in widespread breeding failure and alarming declines in several raptor populations.

▼ Breeding can fail at any stage. Wedge-tailed Eagles (*Aquila audax*) commonly lay two eggs but raise only one young. This youngster shares the nest with an unhatched egg, either infertile or with a dead embryo; in very good years it could have up to two siblings.

N. N. Birks

BREEDING DISPLAYS

▶ Several raptor species establish and maintain their pair bonds through vigorous aerial courtship displays—many obviously advertising the participants' considerable flying skills. Mutual soaring (A) may lead to mock attacks (B) where the lower bird, usually the female, rolls to present her feet as the male swoops by (C). The pair sometimes touch feet briefly, before the male swings up and out of his dive and the female rights herself (D). The sequence may then be repeated.

A

B

BEHAVIORAL ASPECTS OF BREEDING

In migrant populations breeding behavior starts with the arrival of birds from their wintering grounds. If one member of a pair winters in the breeding area, it is usually the male, possibly because he may be unable to breed if he does not secure a nesting territory for the following year. If both partners arrive from elsewhere in spring, the male normally finds a territory and then attracts a mate, though sometimes both partners seem to arrive on the same day. Greater fidelity to breeding sites by males than females is also common in other birds.

Where winters are less severe, breeding pairs remain on their territories all year. Displays, nest building, prey deliveries and copulations may occur sporadically throughout the winter, increasing in spring. Pairs may form at any time during the winter, but this is most likely in fall and early spring, when immigrants arrive to pair with single residents.

BREEDING DISPLAYS

As in many birds, breeding in raptors is characterized by particular displays and calls. These are associated with the formation and maintenance of the pair-bond, and the selection and defense of the nest and nesting territory. It can be difficult to separate these functions because the same behavior may serve both to ward off intruders and to attract mates.

Raptor nesting displays usually involve distinctive flights and sometimes special calls. In nearly every species studied, mated pairs soar together during courtship. In large, slow raptors, such as the *Gyps* vultures, this seems to be the only display between partners. Common behavior during soaring is for one bird (usually the male) to dive at the other in mock attack. The lower bird may roll over on its back, sometimes locking talons briefly with its partner. In some species this foreshadows the exchange of food during incubation, but the "rolling-over" display is also

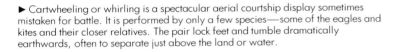

▶ Cartwheeling or whirling is a spectacular aerial courtship display sometimes mistaken for battle. It is performed by only a few species—some of the eagles and kites and their closer relatives. The pair lock feet and tumble dramatically earthwards, often to separate just above the land or water.

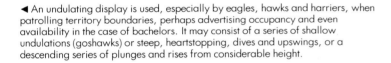

◀ An undulating display is used, especially by eagles, hawks and harriers, when patrolling territory boundaries, perhaps advertising occupancy and even availability in the case of bachelors. It may consist of a series of shallow undulations (goshawks) or steep, heartstopping, dives and upswings, or a descending series of plunges and rises from considerable height.

seen in species that never pass food in the air. In some kites and eagles, pairs that lock talons will tumble through the air in a spectacular "cartwheel" display.

Undulating flights are used for display in several groups of raptors, especially accipiters, eagles and harriers. The displaying bird alternately dives and climbs during flights that may last many minutes and cover considerable distances. In Honey Buzzards (*Pernis apivorus*), undulating flights seem to mark out the territory boundaries of pairs.

The most complex and spectacular displays are seen in the most agile hunters. Some falcons have a rapid "rocking" flight, in which the body is tilted from side to side. The display is combined with fast, shallow wing beats and high-pitched calls which make the displaying bird very noticeable. Displays can occur at great height, and will sometimes end with a breathtaking "V-flight" towards the nest: the bird holds its wings back in a V-shape and plummets downwards at great speed.

Territorial encounters with intruders involve somewhat similar behaviors, and observers are sometimes unsure if they are watching a pair displaying to each other or two neighbors fighting. Rivals often engage in mutual soaring, the defending bird usually being the lower, so that it lies between the intruder and the nest. In more intense fights, birds will chase each other and even lock talons, tumbling to the ground and striking at one another. Such attacks can lead to injury, and are known to have caused deaths in a variety of raptors, including Peregrines, Ospreys, Golden Eagles and European Sparrowhawks.

SELECTION OF MATES, TERRITORIES AND NESTS

The processes of selecting a mate, territory or nest site are poorly understood in raptors because they may happen quickly and are rarely observed. In migratory or short-lived species, changes of territory and mate between years are fairly frequent, so individuals often have choices to make. In sedentary or long-lived species, vacancies in the breeding population are rare, and there may be no alternative for incomers apart from accepting a widowed partner and its territory.

Researchers have been able to examine the outcome of such selection, however, by comparing the frequency with which territories are occupied, or mates of a particular type are paired, with the frequency expected if birds selected at random. Eurasian Sparrowhawks occupy some nesting territories more often, and others less often, than would be expected by chance. The preferred territories are those where

breeding is most successful, and individuals that fail in one year tend to move to a better territory the next. In this species, and probably in many other raptors, nesting territories vary in quality, and individuals seem able to assess this and choose where to nest accordingly.

The more productive breeding by adults, compared to subadults, suggests that individuals may also choose mates according to their age. This is indeed the case in several species where individuals frequently breed as yearlings, such as Eurasian Sparrowhawks and Old World Kestrels. In most years, pairing between adults, or between yearlings, is more frequent, and mixed-aged pairings less frequent, than expected if birds mated at random with respect to age.

CHOOSING A NEST SITE

Once a pair is together on a territory, they have to decide where to nest. Some pairs may have only one suitable site within their territory, but most will have several places where they could make a nest. Which partner chooses the site and builds the nest is not always clear, and may vary from pair to pair in the same species. However, it often appears that the male finds a suitable site, or begins to build the nest, and then tries to attract the female to it. She may help with the final stages of building or scraping the nest cup, and probably has the final choice of where the eggs are laid.

COURTSHIP

From the formation of the pair, or the initiation of breeding behavior, until the eggs are laid, behavior is concerned with defending the territory and nest site, maintaining the pair-bond, preparing the nest and feeding the female to bring her into breeding condition. The division of labor becomes increasingly apparent as males spend more and more time hunting for their mates, who in turn become less active. Both partners may defend the territory early in courtship, but males take the more active role as laying approaches.

Courtship activities are important in synchronizing the breeding of the pair and developing behavior patterns that will be necessary for the successful rearing of young. In many raptors the delivery of prey by the male to the female is especially important. Females cannot lay unless they receive sufficient food, and in some raptors the onset of courtship feeding determines when the pair will start laying. Some males start to feed their mates immediately, whereas others do not do so regularly for some weeks. In this way, male behavior influences whether the pair breeds at all and, if so, when.

Exchange of food may take place on the nest or at a nearby perch. The male signals his arrival by calling softly, and the female may fly from near the nest to meet him and take the food from his claws.

▼ Courtship feeding is necessary for successful breeding in most raptors. Not only does it strengthen the pair bond, but also it helps synchronize breeding of the pair and provides the female with the reserves necessary for egg formation. Sparrowhawks, harriers and some other raptors make a spectacular exchange of food in mid-air.

In harriers and some other raptors, the food pass is a spectacular mid-air transfer: the female flies up to meet the male, rolls onto her back and picks the prey from his talons or catches it as he drops it.

Throughout courtship, partners spend a considerable amount of time displaying to one another. This presumably helps to bind their relationship, and may also help to stimulate the female to lay. Copulations start well in advance of egg laying, and are much more frequent than is necessary for fertilization, so they may also help to bond the pair. In Old World Kestrels, for example, pairs may mate once or twice a day even eight weeks before laying, increasing to about eight times a day when laying starts, and continuing at this rate until the clutch is completed. The high copulation rate may also help male partners to counteract the effects of occasional copulations by the female with other males.

Nest building or preparation occurs in bouts throughout courtship, often in the early mornings. The nest may be started early in courtship, but then added to only during fine weather, and not completed until just before the eggs are laid. In falcons, the nest cup may be scraped well in advance of laying, so the final preparation of the nest requires little effort. The time spent building stick-nests depends on whether a new structure is started or an old nest is refurbished. Species that re-use nests nearly always add some new material each year, and this may serve to advertise that the territory is occupied, as well as help to maintain the structure. In large raptors, new nests are often started by young pairs, but may not be laid in until the following year.

As courtship feeding increases, the female begins to gain weight. This is due mainly to increases in fat reserves, though some of the extra food is stored as protein in the pectoral muscles. The extent of this weight gain varies between species: female Ospreys, for example, increase by only about 65 grams (2 ounces), or 3 percent of their body weight, whereas Old World Kestrels gain the same amount, but this represents nearly 30 percent of their initial weight.

The extra reserves are not merely to enable the female to produce eggs, but are mostly retained during incubation as an insurance against possible food shortages. The stores may then allow females to stay on their nests if their mates are temporarily unable to deliver prey, and can make the crucial difference between nesting success and failure. In European Kestrels, late-laying females gain less weight than early ones and those that show a decline in weight during incubation are likely to desert their clutch.

Large raptors can endure starvation for longer than small ones, and females should need fewer reserves. Some sources of food are more predictable than others. The Ospreys mentioned above had little trouble

N. N. Birks

▲ As an integral part of courtship, the male catches prey and presents it to the female; this display may help her to judge whether he will be a good provider for her and the chicks while she is confined to the nest during incubation and brooding. His willingness to release prey to her is critical. If he is not generous she may refuse to mate with him or even seek another male. Here, a female Peregrine Falcon descends towards a fence post to claim a galah caught by the male.

◄ The culmination of various courtship behaviors is often mating. The male alights on the female's back with clenched feet, and if she is receptive she raises her tail and lowers her head. He lowers his tail down and under hers so that their cloacas meet and sperm is exchanged. The pairs of some species copulate as many as 400–600 times per clutch, far more than required for fertilization. It is thought that such apparent excess helps to maintain the pair bond and also reduces the chance of other males fertilizing the eggs.

Angelo Gandolfi

▲ Once a nest site has been chosen, often by ritualistic escorting of the female around potential sites by the male, nest preparation begins in earnest. This Egyptian Vulture pulls wool from a carcass to line the bulky nest of sticks it has built on a cliff ledge or cave.

▶ Bodyweight changes during breeding. The male sparrowhawk must remain strong and fit throughout breeding so that he can hunt for his family. The female, fed by him, must put on enough weight for egg production. She must then maintain stored reserves to tide her through temporary shortages while she is incubating and tied to the nest.

▼ On a nest fastooned with colorful bric-a-brac, a female Osprey incubates. She is relieved by the male while she feeds on prey he has delivered, and sometimes for longer, but does most of the incubating for the 37 days needed for each egg.

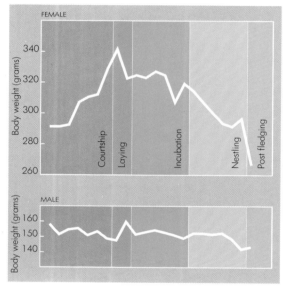

François Gohier/Jacana

catching fish, and females could virtually guarantee an adequate daily food supply during incubation. This is not so for all raptors, however, where heavy rain may result in sudden reductions in the availability of food.

As well as putting on weight, females also develop a brood patch, an area of skin on the belly, rich in blood vessels, that transfers body-heat to the eggs. Females start to lose feathers from their undersides as they gain weight, so the brood patch is well developed when incubation begins. Male raptors do not have a brood patch, apart from the few species where incubation is shared between males and females.

Towards the end of courtship, females spend nearly all day sitting at the nest and are extremely reluctant to fly. The extra weight gives them a labored flight, and they would probably have difficulty in catching food for themselves. This behavior is called "egg-laying lethargy," and is widespread among birds. It may be an adaptation to protect the eggs within the female, which are vulnerable to breakage once the outer shell has been produced.

INCUBATION

In most raptors, the female does nearly all the incubating, the male merely covering the eggs briefly while his partner eats the food he has just delivered. For the female, the long hours of sitting are otherwise relieved only by the periodic turning of the eggs. She does this with her beak, using a sweeping motion that both rotates the eggs and changes their position in the nest. This behavior is most frequent early in incubation, and may prevent the shell membranes from fusing and distribute the heat more evenly over the eggs. Sitting birds may also pull at twigs or other material near the nest cup, building up the rim, which helps to prevent eggs or small chicks being swept from the nest when the female leaves suddenly.

Towards the end of incubation the young can be heard calling from the eggs, and this may warn the female that the hatch is imminent. The young chip at the shell with a growth on the beak (the "egg tooth"), and will normally emerge within 1–2 days. Females are reluctant to leave the nest at this critical stage, even when the male delivers food.

THE NESTLING STAGE

The last egg laid usually hatches several days after the first. Although the spread in hatching within a clutch is considerably shorter than the spread in laying, the asynchrony still means that the youngest chicks are smaller than their siblings. Small chicks can be severely disadvantaged, and may die because they cannot reach food or because they are deliberately killed by their nest mates. Such "Cain and Abel" conflicts are frequent in some eagles which nearly always lay two eggs

▲ An exhausting process, hatching may take several days. It is heralded by a small raised hump on the outer surface of the egg, which the chick eventually opens into a window using a special egg tooth on the top of its beak. From there it works in a circle, cutting a line around the egg until it can push the two halves apart.

◀ After about five weeks in the nest, Black Kite (*Milvus migrans*) nestlings are almost full grown and able to defend themselves against many predators. Here they make a brave but futile attempt to bluff the intruding photographer. In another week they will be ready to fledge, and will fly from the nest if disturbed.

but never fledge more than one chick. Aggression starts soon after the second chick hatches: the older may drive the younger from the nest, prevent it from feeding or simply peck it to death. Fighting subsides when the female is brooding, but she will not attempt to separate chicks that fight while she is standing nearby.

This gruesome behavior may be a way of adjusting the brood size to the food supply; in species such as fish eagles and Golden Eagles (*Aquila chrysaetos*), two young are raised if food is plentiful, but not if it is scarce. However, in several of the *Aquila* eagles, siblicide occurs even when there is plenty of food in the nest. The reason for this apparently pointless behavior is unclear, but laying more eggs than necessary may be an insurance against the first egg not surviving. Direct sibling aggression is less frequent in medium-sized raptors, and apparently absent from falcons and small accipiters, where younger chicks may be out-competed for food but are rarely killed by their nestmates.

During the nestling stage, the male continues to deliver prey, but he hardly ever broods the chicks. The female broods to keep young chicks warm, protect them from rain, or shade them from excessive heat. At first, the male may pluck prey before bringing it to the nest, and will often eat the head himself. The female tears the carcass into bite-sized pieces and feeds these to the chicks. Unlike many birds, raptor chicks have some vision at birth and are able to take prey from their mother's beak, though they can handle only small

scraps at first. Even large raptors are highly dextrous when feeding small chicks, and there is something incongruous in the sight of a huge eagle stooping to offer chicks a tiny morsel of food held in her powerful beak.

A few raptors swallow prey, deliver it to the nest and regurgitate it for the chicks. Vultures do this because their food is torn from carcasses in small, slippery pieces that cannot be easily carried in the feet. Snake eagles also swallow their prey before flying to the nest, and eaglets pull the still-wriggling snake from their parent's mouth. Writhing snakes may be difficult to hold in the feet, or easily stolen by other birds of prey because they dangle below the carrier.

Competition can be ferocious once chicks learn to grapple larger items, and any food not swallowed quickly is liable to be stolen by a

◀ Pressing forward and wailing loudly, these Peregrine Falcon chicks are offered slivers of meat by the female. For falcons, unlike some other raptors, mealtimes are fairly peaceful, if noisy; the chicks all receive a share of the food, and squabbles are rare and minor.

sibling. Chicks eventually learn to dismember prey themselves, and the parents then drop intact items into the nest and leave quickly.

As the male does not normally feed the chicks, some species may be unable to rear young broods if the female dies suddenly. However, widowed males of other species, such as European Kestrels, have been seen to gradually take over the maternal role after a day or so, and a few managed to rear the brood successfully by themselves.

During the first week or so after hatch, the female usually loses any weight she gained prior to laying because she gives most of the food to the chicks, and eats only the skin, intestines and bony parts herself. The loss of weight may prepare her for flying efficiently if she has to help with the hunting, but the extent to which she hunts varies considerably between pairs. At some nests, the female remains at the nest throughout the nestling stage and never hunts for the young. At other nests, the female begins to hunt as soon as the young are no longer brooded, and may make nearly all the prey deliveries thereafter. This variation may depend on the food supply and whether the male can provide enough food on his own.

GROWTH AND DEVELOPMENT OF RAPTOR CHICKS

ANDREW VILLAGE

The rate of growth in some raptor chicks is as fast as any recorded for warm-blooded animals. Small accipiters and falcons can double their hatching weight in one or two days, and reach adult weight in under three weeks. Weight-gain is slow at first, then increases rapidly before leveling off. Many chicks become heavier than their parents, though they usually lose some weight before they leave the nest. Large species tend to grow much more slowly, and may not attain full size until after they leave the nest.

The rapid growth of raptor chicks is possible because of their high-protein diet and because nearly all the energy from food is used for tissue growth, rather than in keeping the body warm. Raptor chicks are covered by a fine down when they hatch, but this is not sufficient insulation, and they must be brooded constantly until a coarser down grows and they have some control over body temperature. This happens at about two weeks of age in small raptors, after which the female will cover the chicks only during heavy rain or when shading them from intense sun in exposed nests.

Development of the different parts of the body proceeds in a fairly fixed order. Newly hatched raptors have large heads, big mouths and protruding abdomens to cope with the food, but small feet and tiny wings which are not needed at this stage. Bone growth proceeds rapidly. The chicks' legs and feet reach full size before the wings, the feathers of which are often not fully grown until well after the young leave the nest.

▲ Both parents, especially the female, tend the chick. Unusual among raptors, the Secretary Bird (*Sagittarius serpentarius*) regurgitates a green mass of (mainly) insects, then feeds it, piecemeal, to her young nestling.

▲ On such a rich diet growth is rapid; by 21 days the chick will have the first of its feathers, the distinctive crest. During the latter stages of its 10–11 weeks' occupancy of the nest the parents rarely stay long.

At most nests, the rate of prey deliveries rises rapidly in the early nestling stage, to match the increasing food requirements of the growing brood. Once the chicks reach full size, their food demands are fairly constant, and the prey deliveries level off. In some cases, the males are able to adjust their hunting effort to the varying demands of different-sized broods, though marked increases in delivery may not be sustainable for long, especially if food is scarce.

THE POST-FLEDGING PERIOD

Young raptors may start to wander from the nest before they are fully able to fly, returning whenever the parents deliver food. They may "practice" flying by flapping their wings vigorously, though the ability to fly is largely innate, and mainly awaits the maturation of the flight feathers. Even after they leave the nest, the young return frequently at first, especially if smaller chicks are still being fed there.

The fledged young spend most of the day sitting near the nest, waiting for their parents to bring food. They call loudly when this happens, and flap their wings excitedly to gain the parents' attention. Fledgings soon learn to fly towards their parents and collect food from them. Exchanges of food are initially on the ground or at a perch, but may eventually occur on the wing, in a fashion similar to the aerial food pass between adults in some species.

The development of hunting skills in raptors is a fascinating, but little studied, aspect of their behavior. There is some evidence that parents encourage their offspring to hunt for themselves by making them work for their food. As juveniles become more proficient at flying, the adults of some species become less eager to give up prey, and will only do so after a prolonged chase. In a few accipiters and falcons, adults have been seen to release live prey near the nest which the young then chase and catch for themselves.

Although hunting behaviors may be largely innate, the skills must be practised to improve coordination. Juveniles may amuse themselves between feeds by chasing each other, making mock dives, or pouncing on inanimate objects such as stones or pine-cones. These objects are grappled with the same movements that will later be used to tackle real prey.

It is difficult to judge how long the young are dependent on their parents after leaving the nest. In small raptors they may stay for two to four weeks, but in large species it may be many months before they become fully independent. Juveniles probably start to disperse because their parents stop feeding them, and the fledged young of some species can be kept near the nest for many weeks if they are fed there artificially. Parents may vary the amount of post-fledging care they give their young, and in some species, late-nesting pairs tend to desert their fledglings sooner than those that rear broods early in the season.

CONCLUSIONS

All raptors must reproduce to survive, and their ecological and behavioral adaptations to breeding are intricate and complex. Although our knowledge of raptor breeding biology has increased enormously in the last two decades, there is still much that we do not understand. This is particularly true of the lesser-known species, many of which are endangered. The breeding season is a good time to collect basic data on such species because birds are tied to a nest and can be more easily observed than at other times of the year. The amateur naturalist and wildlife photographer thus have a real opportunity to make important contributions to our knowledge of raptors and their reproductive behavior.

▲ As heavy as its parents when it left the nest, this immature Brown Falcon takes a rabbit caught by its mother. It will be dependent on its parents for several weeks, sometimes harassing them mercilessly for food, while it gains flying and hunting skills. During locust plagues, prey is easy to catch and plentiful, and the fledglings become independent more rapidly.

◀ After 10 or 11 weeks of rapid growth, Sea Eagle (*Haliaeetus leucogaster*) nestlings are ready for their first flight. They gradually become independent over the next month or so before dispersing. Their first few years are spent in brown, immature plumage, which will change gradually, over about three molts, to the white of an adult.

MORTALITY

CHARLES J. HENNY

Mortality is the death rate or ratio of total deaths to total population per unit of time. Dead hawks, falcons or eagles are not something most people like to hear about. However, the mortality rate can be used by scientists to better understand population variations in any species, and perhaps show weak links or critical points in the life cycle. For example, if we know age-specific mortality rates for a population and the age at which the birds nest, we can estimate the number of young that must be produced each year to maintain a stable population. Population modeling of this type was done in the late 1960s in an attempt to evaluate the impact of DDT on birds of prey. Production was obviously poor in many locations; *normal* production rates were not known so were estimated by modeling.

▲ Banded in the nest, the details of this young Sea Eagle (*Haliaeetus albicilla*) will be sent to a central bird-banding co-ordinating agency. Reports to the agency of future resightings of such known-age raptors, either alive or dead, are the best way to study mortality in wild populations.

▶ An individual number on a metal leg band will identify this immature Peregrine Falcon if it is found in years to come. Information on the age at which individuals die and the cause of their death is essential to the understanding of mortality (death rate) and its converse, longevity (life expectancy), both necessary for sound management and conservation of species.

The study of mortality of birds of prey is in its infancy. Individually marked birds are a prerequisite for most mortality studies. Birds of prey have been captured and flown in falconry for thousands of years, but systematic trapping (using many of the ancient techniques), marking (ringing), and releasing birds back to nature is a relatively new activity. H. Chr. C. Mortensen in Denmark in 1899 is credited with the inception of systematic bird-banding. The bird-banding program in North America has been in operation since about 1920. At least 39 systems in at least 26 countries were in operation by about 1950 and

over 9 million birds were banded. Banding activity has increased rapidly over the last 40 years. Sufficient time has passed and records have accumulated to provide some useful information on certain questions about the mortality and longevity of birds of prey.

LONGEVITY AND MORTALITY RATES

How long does an eagle or hawk live? This question seems relatively straightforward but is difficult to answer with certainty. Two types of information are available: (1) from captivity (zoo and aviary records, and falconry records) and (2)

from wild birds. To obtain useful information from free-living birds requires them to be banded individually for long enough for them to reach their maximum lifespan, and for someone to find the bird soon after it dies and report its number to the banding program. Early reports of eagle or hawk nests occupied year after year led some observers to conclude that the same bird was present and enjoyed an extremely long lifespan, but this was not necessarily true. Prime nesting sites are always in demand and are used by another individual or pair upon the death of the original occupant.

The maximum longevity record for a species is interesting, but it is not nearly as useful to the scientist as age-specific mortality rates or the average life expectancy. Information about the maximum longevity, with some limitations, may be obtained from the general banding of birds. However, to obtain age-specific mortality rates or average life expectancy requires detailed investigations and well-designed studies. Today,

only a few examples of such detailed studies are available in the literature.

Leslie Brown and Dean Amadon, and later Ian Newton, reviewed longevity records for birds of prey in captivity and in the wild. They concluded that the larger species were potentially very long-lived and cited examples of big vultures, condors

▲ Had it not been killed in an avalanche this massive Bearded Vulture (*Gypaetus barbatus*) may have lived for several decades. Although fascinating, such an accident may not be an important cause of death for the vulture population. Other factors, notably starvation, probably claim more lives.

◄ Close inspection reveals the probable cause of death of this hawk. Concave, wasted breast muscles suggest starvation. However, such a hasty judgment may not tell the whole story. While the hawk may have ultimately starved to death, the primary cause could have been disease or poisoning, or even social pressure from other hawks, excluding it from their territories.

and large eagles that occasionally lived for 40–55 years, medium-sized buzzards (buteos) and kites for 20–40 years, and small falcons and accipiters for about 15 years in captivity. Banded birds in the wild occasionally lived as long as the oldest captives, but earlier authors indicated that more time was needed for data to accrue in the wild before longevity records of captive and wild birds could be compared and conclusions made about maximum longevity. Although a small segment of the population lives for a long time, and the maximum longevity record by definition is an extreme case, it is also important to recognize that, in most species, over half of the young fledged will die during their first year of life.

Early work suggested effective physiological time (lifespan) was scaled to body size, and recent work verified that maximum longevity of *birds in general* is related to the bird's mass (weight), i.e. a trend for larger birds to live longer than small ones. However, large-scale banding programs have not been in operation much longer than one lifespan for large birds, and investigators caution that their findings may need refinement in the future when additional data on longer-lived large birds become available. A further complication for longevity studies is band loss by older birds. For some species, the existing longevity data probably reflect band longevity rather than bird longevity.

▲ In general, large raptors live longer than small raptors. Medium-sized, this African Marsh Harrier (*Circus ranivorus*) has a potential lifespan of two or more decades in the wild.

▶ Body size is only one factor that influences life expectancy; prey characteristics, hunting methods, lifestyle and environmental conditions can also be important. The Palmnut Vulture (*Gypohierax angolensis*) scavenges for crabs and fish around waterways. It might be expected, then, that the vulture is less likely to die in a hunting accident than is a swift-flying falcon that must grapple with and subdue prey. However, the vulture's preference for the husks of palmnuts sometimes brings it into conflict with people, and death may be the consequence.

In spite of the preliminary nature of the longevity records, it is apparent that larger raptors tend to live longer than smaller raptors. It follows that species with the lowest adult mortality rates have·the longest lifespan. Newton compiled estimates of adult mortality rates; in general, the largest species had the lowest adult mortality rates, as expected.

The size relationship should not be overemphasized because, as new knowledge becomes available, other factors (food habits and dependability of food, nesting density, migratory characteristics, amount of fat reserves, environmental conditions) can be added to improve our overall understanding of mortality. Some of my early adult mortality rate estimates suggested that Barn Owls at different geographical locations had different adult mortality rates. Barn Owls had a much higher estimated adult mortality rate in northern than in southern United States (50 v. 35 percent). This resident species has one of the lowest fat reserves of any owl, and the literature contains much information about starvation and deaths during periods of severe winter weather and associated food shortages in the northern United States. It appears likely that mortality during these severe weather episodes contributed to the higher adult mortality rate (average of many years) in the northern portion of the Barn Owls' breeding range.

Ed Mackrill/Aquila Photographics Ltd

▲ To avoid the harsh winters of their breeding range, some raptors migrate to milder wintering areas. However, migration has its own hazards. The diminutive Sharp-shinned Hawk (*Accipiter striatus*) traverses unknown territory on its annual migration, exposing itself to starvation and predation by larger raptors.

LONGEVITY RECORDS FOR BIRDS OF PREY

Longevity records based on recoveries of banded birds.
Note for North America: [1]100–250 recoveries, [2]251–999 recoveries, and [3]more than 1000 recoveries.
(There were less than 100 recoveries for the other species listed.)

Species	Weight of females (grams)	Age Year	Age Month	Species	Weight of females (grams)	Age Year	Age Month
North America				**Western Palearctic**			
Bald Eagle[3]	5,244	21	11	White-tailed Eagle	5,572	21	1
Golden Eagle[2]	4,692	17	1	Golden Eagle	5,194	25	8
Black Vulture[3]	2,172	25	6	Short-toed Eagle	1,735	17	4
Osprey[3]	1,568	25		Lesser Spotted Eagle	1,735	26	1
Turkey Vulture[1]	1,467	16	10	Osprey	1,627	24	10
Rough-legged Hawk[1]	1,278	17	9	Northern Goshawk	1,250	19	
Ferruginous Hawk[2]	1,231	15	11	Red Kite	1,135	25	9
Red-tailed Hawk[3]	1,224	21	6	Peregrine Falcon	1,110	16	4
Northern Goshawk[2]	1,137	13		Rough-legged Buzzard	990	10	10
Swainson's Hawk[1]	1,069	15	11	Buzzard	940	25	4
Harris' Hawk	1,047	12	7	Black Kite	850	23	8
Peregrine Falcon[2]	952	12	3	Honey Buzzard	790	29	
Prairie Falcon[2]	801	10	7	Marsh Harrier	669	16	8
Red-shouldered Hawk[2]	643	19	11	Hen Harrier	527	16	5
Northern Harrier[2]	531	16	5	Pallid Harrier	438	13	6
Cooper's Hawk[2]	529	10	6	Eleonora's Falcon	388	6	
Broad-winged Hawk[1]	490	18	4	Montagu's Harrier	370	16	3
Snail Kite	380	7		Sparrowhawk	264	15	6
Black-shouldered Kite	350	6		European Hobby	240	10	9
Mississippi Kite	314	8		Common Kestrel	215	16	2
Merlin[1]	213	7	10	Merlin	212	12	6
Sharp-shinned Hawk[3]	174	9	10	Lesser Kestrel	173	6	2
American Kestrel[3]	120	11	7	Red-footed Falcon	167	12	5
				South Africa			
				Cape Vulture	No data	11	3
Australia-New Zealand				Brown Snake Eagle	2,048	6	10
Wedge-tailed Eagle	3,402	5	11	Wahlberg's Eagle	1,147	11	9
Little Eagle	1,000	10	3	Lizard Buzzard	310	8	7
Whistling Kite	845	10	11	White-eyed Kestrel	272	6	6
Swamp Harrier	762	18	2	**Southeast Asia**			
Brown Falcon	570	10	6	Gray-faced Buzzard	397	8	6
Little Falcon	310	10	6				

INFECTIOUS AND PARASITIC DISEASES

JOHN E. COOPER

Free-living birds of prey can harbor a large number of organisms, ranging from bacteria to biting lice. Many of these organisms are non-pathogenic; that is, they are not a direct cause of disease, but the situation may change if the host's resistance is reduced or the number of organisms increases excessively. As few raptors are gregarious, they are unlikely to be affected by epizootics (epidemics) of disease, except perhaps when they are on migration or gathering together for other reasons. Diseases are not uncommon in captive birds, and there is much documented information on this subject, particularly relating to falconry, which is relevant to understanding the possible role of microorganisms in wild populations.

Perhaps the best documented viral infection of wild raptors is avian pox. Affected birds show plaque or scab-like lesions on the feet and head. Some affected birds appear to recover uneventfully, whereas others die, particularly when the scabs affect their eyes.

Various bacterial diseases have been reported in wild birds of prey and some may be acquired from prey, for example, fowl cholera (*Pasteurella* infection), an important cause of death in waterfowl, avian tuberculosis (*Mycobacterium avium* infection) and salmonellosis.

Protozoal parasites occur in wild raptors but often appear to be of no significance in a normal healthy host. Thus many blood parasites, while of considerable interest, are probably unimportant insofar as populations are concerned. Perhaps the best-known protozoan disease of birds of prey is trichomoniasis (*Trichomonas gallinae* infection) which affects the mouth and throat and was first described in falconers' birds, and given the name "frounce", hundreds of years ago. Despite its importance in captive raptors, there are relatively few reports of trichomoniasis in free-living birds, although (as with other diseases) it is possible that cases are missed. A recent study reports trichomoniasis in Goshawks (*Accipiter gentilis*) in an area of Britain and suggests that this disease may play a part in limiting the spread of the Goshawk in that locality. Helminth (worm) parasites are commonly found in wild raptors. From time to time they are implicated in ill-health or death.

External parasites are also prevalent. Biting lice (Mallophaga) often increase in numbers when a bird is debilitated but rarely cause disease per se. Mites of various types have a greater potential for pathogenicity since many of them suck blood. Myiasis (maggot infestation) is reported occasionally. Hippoboscids, which are blood-sucking flies, are frequently seen on birds of prey and may alarm ornithologists who encounter them—for example, when handling birds for banding purposes. Hippoboscids *do* suck blood (avian, not human) and infestations can contribute directly to ill-health or death in birds, as well as transmitting some of the blood parasites referred to earlier.

There is a complex interaction between wild raptors and the various microorganisms and parasites which live in or on them. Much remains to be learned about these potential pathogens and their significance to raptor populations. In the past it has been assumed that disease is of little importance other than (perhaps) as secondary to starvation. Recently, however, there have been suggestions that pathogens may contribute significantly to mortality, especially in small, isolated populations. This field provides an opportunity for biologists and veterinarians to work more closely together.

▼ Unsightly lesions on the head and feet of this wild Peregrine Falcon, brought to a rehabilitation center, are typical of avian pox. A mosquito-borne viral disease, pox can be seen on featherless parts of the falcon. Although often mild and non-fatal, a severe case can leave a bird unable to hunt. Secondary infection of the damaged skin can also occur.

John E. Cooper

▼ When handling raptors it is not unusual to see a biting louse (Mallaphaga) crawling through the feathers. Specific to raptors, they will not live on people. On a healthy bird they are seldom a problem. However, if the raptor becomes sick or debilitated the lice can take over and cause irritation and feather damage.

John E. Cooper

Jonathan Scott/Seaphot Ltd/Planet Earth Pictures

The procedures available 20 years ago for estimating mortality rates have been questioned in recent years. However, the potential bias (usually, overestimated adult mortality) was present in both the northern and southern mortality estimates. Population models suggested that northern and southern populations could remain stable for Barn Owls with observed production and mortality rates. If the mortality rates were biased high, it would mean that not all adults needed to attempt nesting each year—a point that agrees with data accumulated over the last two decades. The geographical variation in mortality rates within a species range deserves more attention. However, for many birds of prey, no longevity records—let alone mortality rate estimates—exist, and some species have never been banded.

Several excellent long-term raptor field studies have been conducted which include estimates of mortality rates. Ian Newton's study and resulting book *The Sparrowhawk* is the most complete study to date and should be viewed as the model for future detailed investigations. Newton estimated mortality rates in several different ways, thus checking the results of any one method against those from the others. He used information from: (1) recoveries of dead birds in the National Ringing Scheme (data from Scotland, and all data available); (2) known-age birds, banded as nestlings and trapped alive while breeding in study areas and retrapped in subsequent years ; and (3) birds banded as adults of unknown age together with those of known age (increased the sample size from procedure 2) and retrapped. The analytical procedures were slightly different for each data set, but the estimates were remarkably consistent. During the first year of life, the mean mortality rate was estimated at 69 percent for males (weighing 143–155 grams; 5–5.5 ounces) and 51 percent for the larger females (260–325 grams; 9–11 ounces). The annual mortality rate for males after the first year was estimated at 31–33 percent, and of females at 29–36 percent. The oldest male Sparrowhawk, among British banding recoveries, died in its eighth year, and the oldest female in its eleventh year. Newton reported that body mass correlated with survival during seasons of high mortality.

He also reported heavy mortality of newly independent juveniles in August and September, largely due to starvation, although prey were plentiful in the countryside. The starvation was believed to be the result of inexperience. Young birds do not possess the skills of adults in catching and killing prey, and they are also more vulnerable to various mortality factors.

The first-year mortality rate of 50 percent or more seems typical for most birds of prey, while adult mortality rates may be as low as 5 percent (Red Kite) or lower and range up to 50 percent.

▲ Inexperience is the biggest natural killer of young raptors; starvation and accident claim the lives of many immatures. Even success at hunting does not guarantee survival. Catfish tightly clasped in its talons, this immature African Fish Eagle risks its catch being pirated by an older eagle.

Clem Haagner/Ardea London

▲ Early life tends to be harder for males than for females, and fewer survive to breed. Weighing not much more than 80 grams, the tiny male Little Sparrowhawk has less chance of surviving his first year than the female, about twice his weight; perhaps 70 percent of males will die, and 50 percent of females. Even fewer males reach breeding age of two or more. This productive adult female, now at least two, could have first bred at one year of age.

▲ Stretching its wing, this adult Bateleur can afford to relax. Once they have reached adulthood, survival skills honed along the way, most raptors suffer annual mortality rates as low as five percent or less—that is, about 95 in 100 adults survive through any particular year.

► While studies of banded birds are valuable, because the immature plumage of many raptors is different from that of the adult, observation provides another means of estimation of mortality. The pale plumage of this Martial Eagle (*Hieraaetus bellicosus*) immediately identifies it as an immature. The number of pale birds in a population can be counted. If the population is more or less stable, the number of immatures entering the breeding population must balance the number of adults that die.

AGE STRUCTURE OF A POPULATION

The low percentage of banded birds of prey found by the public and reported to banding schemes testify that the vast majority of dead birds escape notice. Newton's detailed study mentioned above, where the investigator retrapped his own banded birds, provides one alternative for obtaining mortality information. Another approach makes use of the fact that many eagles and some larger hawks have subadults that can be identified by plumage. Several subadult age classes can be discerned for some species. If the population remains constant (or nearly so), as many juvenile individuals must enter the breeding population each year as adults are lost. Therefore, field observations of age ratios in the population can be useful. This approach requires a large unbiased sample of observations that is representative of the whole population.

Leslie Brown pioneered the age ratio approach for raptors. Few if any birds had been banded, so the only option was to obtain age ratio observations. He selected eagle species in East Africa that were easy to observe and sufficiently

Clem Haagner/Ardea London

common to provide large amounts of data, and in which it was possible to separate subadults from adults, and to decide their ages with some degree of accuracy. He studied the Bateleur (*Terathopius ecaudatus*), the African Fish Eagle (*Haliaeetus vocifer*), and the African Bearded Vulture (*Gypaetus barbatus*). The Bateleur (1,746 records) included 63 percent full adults, 29 percent 1–2 year olds, 5 percent 3–5 year olds, and 2.2 percent in pre-adult plumage. Brown interpreted this to mean that 97–98 percent of the young died before reaching sexual maturity at 7 years. It also suggests that adults have about a 3.5 percent (39 pre-adults/1,101 full adults) annual mortality rate. The African Fish Eagle (4,217 records) included 84 percent full adults, with 6.3 percent 1 year olds, 3.4 percent 2 year olds, and 6.6 percent early and late subadults. For the Bearded Vulture (478 records), 77.4 percent were full adults, and 22.5 percent were subadults (1 year olds, 2–5 year olds, and 5–7 year olds). To best estimate adult mortality rates with the age ratio approach requires the ability to discern the subadult plumage immediately before it becomes adult plumage.

Peter Steyn

▲ To warm itself, this Bateleur adopts an heraldic pose to catch the sun. Brown plumage and gray face and legs, compared with the striking black, chestnut and white plumage and red face and legs of an adult (opposite), identify the individual as an immature. In one East African study, 37 percent of those counted were not yet in full adult plumage; it was estimated that 97–98 percent of young birds would die before reaching breeding age at seven years.

◀ To both eagle and bird-watcher, the dark plumage and possession of a dark breast and throat distinguish this adult Martial Eagle from the pale immature (opposite). Intermediate age-groups can also be recognized because the change from immature to adult takes several years, the plumage darkening and gaining more spots on the upper breast and throat, which coalesce over time.

Large long-lived species characteristically have deferred maturity (first breed at 3 years or older) and relatively low reproductive rates. The long-lived characteristic helped the Osprey in the northeastern United States survive through the DDT era. The population was reduced about 90 percent in several states, but the surviving individuals provided the base to start rebuilding after DDT residues declined to a level that allowed adults to lay healthy eggs. If the species was short-lived, it would have been extirpated. The recovery will be slow because of the reduced breeding potential in larger long-lived birds; however, some younger age classes that normally would not breed can do so when population densities are low.

CAUSES OF DEATH

It is only in the last few decades that post-mortems have been conducted on sufficient numbers of raptors to determine specific causes of death. It soon became obvious that sick, injured or dead raptors found were not a representative sample of those dying in nature. Those hit by cars, electrocuted at power poles, or shot were more likely brought to a veterinarian or a raptor

rehabilitation center than those sick and dying from natural causes in the forest.

In the United States, much of the autopsy work has been limited to Bald Eagles (*Haliaeetus leucocephalus*), the National Emblem and an endangered species, which has suffered from many human-induced problems. Between 1960 and 1981, 768 Bald Eagles were autopsied and analyzed for various pollutants by the U.S. Fish and Wildlife Service. The analytical procedures improved over the years but the percentage of eagles shot provides a useful guide to the trend over the last 22 years. Shooting remained the most frequent cause of death but the proportion of mortalities due to shooting declined steadily: 1960–65, 59 percent; 1966–68, 41 percent; 1969–70, 46 percent; 1971–72, 35 percent; 1973–74, 28 percent; 1975–77, 20 percent; and 1978–81, 19 percent. The probable cause of death for 293 Bald Eagles found dead or moribund between 1978 and 1981 included: trauma (20%), shot (19%), electrocution (15%), emaciation (11%), infectious disease (6%), trapped (6%), lead poisoning (6%), hit by vehicle (6%), dieldrin poisoning (2%), drowning/emaciation (1%), open/no diagnosis (6%), and others (2%).

▼ Harsh winters take their toll. Even adult Bald Eagles succumb to storms or food shortages. However, shooting, although not as widespread as it once was, remains the single highest cause of death. Autopsies of eagles found dead show that almost 20 percent of America's National Emblem are shot.

Lon Lauber/Oxford Scientific Films

Richard & Julia Kemp/Survival Anglia

Frans Lanting/Minden Pictures

◄ Before the 1970s, powerlines, a convenient perch for the raptor, particularly in treeless areas, often caused electrocution. Research provided the reasons and the remedies, and today many power companies construct new raptor-safe lines or modify old ones.

In the early 1970s, a new effort was made to gain an understanding of raptor electrocutions (primarily eagles). Field studies documented its magnitude and the types of structures involved, and research led to design modifications of transmission line structures. Many types of modification options were available and have been used by power companies in critical areas to reduce raptor electrocutions. The young just learning to fly were killed most often. The electrocution problem is not totally solved, but great progress has been made since the early 1970s in many parts of the world.

Birds of prey reported by Doug Keran and the Raptor Rehabilitation Laboratory at the University of Minnesota provide a source of recent information (mostly the 1970s) on causes of death for raptors found in the Great Lakes area. The species were divided into nine groups and the causes of death placed in several categories. Natural mortality and unknown mortality accounted for only 8.3 and 7.4 percent of the total. Therefore, people were responsible for the deaths of at least 84.3 percent of the raptors in the sample. Shooting killed 20.6 percent. The large slow-moving soaring hawks—Ospreys, buteos (over half

▲ Human-caused mortality of raptors can be inadvertent. The persistent insecticide DDT is relatively safe for human use, and its devastating environmental effects were not anticipated. Many years after its introduction, dramatic and widespread declines in the numbers of some species of raptor alerted the world to one of DDT's most insidious effects. Comparisons of "healthy" eggs (left) with those from contaminated areas (damaged egg, at right) provided vivid evidence that DDT was causing many species to lay thin-shelled eggs unable to withstand incubation, thus killing embryos and preventing young birds from entering the population.

Caroline Atzetmuller/Oxford Scientific Films

◄ Collisions with vehicles account for countless raptor mortalities each year. Species that haunt roadways are most susceptible. The fast, low flight of this European Sparrowhawk (Accipiter nisus) may have resulted in its death on an English highway.

Weldon Trannies

▲ Large, relatively slow-flying raptors are most likely to fall prey to shooters. Once the most persecuted of raptors, this Wedge-tailed Eagle (*Aquila audax*), lying dead on an Australian outback road, escaped the bullet but was hit by a car as it fed on road-killed carrion.

► While human-inflicted mortality is fairly well documented and, at least in some cases, has been remedied, much remains to be discovered about raptor mortality. The handsome Red-tailed Hawk (*Buteo jamaicensis*) is no longer a favored target for American shooters but may someday be the subject of a study on mortality from natural causes.

► For their real or imagined depredations on livestock, raptors were once caught and left to die a slow, cruel death dangling from a vicious steel-jawed trap on a post. Happily, today's traps are usually kinder. This Australian Kestrel (*Falco cenchroides*) will be removed from the trap in minutes, measured and released unscathed.

were Red-tailed Hawks)—and the eagles took the brunt of the shooting pressure although all raptor groups were shot. Traps to catch furbearers in the Great Lakes states were directly responsible for 10.2 percent of the raptor deaths, with Great Horned Owls and Bald Eagles particularly vulnerable. Furbearers are more important in the Great Lakes states than in many regions of the United States. Therefore, trap-induced mortality was probably over-represented in this data set compared to its impact at other locations. When the information was presented to the state legislatures in the early 1980s, laws were soon enacted which banned the use of exposed baits within 7.6 meters (25 feet) of a trap set. Gary Duke, from the University of Minnesota, noted that the numbers of trapped raptors coming into their center declined dramatically after the laws went into effect.

Much of the human-caused mortality was lumped into the catch-all "other" category. Doug Keran's data subset (270 records) included the

category *road kills* which was 83 percent of the "other" category. The road kills were an even higher percentage for buteos and American Kestrels (*Falco sparverius*) and averaged 86 percent for all owls. Clearly the dead raptors found were biased towards deaths incurred by humans—primarily those shot, hit by motor vehicles, and trapped. Birds directly injured or killed by humans are more likely to be found than those birds that die of other causes. The "unknown category," of course, could also include people, pesticides and other pollutants as documented for the Bald Eagle. This biased sample emphasizes human-induced mortality factors, but from another point of view, these are the factors that can be, and in some cases already have been, changed. Mortality from trapping and electrocutions are good examples. Controlling the use of certain highly toxic or bioaccumulative pesticides has some success stories (for example, Bald Eagle, Osprey, Peregrine Falcon); the reduced use and eventual phase-out of lead shot for hunting waterfowl in the United States is in progress. Lead is primarily obtained by Bald Eagles from eating sick or dead waterfowl that ingested lead shot or were shot by hunters. Fortunately, most raptors, including the Bald Eagle, regurgitate a high percentage of ingested lead shot with their pellets (undigested bones, fur, and feathers). Without this pellet-casting trait, the Bald Eagle would probably have become extirpated in portions of its range early in this century long before the lead problem was known.

In summary, we have much more to learn about raptor mortality, especially age-specific mortality and mortality from natural causes. However, information about human-induced mortality can be useful immediately; management steps can be taken to effectively reduce or to eliminate these causes.

John Kiely/Australasian Nature Transparencies

MIGRATION AND MOVEMENTS

WILLIAM S. CLARK

Each spring and autumn people gather at a few specific locations in North America, Europe, Asia, and the Middle East to witness one of nature's greatest spectacles, the migration of diurnal birds of prey. Armed with binoculars and telescopes, they go to watch and marvel at the passing parade of flying raptors. While migration takes place across a broad front, the spectacle is best viewed at the relatively few places where migrating raptors concentrate. At many of these sites tens of thousands of raptors can be seen in a season; at a handful, hundreds of thousands; and at two, over a million.

Movements by birds of prey are of two different types: dispersal and movements necessitated by periodic changes in food. Dispersal is the random wanderings of recently fledged raptors from when they leave or are ejected from their natal areas until they establish their own breeding areas. For some individuals of the larger species, these peregrinations may last as long as six years, but for most, it is less than a year. The movements are in any direction and may take the bird far from its natal area. The young of all raptor species disperse.

Movements of raptors in response to periodic changes of food availability may be further categorized into four classes.

1. *Migration*, the movement on a regular seasonal basis of birds from one area to a different area. Two types are recognized, summer/winter and wet season/dry season migrations.

2. *Local movements*, performed on a regular basis. For example, birds move after the breeding season to areas where prey is available, but where suitable nest sites are not. The distances moved are usually short relative to most raptor migration distances.

3. *Periodic irruptions*, which occur when some or all of a population leave the breeding area for winter during years when there is a low ebb in the cyclic prey abundance.

4. *Nomadic wanderings*, such as when raptors drift from one area to another because of unpredictable food availability, usually moving into an area after sporadic rainfall.

These categories are somewhat arbitrary, and the movements of some species fall in between or encompass more than one.

Migration is the widespread movement of entire populations or subpopulations of birds (including birds of prey) to take advantage of seasonal food availability for nesting. Raptors that have nested in areas with a plentiful food supply in summer but a much diminished supply in winter must leave after their breeding seasons (or starve). Almost all of these species are in the northern hemisphere, and the birds migrate south in the fall to milder temperate, subtropical, or even tropical, climates to spend the winter. In spring they return to occupy their summer breeding territories.

The entire populations of 28 species or subspecies migrate from the breeding range to an entirely different wintering range; in all cases the breeding range is in the northern hemisphere. In 42 additional species, only the northernmost (or southernmost for austral species) individuals that experience food shortage move, with adults usually remaining further north (or south) than juveniles. Sixteen such species breed in North

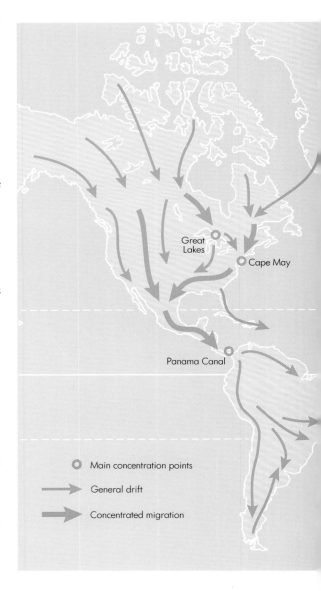

Great Lakes

Cape May

Panama Canal

○ Main concentration points

→ General drift

⇒ Concentrated migration

Neal Smith

◄ A feast for the eye of a raptor watcher. Part of a concentrated stream of raptors that crosses the Isthmus of Panama southward for two to three months each autumn, and returns northward in spring. Some species spend as long as two months on migration and travel 11,000 km (6800 miles). While such examples of predictable mass migration are impressive, many raptors make less spectacular, or less regular, movements just as important to survival.

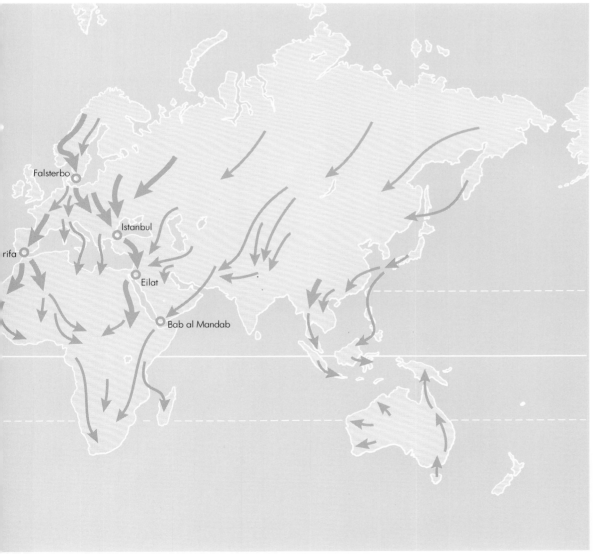

◄ Throughout the world there is an autumnal flow of certain raptor species, either the entire population or particular parts of it, from their breeding grounds to non-breeding areas where food is seasonally available. Although there are obvious points of concentration, where many migrants are channeled into a narrow stream by the landform, precise routes are difficult to detect. The general pattern of raptor migration and the main migration routes are shown. Some species complete only part of the journey, others travel an entire route, from one geographic extreme to the other.

▲ The autumn exodus of Rough-legged Buzzards (*Buteo lagopus*) from their Arctic breeding range, to winter in temperate central United States and Eurasia, varies according to food supply and snowfall. In mild winters, or when vole numbers are high, they stay longer in the north.

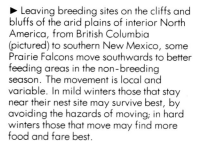

▶ Leaving breeding sites on the cliffs and bluffs of the arid plains of interior North America, from British Columbia (pictured) to southern New Mexico, some Prairie Falcons move southwards to better feeding areas in the non-breeding season. The movement is local and variable. In mild winters those that stay near their nest site may survive best, by avoiding the hazards of moving; in hard winters those that move may find more food and fare best.

America, but only two in South America. Eighteen Eurasian species are partial migrants, with nine additional species in eastern Asia. There are three Australian and four southern African partial migrants. Considering that some species occur on more than one continent, a total of 69 species, or almost one-fourth (25%) of the world's total, make a noticeable fall/spring migration. The fraction of the world's individual raptors is most likely much greater, as northern species generally have much larger populations.

In western Africa, at least six species make significant movements based on predictable annual rainfall cycles. During the dry season they occur in the southern savannas, then move north into the grasslands and desert edge after the onset of the rainy season, and move back when it ends. The reason for their movements is availability of prey. Some of these species breed during the wet season; others breed during the dry season.

After breeding, some adults and juveniles of the Prairie Falcon (*Falco mexicanus*) of North America make local movements of tens to hundreds of kilometers to areas with sufficient prey not occupied during the breeding season because of the lack of nest sites. Prairie Falcons are limited in breeding area by dependence on the availability of suitable nesting cliffs. Some Prairie Falcons must move after nesting because their main prey, ground squirrels, aestivate (pass the summer in a dormant state).

The irruptions of some northern species, for example the Northern Goshawk (*Accipiter gentilis*), are a result of cyclic prey fluctuations. During winters when prey are scarce, many breeding and non-breeding individuals leave the breeding grounds and go south. These irruptions are thus themselves somewhat cyclic.

Nomadic wandering is the least common type of movement. Apparently, only one species appears to be truly nomadic for its entire range, the nocturnal Letter-winged Kite (*Elanus scriptus*) of Australia. Such birds wander erratically in the interior of Australia and apparently breed only when and where their mammalian prey become abundant. Individuals and regional populations of other Australian species, particularly non-breeders, are also somewhat nomadic in the interior. In parts of Africa where rainfall is sporadic and unpredictable, local populations of four, and possibly more, species are nomadic.

Of all the types of movements discussed, spring/fall migration is the most noticeable. Most of the remainder of the chapter refers to this type of raptor movement.

Hans & Judy Beste/Auscape

Jack & Lindsay Cupper/Auscape

◀▲ Australia's nocturnal Letter-winged Kites appear to be truly nomadic. They wander the arid interior and breed only when small mammal prey is plentiful following good rains. Nevertheless, research may one day reveal a pattern to their movements.

MIGRATION

All species of completely migratory raptors breed in the northern hemisphere. To understand this, one only has to look at the location of land masses on the earth, particularly near the poles. Europe, Asia, and North America extend within the Arctic circle, close to the North Pole. Consequently, these northern areas experience large seasonal extremes of weather, with warm summers and abundant prey but cold winters with little prey. The smaller land masses of the southern hemisphere, South America, southern Africa, and Australia, are not nearly as close to the South Pole, and so have less seasonal weather variations. Raptors there do not have to move out for the winter because of prey unavailability. There are no breeding raptors on the Antarctic continent.

What causes the urge to migrate? The onset of migratory behavior has been studied in several species of birds, but apparently not for any raptors. Nevertheless, the mechanism should be similar. It appears that many external factors trigger the urge to move. Photoperiod changes apparently trigger physiological responses in birds that help prepare

them for their journey by storing fat. Then weather factors are the prime stimulus to actually begin and continue migration. Some birds of prey, notably those that make long-distance migrations over terrain where they cannot find food, such as Western Honey Buzzards (*Pernis apivoris*), Swainson's Hawk (*Buteo swainsoni*), and Eastern Red-footed Falcon (*Falco amurensis*) put on extra weight in the form of fat which is used as fuel during the long migration. Most migrants, however, stop and forage for food when the opportunity arises and are able to migrate with smaller fat stores. All migrant raptors stop to drink. Individuals of several species, including Black Kites (*Milvus migrans*), Honey and Steppe Buzzards (*Buteo b. vulpinus*), have even been observed drinking briny water from salt ponds.

Almost all species of raptors make the majority of their migrations by utilizing rising air columns called "thermals." These "bird elevators" allow the soaring birds of prey to rise up above the ground with little effort; they only have to stretch out their wings. Upon reaching height where the thermal runs out, the birds begin gliding in the

▶▲ In fall, much of the European population of Black Kite (*Milvus migrans*) joins the flow of raptors heading to Africa. Some travel, and rest at night, in loose flocks. In Australia they are periodically eruptive, moving from the center towards the coast; some parts of the population may regularly winter in northern Australia.

primary migration direction, again with little or no effort expended, until they reach another thermal, where the process is repeated. The birds thus accomplish their overland migration with minimal expenditure of energy.

Recent studies using radar have revealed that when using thermals in temperate areas, raptors fly at altitudes of between 300 and 800 meters (980–2,600 feet) above the ground. In the tropics, thermals can rise up to 4,000 meters (13,000 feet), and raptors have been encountered even higher. Raptors above 700 meters (2,300 feet) are usually not visible to the unaided eye. In the early morning and late afternoon, thermals are rather weak and the raptors migrate at much lower altitudes. By midday, when thermals are strongest, migrants fly at the greatest altitude, often out of sight. This could explain the "noon lull" phenomenon described by many authors. At some concentration points, particularly peninsulas, raptors cease using thermals, drop in altitude, and begin using powered flight.

Migrant raptors usually move on a regular annual schedule. Some species, like the Black Kite,

migrate early in the autumn; others, for example, the Rough-legged Buzzard (*Buteo lagopus*), move later; and others move throughout the entire season. Spring migration timings are usually the opposite, with early fall migrants moving late, and so on. Most studies on the age of migrant raptors have shown that juveniles make up the bulk of the migration early in the fall, followed later by adults. In the spring, adults precede juveniles.

Do raptors migrate singly or in groups? The simple answer is that they do both, depending somewhat on the species. Some species, particularly harriers and some falcons, almost always migrate as individuals. They are less dependent on thermals and are not prone to be deflected and concentrated by water barriers, so they are usually seen singly on migration. Buzzards and eagles are often encountered in groups, perhaps because they were concentrated into these groups by a water barrier or by attraction to a single thermal; hawks have been observed to make large alterations in their glide direction to join others rising in a thermal. Such movements may be somewhat like people getting on an elevator

Peter Steyn/Ardea London

Ardea London

◄▲ Some migrants, particularly those that soar and do little active flying, are thought not to feed on migration, arriving exhausted. Others stop to forage and drink. The Steppe Buzzard, a migratory sub-species of the Eurasian Buzzard, reaches South Africa in the non-breeding season.

together, the only reason for being there is to go up and not to socialize, However, several authors feel that some of these solitary species form loose migration flocks to aid in finding thermals. A final group, composed of social species, most likely perform most or all of the migration together. Examples are communal species such as Black Kites, Mississippi Kites (*Ictinia mississippiensis*), Levant Sparrowhawks (*Accipiter brevipes*), Turkey Vultures (*Cathartes aura*), Swainson's Hawks, Lesser Kestrels (*Falco naumanni*), Eastern Red-footed Falcons, and Western Red-footed Falcons (*F. vespertinus*). However, individuals of at least one social species, the Eleonora's Falcon (*F. eleonorae*), apparently migrate singly.

Because of the dependence on thermals and the usual daytime activity of diurnal raptors, migration takes place during daylight. However, recent observations suggest that migration of some individuals may continue at night. An observer counting owls at Cape May Point, New Jersey, USA, in the fall observed two Northern Harriers (*Circus cyaneus hudsonius*) flying south long after the sun had set. Observers regularly note a flight of

Merlins (*Falco columbarius*) and American Kestrels (*F. sparverius*) moving across the Delaware Bay from Cape May Point well underway at first light, and Merlins seen to roost in trees at dusk were not there at dawn. One researcher noted that Peregrines (*Falco peregrinus tundrius*), which had radio-transmitters attached, continued to fly over open ocean all through the night. Harriers and falcons have been observed arriving on the island of Malta at dawn after a considerable water-crossing in adverse weather.

Guy Robbrecht/Bruce Coleman Ltd

◄ Although a social species, Eleonora's Falcons migrate singly. Their annual cycle exploits the autumn passage of passerines across the Mediterranean. The Falcons breed between August and October, then set off for Madagascar and mid-eastern Africa.

CONCENTRATION POINTS

Why are large numbers of migrating birds of prey seen at some places? Quite simply because they have been concentrated by the funneling effect of water bodies acting as a "barrier" or because of the attraction of other geographic features such as mountain ridges, rivers, and shorelines.

Thermals form readily over land but are not so readily formed nor are they as strong over bodies of water. Because they lack usable thermals, water bodies act as barriers to many migrating raptors. The magnitude of the barrier depends on the extent of the water crossing and the species of raptor. Some species, particularly falcons and harriers, are less dependent on thermals for their migration and may make long water crossings using powered flight. The Eastern Red-footed Falcon regularly makes a very long flight across the Indian Ocean from western India to East Africa and back every year. Others such as eagles, buzzards, hawks, and vultures, are more dependent on thermals and alter their flight direction to avoid crossing wide expanses of water. Many concentration points are at the tip of a peninsula where the flying raptors are literally funneled, and are then most noticeable. Fall migrants moving south are concentrated at south-pointing peninsulas; spring migrants by north-pointing ones. Raptors can be somewhat concentrated after making a short water crossing from a peninsula or other concentration point. For example, at Djibouti, in northeastern Africa, researchers have watched large numbers of raptors of 26 species arriving across the water from North Yemen to the east. Most raptors moving to Africa from Asia cross the Arabian peninsula on a broad front. The Red Sea acts as a barrier and concentrates the migrants in North Yemen at Bab al Mandab, the mouth of

the Red Sea, where there is the shortest water crossing. While the concentration is not nearly as great in Djibouti as in Yemen, large numbers are nevertheless seen coming ashore from the east.

Concentrations also occur where raptors can find extra lift, such as along mountain ridges where the wind striking the ridge forms deflected streams of rising air. Updrafts are also produced on certain wind conditions along shorelines. The effectiveness of ridges and shorelines is also a

600 m
(1980 ft)

400 m
(1320 ft)

Raptor leaves night roost and flies up to thermal, then soars to height and begins gliding.

200 m
(660 ft)

Gliding hawk s in a thermal an slight adjustme to join it.

Sea level

Altitude

Distance covered: 0

Time: 11.00 am

▶ Falcons and some other raptors can use powered flight to cross water. Other species, more dependent on thermals, crowd across the few points where continents are closest, down peninsulas and across island chains. Migrating Turkey Vultures rest by night and must wait until mid-morning for the thermals on which they rise and continue their journey. Slotted wing tips, each feather acting as an aerofoil, and a large wing area relative to its body weight allow the Vulture to soar with ease.

David A. Ponton

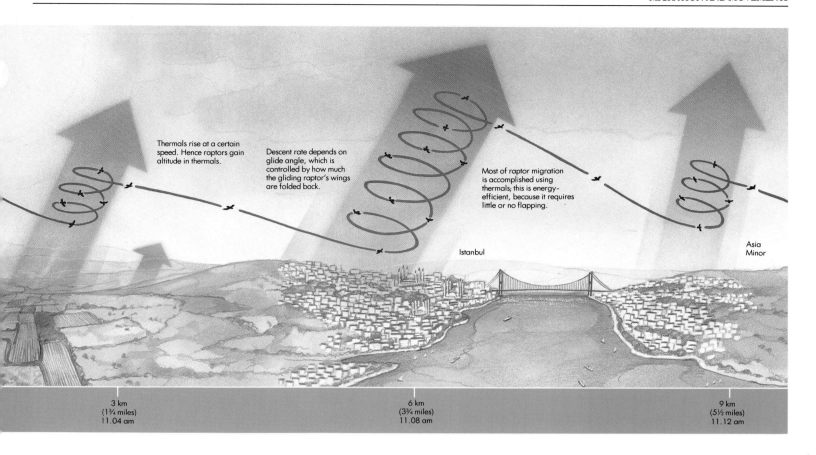

Thermals rise at a certain speed. Hence raptors gain altitude in thermals.

Descent rate depends on glide angle, which is controlled by how much the gliding raptor's wings are folded back.

Most of raptor migration is accomplished using thermals; this is energy-efficient, because it requires little or no flapping.

Istanbul

Asia Minor

| 3 km (1¾ miles) 11.04 am | 6 km (3¾ miles) 11.08 am | 9 km (5½ miles) 11.12 am |

function of their orientation, for if they are aligned in the direction the raptor is traveling, they act also as a "leading line." Raptors follow other noticeable geographic features, such as rivers, which also act as "leading lines" for their migration. Concentration can also occur in very high mountain ranges, where raptors concentrate at passes between peaks. Examples are the passes south of Annapurna in Nepal and several cols in the European Alps and Pyrenees.

Sometimes several of these concentrating factors operate together, as at Cape May Point where the coastal leading line of the Atlantic Ocean leads into a peninsula. Here some of the largest concentrations of raptors in North America are regularly recorded. Another concentration point is in the Pontic Mountains of eastern Turkey, where, in fall, raptors that have been deflected around the eastern end of the Black Sea are further concentrated along several mountain ridges.

▲ Typical raptor migration across the Bosphorus using thermals. As the sun heats the ground, various areas heat more than others and the warmer air above them begins to rise. The raptors spiral upwards on the rising air then glide down to enter another bubble. As the day progresses thermal streets may form, and the raptors may be carried effortlessly along for tens of kilometers.

◄ Sooty Falcons (*Falco concolor*) breed in the Sahara Desert and Near East and some then migrate to Madagascar. They feed on route, unlike some large soaring species. To cross the sea they must use powered flight, more costly in terms of energy than soaring.

O. Langrano/Bruce Coleman Ltd

▶ ▲ Almost the entire population of Swainson's Hawk migrates from western North America to southern or southeastern South America. Some remain to winter in southern Florida. They sometimes travel in peaceful, mixed flocks with Broad-winged Hawks, although both originate from different areas and winter separately.

RAPTOR COUNTS

What is more natural when one is watching the passage of migrating raptors than to ask "how many are going by?" The desire to answer this question is no doubt the origin of most of the world's hawk counts.

One of the first counts was taken at Cape May Point, by Roger Tory Peterson in 1935. He was hired by the Audubon Society to point out to the gunners which raptors, according to the then existing laws, were the "good hawks" (not to be shot) and which were the "bad hawks" (OK to be shot). We have come far since those days, although raptors are still being shot in great numbers around the Mediterranean Sea and other places.

Only in two known locations can over a million passing raptors be recorded during a single season; these are Eilat in southern Israel and the Panama Canal in Central America. The reasons why so many birds pass these two places are that the geographic concentrating factors operate across a wide expanse over which great numbers of raptors migrate. At Panama, virtually all the migrating raptors that leave North America and go into South America, mainly Swainson's and Broad-winged Hawks (*Buteo platypterus*) and Turkey Vultures, pass through this narrow stretch of land twice a year. The Isthmus of Panama is only 73 kilometers (45 miles) wide at this point, and local geographic features further narrow the flight line of passing raptors to an approximately 5-kilometer (3-mile) path.

So many raptors pass by Eilat because of the Red Sea. This water body, over 2,000 kilometers (1,240 miles) in length, acts as a deflection barrier to most raptors returning in spring from Africa to their breeding areas in eastern Europe and western Asia. The migrants fly in a northeasterly direction from winter areas in Africa until encountering the Red Sea. Almost all of them then turn to the northwest and fly along the western shore of the Sea until they reach the point where it splits into the Gulf of Suez and Gulf of Aqaba (across from the tip of the Sinai peninsula). Here most of the raptors cross over the mouth of the Gulf of Suez and continue up the eastern side of the Sinai peninsula until reaching Eilat, at the head of the Gulf of Aqaba. In 1985, over a million raptors

◀▲ Each year a steady stream of raptors, including the Broad-winged Hawk, passes down the Isthmus of Panama. One year more than 2.5 million raptors were counted meticulously from photographs. Later studies from aircraft revealed passage of some species around midday in certain clouds not visible from the ground, and so missed by the camera.

of 28 species were counted passing Eilat.

Concentrations of hundreds of thousands of raptors are recorded regularly at several peninsulas, mountain ridges, and shoreline barriers. Examples are Djibouti in northeastern Africa, Gibraltar/Tarifa in southern Spain at the eastern end of the Mediterranean Sea, the Pontic Mountains of eastern Turkey, Holiday Beach of northeast Lake Erie, and across northern Israel.

Lesser numbers, tens of thousands of raptors per season, are recorded at many concentration locales. These include mountain ridges such as Hawk Mountain in Pennsylvania and the Goshute mountains in Nevada, lakeshore locations such as Duluth (Minnesota), Green Bay and Cedar Grove (Winsconsin, USA), Hawk Cliff (Ontario, Canada), and Beidaihe (Hebei, China), and at peninsula locations such as Cape May Point (New Jersey), Point Diablo (California), Falsterbo (Sweden) and Capes Irago-zaki and Stat-misaki (Japan).

There are numerous locations where small concentrations of hundreds or thousands of raptors are recorded in a season. Because it is an enjoyable pastime, many people stand at a single location every day for an entire season of two or three months and record all the flying raptors they see passing. But why count raptors? What can it tell us? If the count is accurate and the raptors were identified correctly, the total count from an area tells us how many raptors passed. Unfortunately, this in itself is not necessarily a useful number. In cases where there are large concentrations of a single species, the count could be used as a minimum population estimate for that species. For example, most individuals of the Lesser Spotted Eagle (*Aquila p. pomarina*) and Swainson's Hawk pass by a single location in one season. The estimated numbers of the Lesser Spotted Eagle in eastern Europe and western Asia were thought to be only a few thousand pairs. But during several fall counts in Israel, over 150,000 individuals were tallied. This indicates, if nothing else, that the population estimate from the breeding areas was far too low and gives a new minimum value. But this count in itself may also be low, as some individuals are not counted either because they pass too high to be seen from the ground or pass on another flight path.

► A growing number of people count migrating raptors at the better-known concentration points. Such counts have correctly reflected declines in Osprey and Peregrine populations, and subsequent recoveries in numbers. However, accurate identification of a high-flying raptor is not always easy. A knowledge of a combination of distinctive features helps. The diminutive Sharp-shinned Hawk has rounded wings, and a straight cut tip to its tail when gliding. In full soar, the Peregrine Falcon has a characteristic crossbow shape and its fanned tail masks its typically long-winged appearance. Deeply crooked wings distinguish a gliding Osprey. Except for the outer section of the wing, the Mississippi Kite is not unlike the Peregrine in shape. (Here the illustrations are not to scale.)

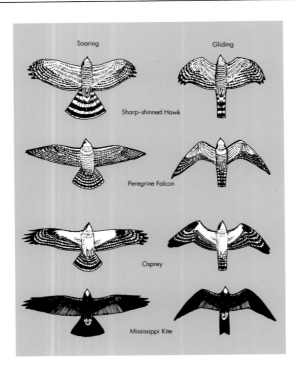

Count data can also tell us something about the relationship of migration to weather conditions. In fall, large counts are associated with northerly (following) winds, rising barometric pressure and falling temperatures, whereas spring counts are greatest on southerly (following) winds, falling barometric pressure, and increasing temperatures. Studies have shown that the number of hawks moving is highest on sunny days, for sun is necessary to form thermals. Rain almost always suppresses migration.

But weather can also affect the count itself. For example, radar studies have shown that migrating raptors approaching Cape May Point fly higher on east winds than they do on west winds. Even if the same number of raptors pass on any given east-wind day as pass on a west-wind day, the count would most likely be higher on the west-wind day. Wind direction can affect the number of hawks counted at a location by affecting the birds' ground speed. A following wind increases their speed over the ground, while a head wind decreases it. So

TOTALLY MIGRATORY RAPTORS

Species or subspecies	Breeding area	Wintering area	Species or subspecies	Breeding area	Wintering area
Osprey (*Pandion haliaetus h. & carolinensis*)	North America; Europe	South America; Africa	Rough-legged Buzzard (*B. lagopus*)	Arctic	Temperate
Western Honey Buzzard (*Pernis apivorus*)	Eurasia	Africa	Lesser Spotted Eagle (*Aquila p. pomarina*)	Eurasia	Africa
Swallow-tailed Kite (*Elanoides f. forficatus*)	USA	South America	Greater Spotted Eagle (*A. clanga*)	Eurasia	Middle East, India
Mississippi Kite (*Ictinia mississippiensis*)	USA	South America	Steppe Eagle (*A. nipalensis*)	Asia	Africa Southern Asia
Gray-faced Buzzard (*Butastur indicus*)	Eastern Asia	Southeast Asia	Booted Eagle (*Hieraaetus pennatus*)	Eurasia	Africa, Southern Asia
Montagu's Harrier (*Circus pygargus*)	Europe	Africa	Lesser Kestrel (*Falco naumanni*)	Eurasia	Africa
Pallid harrier (*C. macrourus*)	Eurasia	Africa, India	Western Red-footed Falcon (*F. vespertinus*)	Eurasia	Africa
Pied Harrier (*C. melanoleucos*)	Eastern Asia	Southeast Asia	Eastern Red-footed Falcon (*F. amurensis*)	Asia	Africa
Levant Sparrowhawk (*Accipiter brevipes*)	Southeastern Europe	Africa	Eleonora's Falcon (*F. eleonorae*)	Southern Europe	Madagascar
Japanese Sparrowhawk (*A. gularis*)	Eastern Asia	Southeast Asia	Sooty Falcon (*F. concolor*)	North America, Middle East	Madagascar
Gray Frog Hawk (*A. soloensis*)	Eastern Asia	Southeast Asia	Merlin (*F. c. columbarius, aesalon, subaesalon, insignis, pacificus,* and *pallidus*)	North America, Caribbean	Central America,
Broad-winged Hawk (*Buteo p. platypterus*)	North America	Central and South America			
Swainson's Hawk (*B. swainsoni*)	North America	South America	Eurasian Hobby (*F. subbuteo*)	Eurasia	Africa
Steppe Buzzard (*B. buteo vulpinus*)	Asia	Africa	Peregrine (*F. peregrinus tundrius/calidus*)	Arctic	South America, Africa
Harlan's Hawk (*B. jamaicensis harlani*)	Alaska, BC	Western USA			

N. N. Birks

more hawks are tallied on a following wind than on a head wind, even if the same number of hawks are flying on both days.

As a rule, counts made in the fall yield larger numbers than do those made in spring. This is no doubt because, all other factors being equal, the fall numbers are swollen by the young of the year, whereas the spring numbers have been reduced by over-winter mortality.

Reverse migration, that is, hawks flying in the opposite direction for the season, has been noted. In all cases, the wind direction was opposite that usually associated with peak flights during that season. Occasionally, when conditions for the best fall raptor flights occur in spring, numbers of raptors are noted at Cape May Point which is known primarily for large fall concentrations. Presumably, the birds moved in from the north, moving opposite to the usual direction.

Some people believe that long-term hawk counts may be used as population indicators. Others argue that there are too many variables involved, such as daily and yearly weather differences, observer differences, and lack of consistency in coverage. Nevertheless, analyses of the count data from Hawk Mountain from 1937 showed, after the fact, the decline of several raptor species in eastern North America, notably the

Peregrine and the Osprey (*Pandion haliaetus*).

In 1973, during the First Hawk Migration Conference held in Syracuse, New York, a new organization was established to promote and standardize hawk counts in North America. The organization was known as the Hawk Migration Association of North America or HMANA. This group is still functioning and puts out a lively newsletter devoted to hawk counting and reports of hawk counts. A standardized form was developed by scientists and statisticians to aid in data collecting. On the form all counts are recorded by half-hour intervals and information about weather is noted.

As more people are attracted to hawk watching and counting, they will no doubt find new locations where concentrations occur. This is particularly true for Asia, where, compared to Europe and North America, our knowledge of raptor concentrations is minimal. Perhaps there are also undiscovered concentration areas in the southern hemisphere, specifically in South America and Australia, like the few known places in southern Africa. In any event, regardless of whether important data are gathered, a growing number of people world-wide will be out with binoculars and cameras twice a year watching and marveling at raptors on migration.

▲ The scientific names of some raptors reflect their migratory habits, obviously noted by early ornithologists; the specific name for Peregrine Falcon, *Falco peregrinus*, is from the Latin for "that comes from foreign parts." But not all subspecies of Peregrine are migratory. Adults of the Australian race (*F. p. macropus*, shown) remain in or near their breeding territory all year.

SOARING RAPTOR MIGRATION THROUGH THE ISTHMUS OF PANAMA

NEAL SMITH

Over the wide bridge of the Panamanian Isthmus, thousands of birds migrate annually. Three of the species that do so employ soaring flight, for long distances (to 11,000 kilometers —7,000 miles) and for long periods (up to 2 months). These are the Broad-winged Hawk (*Buteo platypterus*), the Swainson's Hawk (*Buteo swainsonii*) and the Turkey Vulture (*Cathartes aura*). The major mode of passage of these raptors is diurnal soaring, in which a great portion of their flight energy is extracted from the atmosphere. This energy *is not* uniformly distributed within the airspace but occurs in patches, zones, or waves. Rising columns of hot air are seldom present over water, so soaring migration, for the most part, must be over land. Normally non-social species are thus seen together in enormous numbers during migration. These sources of energy are lacking at night and the birds roost together from about 1700 hours to around 0830 the next day. If it is raining they remain at the roosts by day.

In theory it is possible to count almost the entire world's population of at least two of the raptors, Swainson's Hawk and Broad-winged Hawk, as they enter their non-breeding areas, via the Isthmus of Panama. Their survival there can be assessed from counts on the return, northward flight. In practice it is not so simple. During the months of September through November (the boreal fall and the rainy season in Central and South America) the aerial river of raptors is approximately 12 kilometers (7–8 miles) wide, from the shores of the Pacific (south in Panama) northward. Direct visual counts of such a concentration of raptors are impossible, especially with mixed species flocks. Black and white 35-millimeter photography with long focal length lenses (up to 1600 mm) was a promising alternative. I attempted to take non-overlapping pictures of the birds on a glide rather than when they were in the highly complex thermal columns. The time and date were automatically recorded on the negative. The negative was then placed in an enlarger and projected on white paper which resulted in white specks on a black background. I used a hand counter and a black felt-tipped pen to eliminate all white spots while simultaneously employing the counter. The method was time-consuming, but represented a conservative, archival scientific record. The maximum numbers recorded by this method was in 1985 with 937,400 Turkey Vultures, 811,170 Swainson's Hawks, 788,111 Broad-winged Hawks, and more than 77,116 unidentified raptors. But many hours of observation and flights by me in a glider showed that a significant number of these birds flew inside the clouds and were mostly invisible to ground observers.

The season of northward passage (February–April) is often very different meteorologically from the southward passage, leading to differences in bird behavior. Because the migrants use the shortest straight-line route through Central America, and because of the peculiar bend of the Isthmus, they pass to the north of the southward route. In addition, the Isthmus is under the strong northeast trade winds and thus the birds spread out because atmospheric energy is more uniformly distributed. Thus I know of no practical method to obtain biologically meaningful counts at what is theoretically the most ideal spot for this purpose in the world.

Once the "rivulets of migratory raptors" coalesce at about 20° north on the southward passage, they seem not to eat until they reach their non-breeding areas or run out of body fat. This hypothesis is supported by the absence of feces and pellets at their roosts, by the enormous concentrations of individuals during the diurnal flight and the flight altitudes (normally 1,000 to 2,500 meters; 3,280–8,200 feet) which preclude feeding. The passage times and flight altitudes attained argue that these birds are not simply soaring up with a thermal bubble and gliding forward and down to reach yet another thermal. They are exploiting other complex meteorological phenomena in a manner vastly superior to man-made gliders. The sophisticated energy-saving flight strategies makes these long-distance soaring migrants among the most exquisite fliers of all birds.

▼ For the four-month breeding season the Broad-winged Hawk is found in eastern and central North America. That entire population then migrates to central and northern South America, to return north again in spring. In between, in the West Indies, is a sedentary population.

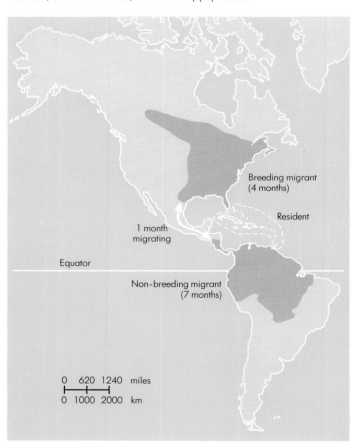

Breeding migrant (4 months)

Resident

1 month migrating

Equator

Non-breeding migrant (7 months)

0 620 1240 miles
0 1000 2000 km

HAWK MOUNTAIN: THE WORLD'S FIRST REFUGE FOR BIRDS OF PREY

S. SENNER

Each fall season about 23,000 migrating raptors may be seen passing over Hawk Mountain, which is on the Kittatinny Ridge in southeastern Pennsylvania (USA). Hawks migrating from the north and northeast follow this and other ridges of the Appalachian Mountains as "leading lines," taking advantage of upward-moving thermal and deflected air currents. Broad-winged Hawks (*Buteo platypterus*) and Sharp-shinned Hawks (*Accipiter striatus*) are most abundant, but, in all, 16 species of raptors are regularly recorded on migration.

Since at least the turn of the century, local residents had gathered each fall at Hawk Mountain to shoot the migrant raptors (especially Sharp-shinned Hawks and Red-tailed Hawks (*Buteo jamaicensis*)). Over the years, tens of thousands of these and other raptor species were slaughtered as they flew low over the rocky promontory that is known today as the Sanctuary's North Lookout.

Scientific publications based on data from raptor carcasses gathered at Hawk Mountain aroused the attention of conservationists, and, in 1934, Rosalie Edge and the Emergency Conservation Committee leased the original property of 564 hectares (1400 acres). She hired a young couple, Maurice and Irma Broun, to become the first wardens of the fledgling Sanctuary. Once they posted the boundaries and patrolled the road to bar would-be shooters, the "battle" for Hawk Mountain was effectively over. In that first fall season, about 500 people climbed Hawk Mountain to watch—not shoot—hawks.

Beyond the boundaries of Hawk Mountain, however, shooting of raptors remained commonplace, and the founders of the new sanctuary quickly began efforts to educate the public about the ecological importance of raptors, and sought legislation to protect them from persecution. In addition, to document the phenomenon of migration at Hawk Mountain, the founders initiated an annual count of migrants—the world's first organized hawk count; this effort continues today.

Historically, Hawk Mountain has played a vital role as a catalyst for interest in birds of prey. As the world's first birds-of-prey refuge, the Sanctuary quickly established itself as an innovative leader in wildlife conservation and education: its education programs have stimulated enthusiasm for birds, conservation, and careers in the natural sciences; its annual hawk counts have spawned hundreds of similar counts and other research on raptors around the world; and its efforts to protect birds of prey from shooters, pesticides, and other threats have achieved lasting results. In 1986 the US President's Council on Environmental Quality reported that the Sanctuary's history "offers a striking example of the role of private initiative in achieving major accomplishments in wildlife conservation."

Today the Hawk Mountain Sanctuary Association has a professional staff working in education, research, and conservation policy. Its program is international in scope and operates on an annual budget of about US$500,000. About 48,000 people visit the Sanctuary annually to watch hawks and other wildlife, to hike and enjoy the scenery, and to participate in a variety of educational programs. The organization is entirely supported by private means—primarily the dues and contributions of its 8,000 members. Through birds of prey, Hawk Mountain and its members contribute to worldwide environmental conservation.

James C. Bednarz/Hawk Mountain Sanctuary

RAPTOR MIGRATION OVER ISRAEL

YOSSI LESHEM

"That path no eagle knoweth, neither hath the honey buzzard's eye seen it" (Job, 28:7).

As long as 3,000 years ago, the Jewish sages noticed the miraculous phenomenon of bird migration over the Holy Land. Only during the past two decades, however, has there been significant progress in the study of this migration. It has emerged that Israel is now one of the best sites in the world—if not the best—for observing raptors in migration.

The map of the main migration sites around the Mediterranean basin, shows that the largest numbers of migrating raptors are seen in Israel. Its location at the junction of three continents (Asia, Africa and Europe) has made Israel an axis of international significance during the annual spring and fall migrations.

For most raptors, large bodies of water, such as the Mediterranean, the Caspian or the Black Seas, are barriers which must be crossed or circumvented en route from Asia to Africa. The raptors of western Europe therefore take the narrowest sea crossing, over the Straits of Gibraltar. A small proportion of European birds crosses the Mediterranean at other points. The majority of birds from northern, central and eastern Europe, as well as large numbers from western Asia and the Caucasus, take the shortest route down the east side of the Mediterranean, through Lebanon and Israel.

Israel's geomorphological features also facilitate large-scale raptor migration. The Syrian–African Rift, which cuts down the entire length of the country, provides perfect conditions for the development of ascending thermals. The rift is narrow in this area, and the great fault scarp of the Judean Desert reach hundreds of meters in elevation. The combination of high cliffs, narrow desert canyons and a high mean temperature along the rift create an ideal migration path for raptors.

The line of the mountains of Lebanon, the Shouf Ridge, the hills of Galilee, Samaria and Judea, run almost parallel to the Mediterranean coastline. This is another reason for the formation of rising air currents, which assist the migration of raptors, storks and pelicans. These migrating birds depend almost exclusively during their migration on rising air currents and thermals.

Thanks to Israel's special location, some record numbers of migrating raptors have been counted, including the greatest number ever seen during one migration season anywhere in the world. In the spring of 1985, over the Eilat mountains, 1,193,228 raptors were counted in 100 days (16 Februray–23 May). The fall surveys have counted over 565,000 raptors in the space of only six weeks annually (1 September–15 October).

Most of the world population of certain species passes over Israel. The dates of passage are well known and relatively regular, so observations may be planned in advance. In the spring of 1985, during the first three weeks of May, 850,000 honey buzzards passed over the Eilat mountains. In the first three weeks of September 1986, 417,000 honey buzzards were counted at Kfar Kasseme, no less than 220,000 in two days.

The world population of Lesser Spotted Eagles (*Aquila pomarina*) had been estimated at only 35,000 individuals. However, in 1983, in late September and early October, 141,000 Lesser Spotted Eagles passed over Israel, *four times* the previous estimate. Seventy-five thousand Steppe Eagles (*A. nipalensis*) passed over Israel in the spring of 1985, and 44,000 Levant Sparrowhawks (*Accipiter brevipes*) in the fall of 1986.

These impressive numbers of birds were observed not only by a network of ground observers but, in parallel, by radar which tracked the massive migration in collaboration with the Israel Air Force. The IAF had suffered severe damage to aircraft from collisions with birds, mainly during the migration season. Improved knowledge of the movements has helped to reduce the accidents.

To see this huge migration, raptor enthusiasts come to Israel in large numbers from all over the world. In 1980 only a few dozen of birdwatchers visited Israel; but in 1988 an estimated 9,000 arrived to watch this unique natural phenomenon.

▼ Cinereous Vulture

Israel Raptor Information Center

The Israel Raptor Information Center (IRIC) has for several years carried out large-scale tracking of migrant raptors, in the spring and fall, using ground-based observations. Since the information collected by observers on the ground is limited, a research project was developed in which a motorized glider tracked the migration of raptors, storks and pelicans.

The motorized glider (OGAR model, produced in Poland) took off in the morning towards flocks of raptors which had landed the evening before. With the aid of radar devices on the ground, the glider was directed to the flock. The glider then accompanied the flock from morning takeoff to the moment it left Israel's borders. Once the glider had joined the flock, the engine was cut off and, along with the raptors, it joined the thermals and soared.

◄ Migration paths of raptors in the fall.

2.09 pm

5.32 pm

▲ Flight path of the glider, described in the text below.

Yossi Eshbol/Israel Raptor Information Center

▲ Many Black Kites appear over Israel in spring on their way to breeding grounds in Europe. In 1977, 26,770 were counted near Eilat.

▼ The altitude of a flock of Honey Buzzards soaring and gliding across Israel, in fall 1986. Bottom line shows land contours and landmarks.

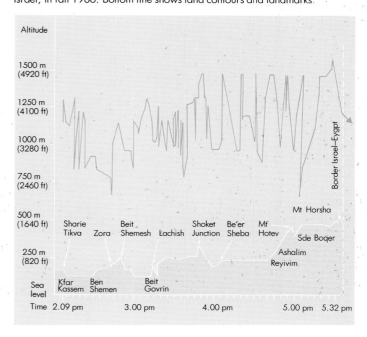

Using this method, we carried out 232 days of flight between 1986 and 1988, accompanying raptors, storks and pelicans. Data were accumulated about flight paths, elevations from the base of the thermal to its top, the distance between the thermals, velocity of bird flight, and weather conditions.

Each day in the fall, we accompanied flocks from the Lebanese border to the Egyptian border, over 250–320 kilometers (155–200 miles). We spent 5–11 hours daily in the glider, with the same flock. Our spring flight paths followed the reverse direction.

Words are hardly adequate to describe the experiences of flying with flocks of migrating raptors. The glider accompanied the birds, wingtip to wingtip, throughout the length of the State of Israel. The only sound during this magical flight was the rush of bird and glider wings, high up in the sky. The birds showed no fear of the glider.

A representative section of flight in the motorized glider took place during the fall migration, on 5 September 1986, together with about 2000 Honey Buzzards (*Pernis apivorus*). The flock was located by approach radar equipment of Ben Gurion International Airport. This equipment directed the glider into a flock over the village of Sha'arei Tikva, 23 kilometers (14 miles) east of the Mediterranean coastline, north of Tel Aviv, at 14:09 hours. The flight ended at 17:32 hours, at Mount Horsha, when the Honey Buzzards entered the area of Sinai and crossed the Egypt–Israel border.

The Honey Buzzards traveled a total distance of 186 kilometers (115 miles) in 3 hours 23 minutes. Their average rate of flight was 55 kilometers (34 miles) per hour. (Wind force was 4 knots, azimuth 300, cloud base at 5500 feet.)

The eagle and Apollo — multifaceted
god who knew the future, made men
aware of their guilt, and purified them of
it — face the future together as they have
since Seleucidian times, 312–64 B.C.
Increasingly, raptors' fortunes are linked
with those of humans.

RELATIONS

WITH MAN

RAPTORS AND PEOPLE

WILLIAM A. BURNHAM

Birds of prey, more than any other group of organisms, have captured our imagination. They have been considered as gods, spiritual messengers, and symbols of strength and courage, but at the same time they have been persecuted through fear and ignorance. Earliest records of this fascination appear in European cave drawings and reappear throughout most of primitive recorded history.

▲ Long perceived as having special powers, raptors have been endowed by the human imagination with religious, mystical and poetic significance. Images of vultures, such as these Gallo-Roman brooches c. 50 A.D., figured largely in ancient civilizations.

► Recorded in a classical mosaic, Zeus, disguised as an eagle, abducts the beautiful Ganymede, son of the king of Troy, to serve as a cupbearer to the gods of ancient Greece.

RAPTORS AND ANCIENT CIVILIZATIONS

The role of raptors in religions of ancient civilizations of Asia and Africa is evident in artefacts unearthed. In Egypt Horus, meaning "Lofty One," was the name of a deity in the form of a falcon. It is thought that the predynastic kingdoms of Egypt had many falcon gods. As hieroglyphs they sometimes represented a king. Falcons were buried in predynastic tombs and worshiped in temples. The eye of Horus was believed to have protective properties and was a popular amulet. The image of the Griffon Vulture (*Gyps fulvus*) Nekhbet, who was the guardian of the king, formed one of the royal crowns of Egypt and could only be worn by a goddess or queen.

Biblical accounts of birds of prey are plentiful. The eagle represented the strength and protection of the Lord as the covenant was offered to Moses: "Ye have seen what I did unto the Egyptians, and how I bore you on eagles' wings, and brought you unto myself" (Exodus 19:4), and later in the Song of Moses: "As an eagle stirreth up her nest, fluttereth over her young, spreadeth abroad her wings, taketh them, beareth them on her wings" (Deuteronomy 32:11). The vulture was seen as a messenger of ill omen: "Set the trumpet to your lips, for a vulture is over the house of the Lord" (Hosea 8:1, Revised Standard Version).

In Greek mythology Zeus, god of the sky, had an eagle which was the only bird believed to live on Mount Olympus. Vultures punished Tityus, son of Zeus, for attacking a sibling, by feeding on his liver. Athene, daughter of Zeus, carried a small owl on her shoulder and was considered very wise—hence the modern cliché, "wise as an owl." The owl appeared on coins from ancient Athens.

C. M. Dixon

◄ The deity Horus, with the head of a Peregrine Falcon, was perhaps the most influential of the many early Egyptian falcon gods. A papyrus, from about 1250 B.C., shows Horus leading Ani of Thebes.

Musée du Louvre, Paris/Giraudon, Paris

◄ A black-figure pottery cup from the sixth century B.C. depicts Zeus, the sky and weather god and chief deity of the Greek pantheon, and his eagle, the only bird believed to live on Mt. Olympus. Such beliefs are clearly based on observation as well as imagination.

RAPTORS IN AUSTRALIAN ABORIGINAL CULTURE: NEITHER SACRED NOR MUNDANE

PENNY OLSEN

Traditionally, Australian Aborigines had a practical view of life. To them the distinctions between sacred and mundane, man and nature, were blurred; religion, social mores and economics were intertwined and directly concerned with everyday living. Raptors were good to eat. At the same time, they were one of the totemic symbols of Aboriginal kinship with the natural world and sometimes featured in religious rituals believed to ensure the preservation of species and the predictability of the seasons. Yet they were not objects of religious adoration. Aboriginal tribe members belonged to both a moiety and a totem either of which could have the name of a raptor—eaglehawk (Wedge-tailed Eagle *Aquila audax*) was popular. This sociocultural system governed such important matters as marriage, sexual access, and social responsibility and behavior; eaglehawks could not marry other eaglehawks but could marry a member of the crow moiety.

Sanctions, particularly the fear of sorcery, upheld religious and social laws. Among certain tribes of Central Australia the medicine men were supposed to have special powers. One of their particular duties was to bring ill upon people who, according to inquest and custom, had committed an offence. Assuming the form of eaglehawks, they traveled long distances at night to visit offending tribes and cause suffering and even death with their sharp talons. To effect quick recovery the attacked tribe's medicine man had to be seen to extract the talons from the unfortunate victims.

Cave, rock and bark painting was practiced by many tribes, and, having no written language, their oral literature was rich. Many stories contain information concerned with survival, or combine lessons on morality and behavior with just-so stories. One tale tells of two brothers, Eagle and Falcon, who went hunting and found some kangaroos in a cave. While Falcon guarded the entrance, Eagle entered to catch the kangaroos. He sent out the thin kangaroos and kept the fat ones for himself. This angered Falcon who lit a fire in the mouth of the cave, scorching the eagle's feathers. The story continues, having condemned selfishness and deftly explained why Wedge-tailed Eagles are black and why falcons do not get on with eagles. Another fire myth, versions of which were told by many tribes from the Kimberleys to the Great Australian Bight, tells of two Black Kite (*Milvus migrans*) brothers who rescued fire which was thrown into the ocean by the selfish Brush Turkey.

Based on observation, Black Kites were thought by some tribes to intentionally spread fire to increase their hunting success, by carrying and dropping burning sticks into dry grass to set it alight. The Aborigines themselves used fire to flush prey and also made use of their knowledge that several species of raptor come from miles away to congregate around a fire and catch animals fleeing the flames. Although fire was used by several tribes to attract hawks, their trapping methods varied. Some simply lit a fire and killed approaching hawks with a spear, throwing stick or boomerang; others concealed themselves in the smoke or among bushes. In parts of the Northern Territory, hawk-trappers built hides: 1–1.5 meter (3–5 feet) diameter horseshoes of flat stones piled about a meter high with a roof of branches and grasses. The trapper lit a small fire outside and hid inside, holding a stick to which a pigeon or smaller bird was attached by a hair belt (string made of human hair or animal fur or feathers) through a hole in the roof. The hawks, initially attracted by the fire, swooped at the lure and were grabbed by the trapper and pulled through the roof. So many Brown Falcons (*Falco berigora*), Black Kites, Whistling Kites (*Haliastur sphenurus*), Wedge-tailed Eagles and other hawks were said to have been caught by this method that the trapper usually finished neck deep in bodies. The hawks were important for subsistence in certain areas and seasons; they were plucked, cooked and eaten and their feathers were generally saved for decorative use in hair belts or ceremonies.

▼ Top: Black Kites hunt insects over a bushfire; this behavior inspired many Aboriginal legends and was used to catch hawks for sustenance. Bottom: Rock paintings by early Victoria River Aboriginal artists celebrate the prominence of eagles in their culture.

Jean-Paul Ferrero/Auscape

Grahame L. Walsh

INCIP LIB·XXXV; VIA ISTE

◀ A twelfth-century French illustration shows a mounted falconer preparing to release his falcon at herons and ducks. Raptors may have been put to such practical use as early as 2000 years B.C. Before then humans may have simply chased them from their kills.

In Rome, Caius Marus, Julius Caesar's uncle, is said to have given each legion an eagle of silver or gold to be carried on a pole with a wreath of victory as a symbol of supreme military strength. Eagles or vultures were widely seen on standards. They were the predominant emblem of emperors and czars. Following the First Crusade, personal arms were adorned with symbols which evolved to family crests used to mark property and vassals. Remnants of this tradition can still be seen today, with birds of prey in prominence. Eagles form the present national emblems of Poland and the United States of America.

RAPTORS AND SHAKESPEARE

Shakespeare (1564–1616) was familiar with raptors and his writings are filled with analogies. In King John he says (Act V, Sc. 2): "Know, the gallant monarch is in arms, And, like an eagle o'er his aiery, towers, To souse annoyance that comes near his nest." He uses the name "kite" as a term of reproach: "You kite!" in Anthony and Cleopatra (Act III, Sc. 13) and "Detested kite!" in King Lear (Act I, SC. 4). He has little more respect for the buzzard in "The Taming of the Shrew" as Petruchio teases Kate: "O slow-winged turtle, shall a buzzard take thee?" Other authors were to follow suit.

RAPTORS AND THE NEW WORLD

In New World cultures also, birds of prey are represented in artefact and legend. The Thunderbird is present throughout North American Indian legends. The form of the Thunderbird is typically a huge eagle or vulture-type bird which exists in the heavens. The bird was believed to cause thunder as it flew, and some tribes considered it to be the Great Spirit itself. Of

lesser size, but of great importance, are the eagles. Eagle dances, ceremonies and societies occur throughout North American Indian legends and culture. Golden Eagles (*Aquila chrysaetos*), the war eagles, were kept for their molted feathers by Pueblo Indians of the southwestern United States. Many tribes used eagle feathers on weapons and head-dresses to symbolize victories and courage or to represent status. Parts of eagles, including feathers, talons, and skulls, remain important in the ceremonial and religious practices of many native American tribes.

The Maya culture in Central America was based on a close association with nature, and animals are evident in many artefacts. Vultures were used as head-dresses for female figures and were probably associated with fertility, as in Egypt. The sun was considered by the Aztecs as an eagle.

◀ An eagle, its body stretched and wrapped with cloth, gave power to its collector. Hallucination was an important element in the religious life of the North American Plains Indian, induced by fasting, isolation and tormenting of the body with skewers. When an animal appeared in a vision as a messenger of the Sacred Powers, it had to be captured and was featured in a medicine bundle.

The Aztec city of Tenochtitlan was founded where the eagle representing the tribal god, Huitzilopochtli, was believed to have landed as a sign. Warriors who attained the greatest honor were members of the Order of the Eagle. The eagle was even one of the twenty signs in their religious calendar.

Today birds of prey are still revered in Latin America. Feet of eagles and hawks can be seen hanging in trucks or buses to ward off oncoming vehicles and danger, as forest animals flee from the feet of the flying raptor. The Waorani, primitive nomadic Ecuadorian people, still keep Harpy Eagles (*Harpia harpyja*) to watch over their settlements, and treasure them for their strength and beauty. They use Harpy Eagle feathers in decorative head and arm bands. Another Amazon tribe, the Amahuaca of Peru, are reported to wipe broth from boiled raptor talons on their bodies before hunting large animals.

CONDORS IN AMERICAN INDIAN CULTURES

NOEL SNYDER

The symbolic importance of the California Condor to various North American Indian tribes has been particularly well documented for California itself, although the bird undoubtedly was once revered by many tribes in other regions too. The Condor was prominent in cave paintings, as a source of bone whistles and ear ornaments, as a source of feathers for various ceremonial purposes, and as a focus of ritual sacrifice ceremonies. Similar practices (involving Andean rather than California Condors) have also been well documented for many native cultures of South America.

California Condors were considered important sources of supernatural powers, and their body parts were used in diverse ways to exercise these powers. For example, shamans of one Californian tribe often used a stick with condor feathers at one end as a healing charm to pass over a sick person's body. In another tribe it was common for shamans to push condor feathers down a patient's throat as part of a ritual to counteract disease. Condor feathers and capes made from condor feathers were also used in dances to celebrate sacred events.

Perhaps the most famous of the condor ceremonies involved ritual killing of captive birds. Variations of this practice occurred in both North and South America. Remarkably dramatic photographs of such a ceremony, involving an Andean Condor in Peru, were published in 1971 by Jerry and Libby McGahan in *National Geographic* magazine. Not all such ceremonies involved the actual killing of condors—in some ceremonies they were set free—but ritual death was certainly a common theme in many regions.

The impacts of condor sacrifice ceremonies on wild condor populations are unknown. In many areas it appears that the numbers of birds affected were too small to have represented major drains on populations. In other places local depressions in condor populations may have occurred.

The ritual importance of condors to native Indian tribes is presently being honored by the naming of all California Condors produced in captivity after Indian sources. Thus Molloko, the first California Condor produced from captive parents, recalls the spectacular "Moloku" (condor) dance performed historically by the Central Sierra Miwok Indians. Similarly, Sisquoc, Sespe, Tecuya, Inaja, and many others, all bear appellations reflecting the close association of condors with human cultural traditions.

▲ Largest flying bird in the world, the immense Andean Condor's wings span 3 meters (10 feet) or more. Not surprisingly, it is the symbol of the modern Peru and also appears on the coats of arms of several other South American countries. Considered the source of supernatural power, Condor cults were important religious elements in the cultural traditions of certain South and North American Indian tribes. Some ceremonies involved ritual sacrifice of a Condor; in others the bird was freed. Even today the bird is revered.

Olivier Pighetti/Sygma

◄ Falconry is thought to have originated in the East at least as early as 700 B.C. Tiles in the Palace of Golestan, Teheran, show the refinement of the art of falconry, as important to fourteenth-century hunters as the bow.

HISTORY OF FALCONRY

No closer relationship has existed between mankind and birds of prey than through falconry, as explained by Roger Tory Peterson (1948).

> Man has emerged from the shadows of antiquity with a peregrine on his wrist. Its dispassionate brown eyes, more than those of any other bird, have been witness to the struggle for civilization, from the squalid tents on the steppes of Asia thousands of years ago to the marble halls of European kings in the seventeenth century.

Falconry, broadly defined as the capture of quarry with trained birds of prey, grew from a method of hunting to a sport. The origin of falconry is lost in the dust of antiquity but it probably began in the Near, Middle, or Far East. Some authors have suggested origins as early as 2000 B.C. but the earliest defendable record is an Assyrian bas-relief (722–705 B.C.). The lifestyle of the nomadic people of Asia was probably well suited for falconry, and use of falcons and eagles may have been a more effective method of obtaining meat than through primitive bows or spears. Falconry was probably practiced in India at a very early period, although the earliest reference does not occur until the second century A.D., and it reached its greatest popularity there after

infiltration of Islamic culture in the fourteenth century. In China, accounts of using falcons in the chase are referenced as early as about 680 B.C. in the kingdom of Ch'u. By the Han dynasty (206 B.C.–220 A.D.), the popularity of falconry had evidently increased, as emperor Teng was said to go often to the imperial forest to hunt with falcons. In Japan the first report of falconry occurs about 720 A.D. The sport was probably also practiced by then in Korea, as a reference mentions a strange bird caught in Korea and used for hunting during the forty-third year of the Japanese emperor Nintoku (355 A.D.). Falconry in Persia and Arabia is believed to have begun very early, although few references exist. Persia was the focal point of falconry in the Near East.

There is no evidence to suggest that falconry was known to the ancient Jews of Palestine, and it was not widely known or practiced in ancient Europe. It does not appear in Greek vase-paintings or Roman frescoes, although both include other forms of hunting. Falconry is believed to have existed in the Mediterranean area by 400 A.D., when an elderly author expressed his desire as a youth to have "a swift dog and a splendid hawk." By the sixth century, falconry had become an integral part of the life of Germanic tribes. Their law stated: "If anybody has presumed to steal another's hawk (*acceptorem*), we command that

▲ Clutching a hawk, a Sumerian is depicted on a stele or stela, a standing stone slab used as a grave marker or in dedication. It is not known what role raptors played in Mesopotamian society, one of the earliest centers of civilized, urban life in the third millenium B.C.

► Eugene Fromentin's "Arabes Chassant au Faucon" is typical of the popular. realistic, sporting paintings of the early nineteenth century. Bright and luminous, it conveys a feeling of suspense and excitement as an Algerian falconer waits to release his Peregrine at the shorebird, with two falcons already in pursuit, flushed toward him by the riders in the background.

Musée Condé, Chantilly/Giraudon. Paris

A. Eaton/Ancient Art & Architecture Collection

▲ A falcon on the lady's fist and another killing a rabbit, surrounded by the hunting dogs used to flush quarry for the bird, proclaim the prominence of falconry in medieval life. The tapestry commemorates a late-fifteenth-century marriage in the Upper Rhein region of Europe. Medieval times saw the heyday of falconry; a significant proportion of the population kept a raptor trained, by reward, to hunt for human need and sport.

the bird itself eat six ounces of flesh from the breast of the thief," meaning the falcon's food would be laid on the thief's chest. Laws also protected nests or trees where nests were located.

The period of 500 to 1600 A.D. saw the zenith of the sport which flourished in the feudal societies of European Christendom and Islam. Social rank largely determined the raptor which could be used, as the Abbess Juliana Berger wrote in the Middle Ages: "An eagle for a emperor, a gyr-

falcon for a king, a peregrine for an earl, a merlin for a lady, a goshawk for a yeoman, a sparrowhawk for a priest, a musket [a male sparrowhawk] for the holywater clerk." Falcons were a part of everyday life and were taken to court, church, or battle alike. During the Crusades, the Christians and Saracens used falcons as peace offerings and articles of trade, and took time out between battles to go hawking. Even Mary, Queen of Scots, is said to have found time during her captivity to fly a Merlin

(*Falco columbarius*). Complaints were even registered by one abbess because nuns were bringing their birds to chapel. Large falconry establishments were maintained for centuries by English and French kings, Russian czars, and the Holy Roman Emperors. To many, Holy Roman Emperor Frederick II of Hohenstaufen (1194–1250) is considered the greatest falconer who ever lived and, for his time, a truly modern monarch. In his famous treatise, which was thirty years in preparation, *De Arte Venandia cum Avibus*, he introduced scientific thinking into writing about birds, and his information is still used by modern practitioners. Many famous historic personalities were avid falconers, from the Mongol Genghis Khan to the shoguns of Japan and the Indian maharajahs. Falconry terms are in many of Shakespeare's plays and incorporated into the everyday English vocabulary. Falconry was an obsession which has been compared to baseball in modern North America.

The advent of effective guns for hunting, clearing land for agriculture, management of game preserves, and a general deterioration of the feudal system are cited for the decline in the practice of falconry in Europe during the seventeenth and eighteenth centuries. The unprecedented reverence offered to raptors in Europe was replaced by the slaughter of adults and chicks and the destruction of nests as they were viewed as competitors for game and as vermin.

Falconry continued to be practiced during this period by a dedicated few. In Europe a few falconry clubs existed such as the Royal Loo Hawking Club of Holland. Accounts of hunting of herons with falcons by the Royal Loo Hawking Club describe long, high-circling flights extending over several kilometers, which were followed by highly organized participants on horseback, much as with fox hunting today. The captured herons were frequently released unharmed, after having a dated silver ring placed around a leg.

VULTURES IN AFRICAN CULTURE

P. J. MUNDY

Thousands of years ago when the Pharaohs ruled Egypt, the Griffon Vulture (*Gyps fulvus*) and Lappet-faced Vulture (*Aegypius tracheliotos*) represented the goddess Nekhebet, goddess of childbirth. Entombed rulers were often adorned with these species to impart magical protection.

Until recent decades, vultures covered the length and breadth of Africa, except for the forest. They were therefore well known to Bushmen, Hottentots and Negroes, but possibly not to the forest Pygmies. Strangely enough, there are few rock paintings of vultures, though we can be sure that Bushmen groups make use of vultures to locate dead animals. Certainly Hottentots esteemed the Egyptian Vulture (*Neophron percnopterus*), because it betrayed the lion on its prey and no doubt too it located Ostrich eggs for them; the vulture was called *ouri-gorab* or white crow. To the Bushmen, animals, although good to eat, were once people and perhaps therefore precious. One folklore tale related how a Bushman married the elder sister in a group of vultures and thereafter had trouble with the rest of them eating his kills of springbok.

Pastoral and agricultural Africans have a number of stories and beliefs about vultures. In Hausaland, it is said that the Hooded Vulture (*Necrosyrtes monachus*) lays two eggs, one of which hatches into a fly. Xhosa boys dread the Cape Vulture (*Gyps coprotheres*), in the belief that it can fight a man. Other tribal groups single out the Lappet-faced Vulture as the king or chief, and the White-necked Raven as its spy searching for a carcass; if the ordinary griffon vultures gather first, they must respectfully await the arrival of the chief (no doubt actually to tear the skin of the dead beast). Gruesomely, the Zulu kings Dingaan and Shaka got rid of people after killing them by

S. C. Bisserot

▲ The Hooded Vulture, here feeding with Cattle Egret (*Ardeola ibis*), commonly scavenges around villages and towns of southern Africa and cleans up all sorts of refuse. Hausaland legend has it that the vulture lays two eggs, one of which hatches into a fly. In fact, it lays only one egg.

throwing them to the large and hungry vultures, which became known as Shaka's birds (*izinyoni zikaShaka*).

There is a common belief in southern Africa that vultures can dream of the whereabouts of a carcass. Thus if you eat vulture brains you will be able to foretell the future. With urban influence, future events have taken on a monetary significance, for example horse racing or football pools, and this accounts for the recent and regrettable mass poisoning of these birds.

FALCONRY NOW

Limited information exists on falconry in the Middle and Far East during the seventeenth through nineteenth centuries. Generally, the sport appears to have continued at a reduced level but it remained fairly common in Arabia and Mongolia into the twentieth century. The twentieth century saw falconry reach North America on a very limited basis after the end of World War 1, but not until the second half of this century has the popularity of the sport again begun to rise. In 1982, T. Cade reported that "falconry has never been more popular than it is today." Worldwide, he believes that there are between 10,000 and 20,000 practitioners, primarily in the Middle East, Europe, and North America, with lesser numbers in South America, Australia, New Zealand, Africa, the Asiatic part of the Soviet Union, Korea, Japan, and the Indian subcontinent.

In some countries, the growth in popularity of falconry has resulted in increased regulations to ensure that the take of raptors for this purpose does not seriously deplete wild populations. Strict regulations, sometimes initiated by falconers, exist in many countries, controlling not only the take of raptors from the wild, but how they are maintained and flown. Usually, mandatory tests must be passed before a raptor may be taken, and the level of falconry experience determines what species may be used. An analysis by scientists of the Wilson Ornithological Society on the effect of falconry on raptor populations in North America revealed no detectable negative impact. Similar statistics compiled for birds taken from the wild and flown in falconry in Great Britain showed that over 40 percent of the total number birds were eventually lost to the wild and another 30 percent were intentionally liberated.

Roger Tidman/NHPA

▶ A man, his falcon and dog on a lonely moor—the romantic image of falconry. After more than a century of decline, the 1950s saw an increase in popularity of western falconry. There are now several falconry clubs in Britain alone and many in North America. However, not all countries legalize falconry, Australia and Sweden among them.

▶ Falconry makes the much-admired remoteness of a raptor accessible. The relationship between a falconer and his bird, in this case the coveted Peregrine Falcon, is the most intimate of all human association with raptors.

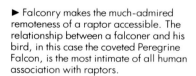

Mike Birkhead/Oxford Scientific Films

Falconers' organizations exist on many continents, but most notable are the British Falconers' Club, the North American Falconers' Association, and the International Association for Falconry and Conservation of Birds of Prey. These organizations have been responsible for providing many of the guidelines and conditions for current laws regulating the use of birds of prey for falconry. Until recent decades falconers were frequently the only ally of raptors and much of the statutory protection is a direct result of the falconers' commitment to preservation of birds of prey. Falconers are, for the most part, strong conservationists, but like any cross-section of humanity, there are individuals whose primary concern is personal gain whatever the cost.

To train a bird of prey requires time, patience, sensitivity, and ingenuity. Depending on the type of raptor and the falconer's situation, it may also require a comfortable income to purchase suitable housing for the raptor and other necessary equipment. Today such accessories may include

radio equipment to track the falcon during long flights, a suitable vehicle, well-trained hunting dogs, travel funds, and even perhaps the rental of a grouse moor in Scotland. The training and care of a raptor is a daily effort which literally requires thousands of hours annually. It is not possible to set the falcon aside like a shotgun or flyrod, to be used as time permits.

Not all species of birds of prey are used or even suitable for falconry. In the purest sense falconry refers only to the use of true falcons of the genus *Falco*, of which the Peregrine is the most popular. Individuals who hunt with hawks and eagles are more strictly called austringers. Traditionally, the medium-sized and large falcons are the favorite species for use in open country against birds. For more wooded areas, the true hawks, genus *Accipiter*, such as the Goshawk, are well suited. Typically, hunting falcons are encouraged to circle high overhead before the game is flushed. However, falcons may also be released from the fist once the quarry is seen, a

Popperfoto

▲ An old photograph records the Mongolian trade in falcons, hooded to calm them. Destined for Peking, they were usually young Peregrine Falcons taken on their first migration. The art of taking quarry with a trained raptor, not always a falcon, was probably conceived and refined in China.

▶ A young Bedouin is taught falconry in the manner of generations before him. Arabia's isolation and harsh climate kept falconry alive if only to catch food to supplement the thin diet. The oil boom may have opened up Arabia, but many wealthy modern Arabs still return to the desert, to the roots of their cultural heritage, to hunt with hawks.

Nick Gordon/Ardea London

practice common in Arabia. Arab falconers may even bind several of the falcon's flight feathers together to prevent it from high circling.

Hawks and eagles are typically carried until quarry is flushed, then there is a direct and usually short flight. In the southwest Soviet Union and Turkey, locals trap migrating Sparrowhawks and rapidly train them to capture migrant quail. After the short migration season the hawks are released. The use of eagles for hunting foxes and wolves has been practiced for centuries in Tartary and Mongolia. These very large Golden Eagles are carried on horseback and released when the animal is seen. A bird which has become very popular in the last decade in North America is the Harris' Hawk (*Parabuteo unicinctus*). This species is flown from the fist after rabbits or hares, and

several falconers may release their birds at the same time when quarry is flushed. This is usually possible with the Harris' Hawk because of its sociable nature.

Falconry has been employed in other ways, such as scaring birds from airfields to prevent the possibility of their colliding with aircraft. This practice has been successfully used in North America and Europe for many years. More recently, plans were announced to hire a falconer to frighten gulls from the new $500 million SkyDome sport arena with its retractable roof in Toronto, Canada. In his novel *The Gift of a Falcon*, author Kent Harrington went to the extreme of having a trained falcon carrying a bomb to an Arab king. A branch of the United States intelligence service once attempted to use trained falcons for locating downed pilots.

Learning falconry is very similar to learning how to fish. In the beginning the novice has difficulty just mastering the equipment, let alone making the first catch. Once the techniques are better understood, the focus shifts to the quarry, and once the first is caught, numbers become very important, including how many can be caught in a day or in a season. The size of quarry then becomes the focus—the larger the better. As the practitioner becomes more attuned with the environment, the height of flight and manners of the falcon, like the cast of the line and delivery of the fly to the surface of the pool, become more significant.

FALCONRY IN ARABIAN CULTURE

KENTON E. RIDDLE

Arabian falconry remains essentially unchanged in form and style, being practiced today much as it was by the bedouin centuries ago. Traditional training and hunting techniques are fast and regimented . . . designed to reduce an art form to basic elements consistent with success. The motivation to hunt and provide meat for the table remains firmly entrenched, although crucial subsistence requirements no longer exist. Sanctioned by the Koran, the Arab passion for hawking is practiced with almost religious zeal. Changing times and wealth from oil revenues have provided the means to transform modern falconry hunts into ostentatious social affairs. Today, falconry is the single most important event that brings Arab tribes back into the desert with kin and countrymen to strengthen bonds, and to seek adventure and communion with the past.

Falconry and related activities wax and wane with the seasons. In the fall, falcon trapping resumes on traditional migratory routes. There is a groundswell of enthusiasm as birds are sought out, examined, and purchased in local falcon markets. Hunting expeditions during the winter months are reminiscent of those of Genghis Khan as large groups of men and falcons join the entourage of sheikhs for magnificent journeys into the desert seeking Bustard, Stone Curlew, and Desert Hare, principal quarry of the Arab falconer. Social barriers fade as men of diverse backgrounds come together, falcon on fist, and sit by desert campfires to reminisce about hunts of old, argue the qualities and attributes of a particularly superb falcon, or recount exciting or humorous anecdotes of the day's hunts. Washed down with draughts of Arabic cardamom coffee, tea, and spiced camel milk, the stories flow through the evening and late into the night.

Early morning will find the hunters moving through the desert at a relentless pace. Falconers no longer hunt from camels but employ customized four-wheel-drive vehicles for transportation. The intensity of the hunt is evident as trackers concentrate on patterns in the sand, searching for signs of quarry, while they cruise at more than 40 km/h (30 mph). Falcons are unhooded and flown directly from the fist at sighted quarry while the hunters, now mere spectators, race to keep the flight in sight. Fortunate falconers and their charges will be afforded a kill before darkness blankets the desert. Singing ancient tribal songs to boost their spirits, the falconers return to comfortable and resplendent encampments.

It is an enthralling otherworld which merits preservation for future generations of Arabs. There are many indications of sufficient concern to ensure its survival. Pre-eminent falconer, His Highness Sheikh Zayed bin Sultan al Nahyan, President of the United Arab Emirates and Ruler of Abu Dhabi, has encouraged conservation efforts to preserve the wildlife and quarry which are vital to the practice of falconry. Reduced hunting pressure, closed seasons in some areas and for selected species, and captive breeding to restock the endangered McQueen's Bustard, are programs recently implemented. Sheikh Zayed's sponsorship of an ultra-modern veterinary

Hans Christian Heap/Planet Earth Pictures

▲ A falconer tends a Saker (*Falco cherrug*), long favored by the Arabs for their stamina, versatility and tolerance of soaring desert temperatures, at Riyadh, Saudi Arabia. Today the four-wheel-drive vehicles that have replaced camels damage the fragile desert, and the McQueen's Bustard, prized quarry, is endangered. The centuries-old hunting tradition still continues, but its survival depends on conservation of habitat, prey and falcon.

research hospital for falcons is a far-sighted conservation effort resulting in improved clinical care for the falcons, client education programs, and avian veterinary research. Other Arab countries have established similar programs, including a number of captive breeding projects which are producing excellent falcons for training. Taken as single events, these efforts may appear to have little significance or lasting value, but the die has been cast and few Arab falconers would relish the thought of falconry becoming extinct. The existential imperative to care for a unique falconry heritage may simply be too strong to ignore.

THE FASCINATION OF FALCONRY

Why have people been so fascinated and enamored by falconry? This is difficult to explain, but I will attempt to illustrate the fascination from my own experience. The Gyrfalcon (*Falco rusticolus*) is considered to be the most powerful of all falcons, but you would not have known that, looking at my downy, white, three-week-old eyas "Sage." However, the down was rapidly lost and replaced by gray feathers that were the color of the western sage shrub. By the time the blood had left her primaries, she had taken her first flights during our daily trips to the open grasslands of Colorado. She, like my two pointing dogs, had become a friend and companion. As the days passed, her strength and stamina grew, and many evenings were spent with her eating the best of my training pigeons as the sun sank over the golden grasses and wheat of late summer. With the first frosts she was introduced to wild quarry. Most quarry birds, like her, were inexperienced, and flights were more the outcome of luck than skill. By winter the months of training began to show rewards, and the awkward eyas began to change both physically and mentally. Although she remained tame and seemed to enjoy my companionship as much as I

hers, a seriousness and purpose were evident when the hood was removed and she was cast to the sky. She now understood the game and knew that a motionless dog meant a bird to chase once I moved to flush, and her greatest advantage was to be high in the sky upwind of the quarry. All potential prey were now gone from the frozen grasslands, our trips were longer and shared with another falconer and his bird as we tented in the rolling hills, the home of the largest North American grouse. Nothing I have experienced in life is so intensively focused and exhilarating as the flush of grouse in front of a rigid pointing dog, with the wind roaring through the feathers and bells of a plummeting falcon. Predator and quarry were honed by evolution over thousands of years in a natural act which is a common occurrence in nature but of which I am now an active and vicarious part. It is a moment to be revisited and enjoyed in the mind's eye a thousand times, and to be shared over endless campfires. Falconry is an immortal bond between man, bird, and nature, which has extended over centuries and continents and beyond races and politics, and when my falcon stoops from the heavens it matters not if I am a common man or Genghis Khan!

▶ A cadger carries a brace of hooded falcons on a portable perch (cadge) hung from his neck, for the mounted nobleman. Hunting scenes such as this by Jan Wynants were popular subjects for nineteenth-century artists, and reflect the fascination of falconry as well as its practicalities.

▶ At the Falconry Centre in England, a White-bellied Sea Eagle (*Haliaeetus leucogaster*) is readied for release. Various species are flown in public displays aimed at increasing interest in and understanding of raptors.

Michael Freeman/Bruce Coleman Ltd

BREEDING OF RAPTORS IN CAPTIVITY

Except for the development of guns, no other event has had such a dramatic effect on falconry as the large-scale breeding of raptors in captivity. Captive breeding of birds of prey happened more by chance than intention until less than 20 years ago. Even into the early 1970s many aviculturalists and naturalists felt that raptors could not be bred in captivity. Since then there has been a growing number of individuals, predominantly falconers, successfully breeding birds of prey. Species bred for falconry are primarily the large falcons and a few hawks. In 1987, in the United States, the North American Raptor Breeders' Association reported 236 licenced propagators with 1,682 raptors of 13 species, including a variety of hybrids. Peregrine Falcons (*Falco peregrinus*) comprised 37 percent, Harris' Hawks 26 percent, hybrids 12 percent, Prairie Falcons (*F. mexicanus*) 10 percent, and Gyrfalcons 7 percent. The remainder of the species

USE OF VULTURES TO DISPOSE OF HUMAN CORPSES IN INDIA AND TIBET

DAVID C. HOUSTON

The thought of using wild animals to dispose of human corpses is guaranteed to send a shiver down the spine of most people in the Western world. But this method of funeral rite has developed in many unrelated human societies. It particularly applies to peoples living in rocky, barren parts of the world, where there is insufficient depth of soil for safe burial, or sufficient timber for cremation. A speedy and civilized way of disposing of the dead is difficult to find in these conditions and the use of wild animals is almost the only option. Most cultures have a revulsion against wild animals, such as wolves, hyenas or dogs, feeding on human corpses, and take considerable pains to prevent this happening. But vultures, with their quick, clean and efficient feeding are widely accepted, and their soaring flight has obvious associations with the release of the spirit.

Human dead were exposed to vultures in ceremonies among several American Indian tribes and other primitive societies, but today it is a common practice only in Buddhist Tibet and among Parsees in India. In a Tibetan burial the body is carried by a professional corpse carrier to a high, rocky area outside the village. There the mourners dismember the corpse, often including the breaking of the bones into pieces, so that they can be totally consumed by the birds. Tibetans believe that the body, without its soul, has no significance, and this form of burial leaves no trace of the body after death. A far more elaborate form of funeral rite has been developed by the Parsees, followers of the Zoroastrian faith, which is one of the oldest religions in the world dating back some 3,500 years.

Although originating in northern Persia, Parsee communities are now found all over the world with a particularly large and thriving one in Bombay in India. To Zoroastrians death represents the temporary victory of evil and is a place where demons are present. They believe that fire, earth and water are sacred creations of God, and must not be polluted with the evil represented by death. God, they believe, created vultures specifically to devour corpses, and this natural form of disposal limits the spread of evil. Corpses are carried by special bearers into "towers of silence," which are round structures screened by a high stone wall but open to the sky to allow the vultures to descend. Nobody except the bearers is allowed to

Luo Xiaoyun/Sygma

▲ In the barren Tibetan landscape, where burial or cremation is impractical, vultures quickly and cleanly dispose of the dead. This is believed to free the spirit from the body and return it to heaven, symbolized by the soaring vultures.

enter these special areas. While the birds are feeding the relatives pray, and then observe special ceremonies for the following three days while the soul is awaiting judgement. These death ceremonies take place in beautifully maintained flower gardens, with fountains and strolling peacocks, and elegant buildings for the mourners as well as the "towers of silence," screened by tall trees. They create a totally restful atmosphere that contrasts markedly with the frantic traffic of the Bombay streets outside the walls.

To people living in a part of the world where vultures are an accepted part of life, it is an entirely natural way of corpse disposal and totally in keeping with their religious beliefs.

held accounted for no more than three percent of the total. Hybrids, created chiefly through the use of artificial insemination, are commonly produced. In some countries laws require hybrids to be reared in isolation from other birds and in association with humans. This results in a type of behavioral sterilization believed to prevent the hybrids from breeding with parent species should they be lost to the wild. Captive breeding has provided falconers with a ready source of raptors, especially Peregrines, Gyrfalcons, and other species difficult to obtain from the wild. Already individual falconers are beginning to breed selectively for desired characteristics. In 1982 over half of the large falcons being used for falconry in the United States were captive bred, and although no accurate figure exists, this proportion has risen since then.

Raptors are being bred not only for falconry, but for conservation, which was in fact the primary purpose behind the development of captive breeding techniques. The idea was to restock large areas from which falcons and other species had been eliminated by organochlorine pesticide use in the 1950s and 1960s. Most important has been the Peregrine Falcon. In the United States since 1973, The Peregrine Fund, Inc.—a non-profit conservation organization which operates the World Center for Birds of Prey in cooperation with the Santa Cruz Predatory Bird Research Group—has hatched over 3,300 Peregrine Falcons and released over 3,000 young to the wild in 28 states. Breeding and release of Peregrines is also done by other biologists in the United States and in Canada and Europe. Over 20 species of falcons have now been bred in captivity, and, besides the Peregrine, the Aplomado Falcon (*F. femoralis*), Bat Falcon (*F. rufigularis*), Prairie Falcon, and the Mauritius Kestrel (*F. punctatus*) have been released and established in the wild. The Aplomado Falcon existed in the southwestern United States until about 1950 when it was lost from a combination of habitat change and DDT-caused reproductive failures. The Mauritius Kestrel is a small falcon which exists only on the island of Mauritius, in the Indian Ocean and once the home of the now extinct Dodo (*Raphus cucullatus*). Primarily as a result of captive breeding, the falcon has increased from no more than six known individuals to nearly a hundred.

Many raptors other than falcons are being bred in captivity. A variety of hawks, buzzards, eagles, and condors have been reared. A partial list includes: the Bald Eagle (*Haliaeetus leucocephalus*), Golden Eagle, Bateleur (*Terathopius ecaudatus*), Harpy Eagle, Ferruginous Hawk (*Buteo regalis*), Red-tailed Hawk (*B. jamaicensis*), Harris' Hawk, Bearded Vulture (*Gypaetus barbatus*), Griffon, Andean Condor (*Vultur gryphus*), and California Condor (*Gymnogyps californianus*). The difficulty of propagation varies greatly from one species to

Nick Greaves/Planet Earth Pictures

◄ A Peregrine Falcon perches on a gloved fist in Zimbabwe. There, only a few licensed A grade falconers can keep a Peregrine. Concerns over pesticide contamination of wild populations led falconers and biologists to initiate a captive breeding program.

another. For example, the condors readily breed in captivity, while accipiters, such as the Goshawk (*Accipiter gentilis*) and Cooper's Hawk (*A. cooperii*), require more care and precise conditions. As a group, owls seem to breed easily in aviaries.

Raptors that are common in the wild and breed readily in captivity are occasionally bred for research. American Kestrels (*Falco sparverius*) have been bred and used for laboratory research into the effects of toxic chemicals on predatory birds. Use of surrogates for research is common practice, and many of the techniques used for breeding of endangered species were first tested on more common species. Some birds used for research are received from rehabilitation centers which accept injured raptors and attempt to recondition them for release. Rehabilitation of injured raptors has become common in North America and Europe. It serves a humane function, but does little to benefit wild populations.

W. Burnham

Frans Lanting/Minden Pictures

▲ Captive-bred Peregrine Falcon chicks in a brooder will later be released to bolster wild populations decimated by human activities, or retained for use in falconry or as breeding stock.

◄ A hybrid Peregrine Falcon–Gyrfalcon, produced by artificial insemination, is tethered to a block perch. Care is taken that it does not become lost to the wild and breed with the parent species.

CURRENT INTEREST IN RAPTORS

Interest in birds of prey for observation and research by both amateur and professional biologists has dramatically increased in the last two decades. Raptors are now some of the most highly sought after species by the ever-increasing number of bird-watchers worldwide. Some enthusiasts will travel to very remote areas solely on the chance of catching a glimpse of some rare eagle or falcon. No less than a mania for urban-nesting Peregrine Falcons exists in North America. In 1989 there were 32 pairs of Peregrines known in 22 cities in the United States, and there is growing demand for additional releases to establish more pairs. Conferences devoted to birds of prey have greatly increased, and in North America more people attend the annual Raptor Research Foundation meeting than the American Ornithologists Union meeting. The scientific literature on birds of prey has increased enormously and popular literature follows suit.

Birds of prey have captured the heart and mind of people around the world. There is no simple answer as to why, but the intelligence of these birds, their grace, beauty, and awesome ability in flight contribute to that fascination. To see them bound by neither land nor air as they climb, roll, loop, and dive in display, or take their food from the sky or land as simply and unemotionally as a man plucks a grape from a vine is no less than inspirational. It is equally inspiring to see a falcon defend its home and young against threats many times its size with such courage, risking injury and death, and moments later delicately nudge a helpless chick under its warm breast. That independence, freedom, and courage cannot help but stir people's imagination.

▶ An ever-growing number of people simply enjoy the sight of a wild raptor in its element. As environmental consciousness sweeps the world, birds of prey have acquired yet another symbolic mantle—they represent a secure, unspoiled, unpolluted future.

WHAT'S IN AN IMAGE: EAGLES IN ADVERTISING

JERRY OLSEN

Eagles have long been admired for their great strength, keen eyesight and enviable powers of flight. Their image has often been used by strategists as a symbol of real or imagined power. The ancient Romans, various German empires, Poland, Spain and Mexico are among the many who have a symbolic eagle on their coat of arms. Barclay's Bank, and countless other companies, proudly display eagle emblems to the world, signifying power and security. Eagles still represent military prowess, as they have for centuries: "Corporal Courage," Wedge-tailed Eagle mascot of the Australian Army's Second Cavalry Regiment, is carried on parade as a symbol of the regiment's reconnaissance role.

Advertisers are well aware of the impact of eagles. That is how Robert Bartos and I found ourselves, one foggy, gray morning, arriving at a film location with Robert's Wedge-tailed Eagle. Two solid days of filming was later cut down to one thirty-second, $A120,000 jeans commercial. When asked why considerable time and energy went into filming the eagle, director-producer Ian Fowler replied: "The AMCO trademark is an eagle, a powerful symbol of dominance. The association between an unshackled, flying eagle and freedom is simple and effective."

The advertisement does successfully equate a jeans-wearing lifestyle with freedom. Across several million TV screens images of an independent young man pulling on his jeans and escaping the confines of a job and the city in his yellow convertible are juxtaposed with those of the eagle bursting from a "cage" to fly free. On the soundtrack a rock group sings: "Born to fly, born to get away like an eagle. I was born to fly."

▲ The origins of Barclays Bank and its eagle crest go back to the early eighteenth century when the founder company moved into a building identified by a sign bearing a black spread-eagle. Then, few people could read, and business houses used pictorial identification so their customers could find them easily. In 1937 the bank made the eagle its official heraldic emblem, adding three crowns from another of its early properties to distinguish it from the many other eagle insignias. Eagles remain one of the most popular and dramatic of all crests, a metaphor for a company's supposed qualities—strength, reliability, power, mastery of the elements.

HUMAN IMPACTS ON RAPTORS

IAN NEWTON

More than most other types of birds, raptors have suffered from human activity, so that, in most developed parts of the world, their numbers are now only a fraction of what they were 100–200 years ago. Three main factors have contributed to population declines—habitat destruction, deliberate persecution and poisoning by agricultural pesticides. Habitat destruction has been going on ever since people began to cultivate crops, but has accelerated in recent times, as ever more forests have been felled, wetlands drained, and grasslands plowed. Deliberate persecution of large raptors was practiced initially to protect domestic animals, but such practices greatly intensified and spread to smaller species, following the development of breech-loading guns in the 1840s, and the subsequent growth in small-game hunting. The problems created by pesticides and other toxic chemicals are relatively recent, dating from the development of DDT and other synthetic chemicals for crop protection from the 1940s onwards.

George I. Bernard/Oxford Scientific Films

► Humans have a profound impact on the landscape, often markedly changing the habitats of raptors. From a TV aerial an Old World Kestrel surveys its suburban territory. While some of the smaller raptors can reclaim part of their former territory by adapting to urban life, their numbers rarely reach those in more natural areas. Those that do adjust delight city dwellers.

Angelo Gandolfi

HABITAT DESTRUCTION

Most raptor species are restricted to particular kinds of habitats, and within these habitats, their numbers are limited by the availability of nesting places and, more importantly, by the availability of suitable prey species. Hence, any form of human land use, which degrades or destroys a natural habitat and its associated prey populations, can cause a decline in raptor numbers. Although certain raptor species can live in cultivated and other modified areas, even cities, providing that suitable prey are available, their numbers in such areas seldom reach the levels found in more natural habitats. In most parts of the world, these habitats tend to be poorer, in both species and individuals, than natural ones. Moreover, the larger species will persist chiefly in the more natural habitats, with mainly smaller species in cultivated areas.

In general the more intensively the land is used for stock or crop production, the less wildlife it supports, at least on a year-round basis. Among open habitats, for example, natural grasslands hold more prey than the similar areas used for ranching, and ranchlands in turn hold more prey than cultivated lands. Annual plowing greatly reduces small mammal populations by eliminating their food and cover, and thus renders croplands of limited value to mammal-feeding predators. Take, for example, the North American prairies, and compare the richness of predator and prey populations in regions under natural grass with the poverty of their equivalents in regions under wheat. In wooded habitats, natural areas of varied structure and tree composition generally support more wildlife than do managed, uniform stands of conifers or eucalypts. The result of such transitions is either to destroy completely the original habitat structure, or to reduce the prey supply to such an extent that it can no longer support raptors at anything near their former numbers. Modern land-use practices tend increasingly to simplify habitats, and to channel large parts of the annual production into crop plants or domestic stock, leaving little for wildlife. Thus each step towards more intensive human land use has a further cost in wildlife terms.

Some recent studies have actually documented the decline or disappearance of raptor populations, coincident with an intensification in land use. For instance, in Zimbabwe, Black Eagles declined over several years from 26 to 14 pairs in an area of heavily used tribal land, but maintained their numbers in a neighboring protected area.

▼ A vulture perches on a German rooftop, not awaiting the death of the occupant of the house, but anticipating the call of its master, a falconer. Larger raptors only survive in the wild in parts of Germany where human activity is low.

Stephen Dalton/NHPA

▲ The African Harrier Hawk (*Polyboroides radiatus*) has curious double-jointed legs for reaching into caves and tree hollows to grab bats and nestling birds. It frequents light woodland and savanna, and human impact has to some extent been beneficial. It thrives where patches of woodland and cultivation form a mosaic.

▼ Persecution and clearance of preferred damp forest habitat is thought to have reduced the population of Greater Spotted Eagle (*Aquila clanga*) by perhaps one half. The Eagle is found from Finland to eastern Siberia, extending south to Hungary and northern India. Such a wide distribution can hinder conservation efforts, as no one country wishes to accept responsibility, and agreement can be difficult.

Habitat destruction takes different forms, some more subtle than others. Sometimes habitats are destroyed completely, as when forests are felled or marshes drained and replaced by cropland. Most of the original species can no longer live there, but may be replaced by a small number of commoner species associated with cultivated land. Alternatively, a former widespread habitat may be fragmented, as when a forest is almost completely removed, leaving isolated patches here and there. The continuation of many forest-dwelling species depends largely on the size and isolation of the patches; local extinctions become increasingly likely if the patches are small (supporting only small populations) and at long distances from each other (reducing the chances of

movements between patches). It is theoretically possible that certain species could die out completely, solely because of the fragmentation and isolation of their population units, even though the total amount of habitat is sufficient to sustain large numbers. Thus biologists are increasingly coming to realize that, to facilitate the long-term persistence of populations, the same amount of habitat is better preserved in few large patches than in many small ones.

Another form of habitat destruction is more subtle, as it involves the long-term degradation of a former habitat by land-use practices which lead to reduced prey supplies. Examples include the use of natural grassland for the intensive grazing of domestic stock, so as to reduce the numbers of rabbits and rodents that raptors can eat; the removal by human hunters of small game animals otherwise available to raptors; or the conversion of natural mixed forest to even-aged plantations of one tree species. In such cases, the habitat may seem superficially similar, but lack the prey necessary to support raptors.

Even quite small changes in forestry or agricultural procedures can have big effects on raptor food supplies. Vultures and other carrion-feeding birds that survived the change from wild to domestic animals have recently experienced a big reduction in food in many regions because improvements in veterinary medicine have reduced the mortality of cattle and sheep on open range. In some countries the problem is accentuated by laws which require the immediate burial of carcasses, for disease control. Only in remote mountain areas, where stock is less accessible, has the supply of carrion, and its dependent vulture populations, been maintained.

One of the problems of conserving birds of prey is the large areas of land that they require, compared to many other animals. This results from their predacious habits, near the tops of food chains. The amount of land needed to conserve raptors varies with the body size of the species concerned. Small species, such as kestrels, require 1–3 square kilometers (0.3–1.2 square miles) per breeding pair, while some large eagles extend over more than a 100 square kilometers (40 square miles) per pair. Perhaps the extreme is shown by the Bearded Vulture (*Gypaetus barbatus*), in which pairs were found during the course of the year to range over areas of around 4,000 square kilometers (1500 square miles), though these ranges overlapped greatly between neighbours.

While some national parks are large enough to sustain isolated populations of large raptors, in the long term the survival of such species over much of the world will depend on land areas outside parks. In effect this means sea coast, or grazing or forest land where wild or domestic animals are available as prey, and where no poisoning of predators is done.

Anup Shah/Planet Earth Pictures

Eric & David Hosking

On a world scale, then, habitat destruction has already accounted for bigger reductions in raptor and other wildlife populations than has any other factor. And with the continuing growth in human population and development, it is still the most serious threat in the long term. However, not all human activities on the land are detrimental to birds of prey, and sometimes, as certain species decline, others increase. Over much of the northern world, the initial destruction of tree cover to make way for cultivation would have favored open country raptors at the expense of forest ones, and, in parts of the western United States, the White-tailed Kite (*Elanus leucurus*) has spread in recent years, associated with this continuing process. Several other species have spread across the great plains in America as a result of tree planting, which has provided nest sites. In parts of Europe, Peregrines (*Falco peregrinus*) probably owe their present high densities to the popular interest in pigeon racing, which ensures a ready supply of prey in regions scarce in wild food. The kites and other scavenging raptors that abound in some tropical and subtropical towns could not be maintained without garbage and other human waste. But like similar populations in Europe in past centuries, these can be expected to disappear as urban hygiene improves.

Human management of water resources also has varying effects on raptors. Wetland areas are destroyed not only by specific drainage operations, but also in arid areas by the general lowering of water tables, due to over-use of water

in towns and croplands. In Arizona, Black Hawks (*Buteogallus anthracinus*) formerly bred in abundance along several major rivers, but are now confined to a few stretches where surface water still flows year-round. On the other hand, the construction of dams and reservoirs has facilitated the spread of Ospreys (*Pandion haliaetus*) and Bald Eagles (*Haliaeetus leucocephalus*) in other parts of the United States. In Oregon in 1976, nearly half the known Osprey nests were associated with reservoirs.

▲ Open country suits the Red-backed Hawk (*Buteo polyosoma*). In natural grasslands it hunts guinea pigs. Clearing for farmland opens up new habitat, and domestic animals, here a goose, can prove an easy meal.

▼ The Barred Forest Falcon (*Micrastur ruficollis*) of South America seldom leaves the forest. Still quite common, it is unlikely to survive if humans continue to clear its rich tropical and subtropical forest habitat and reduce it to low-quality grazing land.

G. Ziesler/Bruce Coleman Ltd

PERSECUTION OF RAPTORS

Some raptor populations are held below the level that the habitat would support by human persecution or toxic chemicals. Particularly in Europe, many raptors owe their present low status to past overkill, from shooting or poisoning. It is difficult, in these days of conservation, to appreciate the scale of persecution only a few decades ago. But because some raptors eat lambs, poultry or gamebirds, they have been killed in millions. The tremendous effects of this slaughter on populations are seldom doubted, but little documentation is available. This is partly because in Europe and North America most reduction of numbers occurred between 1850 and 1900, before biologists were interested in recording it, and in recent years, killing has become illegal in many countries so, practiced subversively, it is hard to study. To protect domestic stock, the killing of raptors was officially encouraged in parts of Europe as early as the sixteenth century, by payment of bounties. But this seems to have been sporadic, and to have had no marked or long-term effects on populations. It was with the rise in small-game management in the nineteenth century that persecution reached its peak, and spread to the smaller species. Game shooting increased in popularity with the introduction of pheasant rearing, and increased again with the improvement of the shot gun, from muzzle-loader to breech-loader. The objective, of total elimination, was achieved for some raptor species over large areas.

Whether large-scale killing of raptors leads to population decline depends on whether the killing replaces the natural mortality or adds to it. Thus if the increased mortality from shooting is offset by reduced mortality from natural causes, so that the number of birds which die each year is about the same, then the population will not decline. But if the mortality from shooting, or from a combination of shooting and natural causes, exceeds that which would otherwise occur from natural causes alone, then the population will decline. In practice, much depends on when the killing occurs. Its effect is likely to be minimal in the months following breeding, for the population is then at its seasonal peak, and contains many juveniles which would die anyway before the next breeding season. In such cases, the shooting has to be exceptionally heavy, if it is to do more than to merely crop an expendable surplus. The effect of killing is greatest if it is done at the start of a breeding season, when the population is then at its seasonal low, and after most natural mortality has occurred. Then shooting not only adds to the natural mortality, but also concentrates on the breeding adults, the most valuable sector of the population, so that decline is rapid.

The vulnerability of any species depends partly on how easily it can be killed. Some species

► High technology and nature juxtapose happily in this deceptively tranquil scene. On an artificial platform, an Osprey cares for its chicks. Behind, as a space shuttle blasts off from Cape Canaveral its flare lights up the sky. With help, Ospreys in the USA have adjusted to life among boats and noisy holiday-makers on lakes and beaches. In Britain they tend to prefer more remote places.

Mike Price/Survival Anglia

PERSECUTION OF THE WEDGE-TAILED EAGLE

MICHAEL G. BROOKER

Few other raptors in the world have been persecuted as severely as the Wedge-tailed Eagle (*Aquila audax*). For almost 100 years it was considered vermin in some parts of Australia and monetary bonuses were paid for proof of slaughter in the form of bills, claws or even eggs. In just two states, comprising about 55 percent of the total land mass of the continent, at least 120,000 birds were killed during the decade 1950–59 in an effort to reduce stock losses.

Although sheep have been in Australia since the end of the eighteenth century, reports of eagle damage to lambs were few before 1860. After this time, labor shortages on the land (accentuated by gold rushes) resulted in gradual changes in sheep husbandry from a labor-intensive system using individual shepherds to an open-range situation with less supervision. In addition, rabbits (*Oryctolagus cuniculus*) were introduced successfully into Victoria in 1859 and had colonized most of the sheep country in southeastern Australia by the 1880s. As a result rabbits became a major food item for Wedge-tailed Eagles, replacing some native mammalian prey species, which themselves were becoming less common with the changes in land use and which may never have been as numerous or as readily available as the rabbit. These changes in food supply may have facilitated an increase in eagle numbers.

Methods of killing eagles varied from a tethered white rooster surrounded by leg traps to shooting birds from light aircraft. One of my earliest childhood memories is of a large black eagle flapping heavily past my head, with a trap attached to its leg. Poisoning was probably the most successful method. For example, 1,060 eagles were poisoned on one sheep station

▲ More than simple protection of livestock, the bodies of scores of Wedge-tailed Eagles, shot and strung up, reflect an attitude prevalent at least until the early 1970s when Australia gave the eagles legal protection.

in Queensland during an eight-month period in 1903.

The resilience of the Wedge-tailed Eagle in the face of almost a century of severe persecution augurs well for its future, especially now that the Eagle is fully protected in most parts of Australia. Its survival is attributable, in part, to the cushioning effect of the introduced rabbit as a plentiful alternative prey, to its diverse diet which includes carrion, and to the fact that large parts of its range have remained unoccupied by humans.

are fairly tame and easy to shoot; others use conspicuous perches and are easy to catch in leg traps; while yet others eat carrion, so are easy to poison. In general, it is the carrion-feeding species that have suffered most, because they can be killed in large numbers with minimum effort. Some birds are killed deliberately in this way, and others incidentally during poisoning campaigns aimed at mammalian predators such as wolves or jackals. Large species are more susceptible to the effects of persecution than small ones, because they live at lower densities, have lower breeding rates and take longer to reach breeding age. Following a 50 percent kill, a slow-breeding vulture population could take more than a decade to recover, whereas a fast-breeding kestrel population could be back in a year or two. In the long term, therefore, it is the small fast-breeding species that are most resistant to sustained killing. A third factor influencing vulnerability is the size and distribution of the population to begin with. Any small population which is localized in a restricted habitat is more easily eliminated than a large population that extends into wild country where it is hard to reach.

EFFECTS ON POPULATIONS

Evidence for the effects of persecution on populations comes from (1) records of numbers killed; (2) correlations between changes in killing and changes in population; (3) recoveries of ringed birds; and (4) studies of birds found dead.

NUMBERS KILLED

The payment of bounties for dead raptors has often meant that good records have been kept of the totals killed. The numbers can be impressive, as the following examples show:

● In Alaska, in 1917–52, rewards were paid for 128,273 Bald Eagles.

● In Norway, in 1846–1900, rewards were paid for 223,487 birds of prey, which included 61,157 Golden and White-tailed Eagles (*Aquila chrysaetos* and *Haliaeetus albicilla*) up to 1869, dropping to 27,319 eagles in 1870-99. As late as 1963, bounties were paid on 168 eagles.

● In Germany, in the Nordrhein-Westfalen districts in 1951–68, 210,520 raptors were recorded killed; in Lower Saxony in 1959–63, 38,432; in

Richard Vaughan/Ardea London

Schleswig-Holstein in 1960–68, 37,792; and at Hessen in 1951–67, 61,353.

● In Scotland from a single estate at Glengarry in 1837–40, 98 Peregrines, 78 Merlins, 462 Kestrels, 285 Buzzards, 3 Honey-Buzzards, 15 Golden Eagles, 27 White-tailed Eagles, 18 Ospreys, 63 Northern Goshawks, 275 Red Kites and 68 harriers were killed, making a total of 1,392 birds of prey.

▲ Turkey Vultures, one of the "buzzards" that loom ominously overhead in many Western movies, align themselves to the morning sun on a Florida street lamp. Common and often associated with humans, they roost on buildings and other man-made structures, and feed on human rubbish and other waste.

◄ African White-backed Vultures (*Gyps africanus*) often clean up in and around African villages. Here several feed together on a giraffe carcass. Although generally well thought of by Africans, such habits make them vulnerable to deliberate poisoning.

Rafi Ben-Shahar/Oxford Scientific Films

From statistics such as these, it has been estimated that, in the 20 years to 1970, several millions of raptors were killed in Europe by game-bird hunters alone, with especially large numbers in France and Germany. The sheer magnitude of such figures has led some people to doubt them, but they are repeated in similar order in region after region, and in each case feet or beak were required as proof of killing. The annual figures for particular areas often exceeded the number that could live there at one time, a testimony to the effects of movements or to the existence of nearby undisturbed populations from which recruits continually came.

In other lists, there was no obvious decline in the totals over many years, which suggests that in these areas the hunters were merely cropping the populations concerned and causing no long-term decline. This is indicated in some official statistics from Austria, which show that in 1948–68 premiums were paid annually on about 12,000 to 20,000 birds. Likewise, the destruction of 6,000 goshawks per year in Finland is also thought to be causing no long-term decline, but most of these birds are juveniles that are killed in the few months after fledging.

CHANGES IN PERSECUTION AND POPULATION STATUS

Further evidence for the effects of persecution on populations came in some areas when the killing was reduced, enabling numbers to rise again. This has been evident in several British species in recent decades, notably the Buzzard (*Buteo buteo*), which now occupies four times the area that it did a century ago. Moreover, all British raptors increased temporarily during the 1914–18 and 1939–45 wars, when many of their killers were away fighting a different adversary.

RING RECOVERIES

Compared with most other birds, not only are more ringed raptors recovered, but many of the recovered birds are reported as shot or trapped. For the common British species, the percentage of ringed birds that were later recovered varied from 7 percent to 14 percent and the proportions of these reported as killed up to 1954 was as high as 68 percent depending on species. The proportions recovered were greater than those for some waterfowl and game birds exposed to proper hunting seasons, and for recognized pest species. After 1954, when protective legislation came in, the proportions reported as killed declined. This drop may have been genuine, or it may have been due to many people omitting to report the birds they had killed, or falsifying the cause of death.

▲ Commensal with humans throughout the neotropics, Black Vultures follow the spread of human influence on the natural environment. They thrive on open garbage dumps and other human waste, but improved sanitation and hygiene, better veterinary care for livestock and burial of the bodies of dead beasts may one day reduce their food.

The numbers alone tell us little about the effect of this slaughter on populations, except that in some cases they must have represented at least the bulk of the local stock. Comparing the figures of the present century with those of the previous, the main difference is in the reduced representation of eagles and other large species. That this was due to the culling itself is supported by the large initial kills, followed by a steep decline as the scheme continued. Thus, the Scottish Glengarry figures included at least four species which were no longer present a century later, but for which the habitat still seemed suitable (two have since returned). Evidently there have been long periods in recent European history when raptor numbers in many areas were well below what habitats would support.

Similar analyses of European recoveries revealed regional variations in shooting pressure. Among kestrels ringed as nestlings in Holland, intentionally killed birds formed 82 percent of all recoveries from Belgium and France, but only 10 percent of those from other west European countries. The mean annual mortality calculated from the two sets of recoveries was significantly different, at 59 percent and 44 percent. In some species, the recoveries implied a difference in wariness between young and old birds, in that more of the birds recovered in their first year had been shot or trapped than of those recovered in later years.

In eastern North America, recoveries from at least three species have suggested a reduction in shooting in recent years, and in two of these, a

Richard & Julia Kemp/Survival Anglia

lessening in the overall mortality. Cooper's Hawk (*Accipiter cooperii*) is commonly known as the "chicken hawk" and has long been a favorite target. Ringed nestlings that were recovered in their first year dropped from 21 percent in 1929–40 to 10 percent in 1941–57, but the proportion of these reported as shot remained about 74 percent throughout. These recoveries gave estimates of the annual mortality for first-year and older birds of 83 percent and 44 percent for the years up to 1940, and of 78 percent and 34 percent for the years after 1940. In the early period the heavy hunting pressure could only have caused population decline, a trend which was confirmed from long-term counts at migration stations.

In the American Kestrel (*Falco sparverius*), diminished shooting pressure was associated with a significant drop in the overall juvenile mortality

from 69 percent in 1935–45 to 61 percent in 1946–65, but not in the overall adult mortality, which remained the same throughout. In the Red-tailed Hawk (*Buteo jamaicensis*), shooting pressure had always been slight, and an apparent drop in recent years had no effect on the overall mortality of either juveniles or adults, as calculated from the recoveries.

Hence, ringing recoveries have shown the importance of persecution in the overall mortality of raptors compared to that of other birds, as well as differences in the importance of shooting between particular species, regions and age groups. For some regions, they have also confirmed that shooting pressure has dropped in recent decades and that, in certain species, diminished shooting has led to reductions in overall mortality.

▲ Generally valued because it eats the snakes so feared by humans, the Short-toed Eagle (*Circaetus gallicus*) has benefited from some clearing as it prefers semi-open country or bush to forest.

199

▶ Ravelled in a mist net, trapped for banding and release, a Sharp-shinned hawk (*Accipiter striatus*) shows how easily raptors can collide with man-made structures. Unable to see the fine netting, they become entangled. Wires, discarded fishing line, netting, even clear glass windows all present similar, almost invisible, hazards to raptors.

▼ In Britain, human impact on Eurasian Sparrowhawks is clear. Early persecution, mainly by gamekeepers, prevented many from breeding. War brought a decline in gamekeeping and a spectacular increase in successful breeding. Post-war, persistent pesticides caused an all-time low. More recently, banning of pesticides and reduction in persecution have allowed a recovery. (The index is the percentage that nestling Sparrowhawks formed of all nestling birds ringed in Britain each year.)

STUDIES OF CARCASSES

The role of persecution in the overall mortality of raptors is also shown from birds found dead or dying. In an American study, 231 Bald Eagles found dead were received for autopsy during the period 1966–74. A minimum of 43 percent had been shot, poisoned or trapped, making persecution the major single cause of death. Other birds died from pesticide contamination or from natural factors. In a second American study, 23 percent of 850 birds of prey found moribund had been shot and another 15 percent trapped.

Such figures show that a high proportion of the deaths of birds examined by biologists can be attributed to direct killing by humans. Whether

they are representative of all deaths depends on how typical a sample was found. One can easily imagine that in the same areas some birds might die in ways which would make them unlikely to be found (for example killed and eaten by predators). This would mean that the role of persecution in the overall mortality would be exaggerated. Ring recoveries suffer from the same drawbacks, but both sources of information give useful comparisons with results from other birds. They also show the prevalence of persecution on sparse raptor populations, many of which were "protected" by law.

THE SHOOTING OF EAGLES FROM AIRPLANES

Wherever eagles live alongside sheep, they feed from dead sheep and lambs, and also kill some live lambs. This is true for the Golden Eagle in parts of Europe and North America, the White-tailed Eagle in Norway and Greenland, the Wedge-tailed Eagle (*Aquila audax*) in Australia, and the Black and Martial Eagles (*A. verreauxii* and *Hieraaetus bellicosis*) in southern Africa. The killing of birds that often follows reached a considerable scale in western Texas and southeastern New Mexico after the discovery that Golden Eagles could be shot down from airplanes. Over a period of 20 years until it was banned in 1962, 1,000–2,000 eagles were shot annually in sheep ranching areas.

The ranchers got together to finance the operations which were performed by a small number of pilots, operating from airports throughout the area. Lambing occurred at different dates in different regions, and a few days before a flock was scheduled to lamb, the rancher would arrange for a "shoot-out." This would continue over several days until virtually all eagles had been removed from a large area, extending beyond the ranch into the surrounding country, up to 240 kilometers (150 miles) from an airport.

As the eagles were removed, others began drifting in from neighboring areas, so it was usual to conduct a second shoot-out two to three weeks later. The total numbers killed in an area greatly exceeded the number present at any one time. Since these birds were winter visitors, it was not possible to assess the effect of the killing on breeding populations, but, with such large numbers involved, it could clearly have drained the population of a considerable area.

OTHER HUMAN DISTURBANCE

Compared to killing, the effects of other human interference on raptors may seem slight, but in fact human presence is becoming increasingly important in rendering suitable habitat unattractive to raptors. This presence is often in the form of tourism or recreation, as an increasingly mobile public intrude on wilderness and other areas

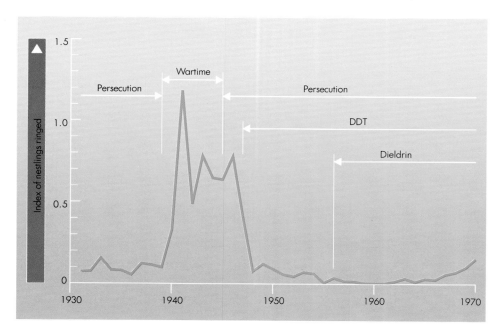

W. Perry Conway/Tom Stack & Associates

which were previously undisturbed. One of the best studies of the effect of continued human presence was in a forest which overlapped the Dutch–German border, roughly half and half. Forest management was similar on each side, but there was much greater human activity on the Dutch side, with more roads, more houses, more holiday cottages, and more recreation generally. Correspondingly, only four pairs of large raptors bred on the Dutch side in 1969, compared with 37 on the German side.

If the general level of persecution were lower, however, the behavior of raptors may well change, making them more prepared to nest close to people. There are indeed already signs of this in that, with increased protection, some species are for the first time colonizing towns and cities in many parts of the developed world. These

adaptable species include Peregrines and Merlins in North America and Northern Goshawks and Sparrowhawks in Europe.

Mike Birkhead/Oxford Scientific Films

▲ Golden Eagles (*Aquila chrysaetos*) have declined in numbers from the 19th century. They are threatened by shooters, trappers, poisoners and the encroachment of suburbia, but where given protection they can maintain stable, even increasing, populations. Unlike the Bald Eagle, they will roost and nest on powerlines.

◄ A few adaptable raptors live their lives in the concrete canyons of big cities. The Old World Kestrel (*Falco tinnunculus*) will lay its eggs on the grit and gravel on the sheltered ledge of a building as long as there is some wasteland or park nearby for hunting.

BALD EAGLES AND SALMON

B. RILEY McCLELLAND

Of the eight species of sea and fish eagles (genus *Haliaeetus*), only the Bald Eagle (*H. leucocephalus*) occurs in North America. Throughout much of its range in Canada and the USA, this species is migratory, often congregating at sites of seasonally abundant food. At the Chilkat River in Alaska, and the Squamish River in British Columbia, 2,000 or more Bald Eagles gather at autumn spawning runs of anadromous salmon.

For 50 years landlocked Kokanee Salmon (*Oncorhynchus nerka*) have attracted as many as 600 migrating eagles to a creek 4 kilometers (2.5 miles) long in Glacier National Park, Montana. Kokanee, a Pacific Ocean species not native to the Glacier Park area, were introduced in the early 1900s. In autumn 1939, the first eagle congregation was recorded. Although not a "natural" event, it may have inadvertently mitigated, to a small degree, the loss of thousands of kilometers of historic spawning habitat to dams in western North America.

In Glacier Park, spawning runs of more than 100,000 salmon have occurred in some falls. Amid the abundance of food, up to 40 eagles perch in a single tree and more than 400 roost communally in old-growth forest several kilometers from the foraging area. Adult eagles swoop on salmon floating on the surface of deep water. The youngest eagles (maturity is acquired in 4 to 6 years), not yet having developed efficient prey-capturing skills, wade to dead salmon easily accessible along the shore. When food is scarce, young eagles attempt to steal from other eagles.

Radio-transmitters attached to eagles' tail feathers enabled a Glacier Park research team to learn that these birds come from as far as 2,000 kilometers (1,240 miles) north of Glacier (the Northwest Territories, Canada) and eventually continue up to 1,000 kilometers (620 miles) south to wintering areas in the western United States. The vicissitudes of prey availability for migrating eagles are revealed by the recent history of the Kokanee in Glacier Park. Salmon numbers declined precipitously from 118,000 in 1985 to 340 in 1987. The peak count (single day) of eagles fell from 520 to 47 during those same years, illustrating the great dependence of the eagles on food availability.

Collapse of the Kokanee fishery probably resulted in part from the introduction of a crustacean (*Mysis relicta*) that competes with Kokanee for food. Overfishing and the expanding populations of non-native predatory fish, such as Lake Trout (*Salvelinus namaycush*), also may have been a factor. Recovery of the Kokanee population is unlikely, and without the salmon, large numbers of Bald Eagles will no longer gather in Glacier Park. They will search other rivers and lakes for fish or crippled waterfowl, and they will soar over fields looking for rodents, jackrabbits, and the remains of dead wildlife and livestock. Juvenile eagles, on their first migration, may be especially stressed. Food will be less concentrated and the eagles will be more vulnerable to shooting, poisoning, trapping, and collisions with vehicles than at Glacier National Park, where they received protection under nearly constant vigilance.

▼ A early US president, Benjamin Franklin, deplored the country's national symbol, the Bald Eagle, for its "bad moral character", reflecting the dichotomy of opinion, less evident today although human impact is larger.

Lon Lauber/Oxford Scientific Films

Tim Shepherd/Oxford Scientific Films

PESTICIDES AND OTHER TOXIC CHEMICALS

Although most kinds of pesticide in large enough doses will kill birds of prey, it is only one group, the so-called organochlorine pesticides, that have reduced populations over large parts of the world. These compounds include DDT, and cyclodienes such as aldrin, dieldrin, endrin and heptachlor. Besides being toxic, these chemicals have three main properties which contribute to their effects on raptors and other wildlife. First, they are extremely stable, so that they can persist more or less unchanged in the environment for many years. Second, they dissolve readily in fat, which means that they can accumulate in animal bodies, and pass from prey to predator, concentrating at successive steps in a food chain. Predatory birds, near the tops of food chains, are especially liable to accumulate large amounts. Third, at sublethal levels of only a few parts per million in tissues, some organochlorines can disrupt the breeding of certain species. They are also dispersed in the bodies of migrant birds and insects, or in wind and water currents, and can thus reach remote regions. So widely were these chemicals used that none of the large numbers of bird species analyzed in the 1960s in Europe and North America was found to be free from organochlorine residues; however, the biggest concentrations were found in predatory birds.

Effects on raptor populations have been noted wherever these chemicals have been used on a

large scale, including most of Europe and North America, parts of Australia, Asia and Africa. Not all species are affected to the same extent, and in particular regions declines are generally more marked in bird-eating than in mammal-eating species. This is partly because mammal-eaters feed on herbivorous prey (a food chain with two steps), whereas the bird-eaters live largely on carnivorous prey (a food chain with at least three steps). It is also partly because birds in general are less able to break down organochlorine residues in their bodies than are mammals, so that at any one time they tend to contain more. Also, many birds range more widely than mammals, so have greater chance of direct exposure to pesticides. All these differences mean that in any one region, any raptors that eat birds are likely to accumulate more organochlorine than are raptors that eat mammals. In some areas, populations of fish-eating raptors, such as Osprey and Bald Eagle, were also affected. This is because some fish accumulate organochlorines to high level, extracting them not only from their food, but also from the water during respiration, as they pass huge volumes over their gills during the course of each day.

Different organochlorines affect raptor populations in different ways. DDT, and its metabolite DDE, are of relatively low toxicity to birds, and their main impact is on reproduction. DDE causes shell-thinning (leading to egg breakage) and embryo deaths, thus lowering the

▲▼ Broadscale use of DDT and other organochlorines brought a revolution in farming practices, but it was the discovery of their insidious effects on wildlife, particularly raptors, that heralded the environmental revolution.

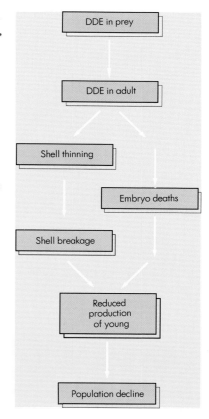

breeding rate. If this reduction in breeding is sufficiently marked, too few young are produced to offset the usual adult mortality, and the population declines. The cyclodiene compounds, such as aldrin and dieldrin, are much more toxic than DDE, and have caused population declines primarily by increasing the mortality rate above the natural level. The relative contributions made by reduced reproduction (from DDE) and increased mortality (from cyclodienes) to population declines in raptors have evidently varied from one region to another, depending on usage patterns. In much of Europe, declines in Sparrowhawk and Peregrine numbers in the late 1950s were so rapid they must have been due mainly to additional mortality. In parts of North America, however, regional extinctions of Peregrines were probably due chiefly to a reduction in the breeding rate caused by DDE. This is the only chemical known to cause a significant population decline by means other than mortality.

As the use of DDT, dieldrin and other organochlorines have been progressively curtailed, residues in raptor eggs and tissues have declined, and populations in Europe and North America have partly or entirely recovered. This is not true in other parts of the world, however, where the use of these chemicals continues, or even increases.

Other types of pesticides have also killed large numbers of birds, including raptors, but so far as is known, have not caused widespread and lasting population declines. Some organophosphorous compounds are especially lethal, and in one two-month period in Holland in 1960, 27,000 birds were found dead and dying around newly sown fields, associated with the use of parathion, and the total number killed was probably nearer 200,000, including eight species of raptors. In parts of Africa, large numbers of raptors are said to die during control operations against the grain-eating bird, Quelea, in which parathion is sprayed from aircraft. Some carbamate pesticides, notably carbofuran, have also been implicated in raptor mortality in parts of North America. In addition, certain rodenticides are known to regularly kill raptors, through secondary poisoning (eating poisoned prey). In the 1960s, widespread declines in the raptor populations of Israel were attributed to extensive use of thallium sulfate, as a rodenticide, while in more recent years in several countries new anticoagulant rodenticides have killed various raptors and owls.

From time to time other toxic chemicals have been implicated in raptor deaths. They include some heavy metals, such as mercury and lead. In several countries effluent from chloralkali plants is a major source of mercury pollution in the aquatic

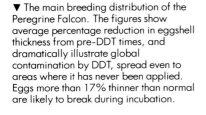

▼ The main breeding distribution of the Peregrine Falcon. The figures show average percentage reduction in eggshell thickness from pre-DDT times, and dramatically illustrate global contamination by DDT, spread even to areas where it has never been applied. Eggs more than 17% thinner than normal are likely to break during incubation.

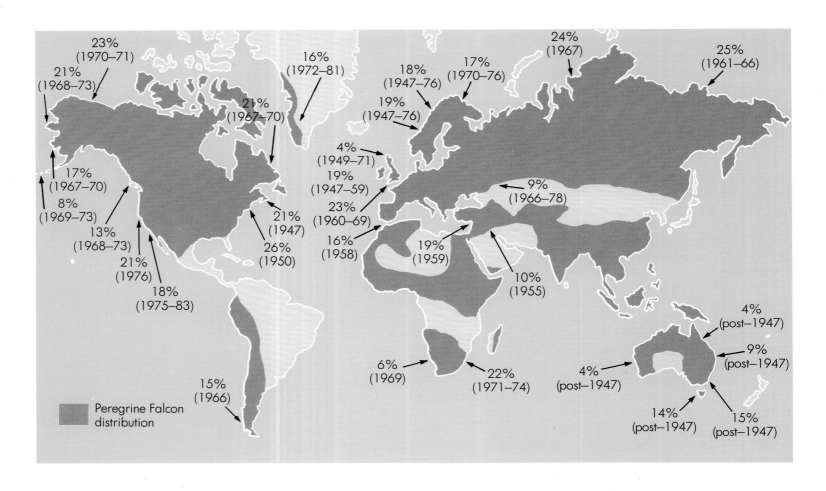

Peregrine Falcon distribution

environment, while certain pesticides are a major source of mercury in the terrestrial environment. Mercury has often been found to kill birds outright, especially when used as alkyl-mercury in seed dressings. Casualties have included mainly granivorous birds, but also many others, including the raptors that fed on the corpses. In the Dutch province of Zeeland, in one year, 103 raptors and 111 owls were found dead from this cause. The widespread killing of such large numbers presumably contributed to the general decline of European raptors in the 1950s and 1960s. The problem with mercurial fungicides was especially marked in Sweden.

Some carrion-feeding raptors in North America have suffered from lead poisoning. This metal is ingested, as bullet fragments or shot, from the scavenged carcasses of deer or waterfowl, which are shot but not recovered by hunters. Lead poisoning may even have contributed to the decline of the California Condor (*Gymnogyps californianus*), now extinct in the wild.

In conclusion, therefore, there are at least five different ways in which the raptors of particular regions have been poisoned to near extinction in the years since 1950: (1) deliberate destruction through use of poisoned meat baits, as for several species in parts of Europe and southern Africa; (2) incidental destruction through raptors taking poisoned meat baits intended for other predators, such as wolves or foxes in parts of Europe; (3) secondary poisoning through raptors taking poisoned prey, such as rodents in Israel; (4) secondary poisoning through raptors taking prey that had themselves been poisoned incidentally during attempts to control some other pest, as when seed-eating birds took grain treated with insecticides in various parts of Europe and North America; (5) secondary poisoning resulting from food chain contamination with persistent organochlorine compounds, which increased mortality, reduced breeding success, or both, in large parts of the developed world.

In any one region, more than one factor has sometimes been involved, and particular raptor species may have declined because of different factors in different regions. When the above events are added to the effects of habitat destruction, shooting and other direct persecution, it is sometimes hard to specify for a given population which factor was most important in causing decline. In particular areas, populations have generally increased somewhat between the periods of successive declines, but increasingly since 1950 populations over large areas have been held by chemical means well below the level that the environment would otherwise support. The biggest problems have come mainly from the use of chemicals which are non-selective, persistent and cumulative. Although the situation has improved greatly since the 1960s, and our

knowledge of the dangers of toxic chemicals is now much greater, it would be unrealistic to expect that such problems will not recur. Meanwhile, however, the raptor populations of Europe and North America are currently experiencing a period of almost unrestrained recovery from pesticide impacts.

▲▼ Strychnine and other poisons are used in carcasses, both legally and illegally, to control foxes and dingoes, but sometimes scavenging raptors like the Whistling Kites (above) are killed. The dead California Condor (below), found in 1984, probably represented 20% of the entire wild population.

RAPTORS AND POWERLINES

JOHN LEDGER

J Robert/Jacana

▲ A mixed blessing, powerlines provide sturdy roosts, hunting perches and nest sites for raptors but their thin wires are hazardous obstacles to fast fliers.

Electricity is the driving force of the twentieth century, allowing us unprecedented industrial development, resource exploitation, communication, data processing and living standards. The next century will see electricity reach the furthest corners of the globe, bringing light, warmth and communications.

The most cost-effective way of getting electricity from source to consumer is by overhead wires—the "powerlines" that festoon most developed countries. Tall high-voltage transmission lines span the long distances between substations, from which medium-voltage distribution lines radiate to feed local low-voltage reticulation lines to end-users.

Raptors have mixed fortunes when powerlines cross their paths. Some collide with the wires and are killed instantly, or suffer mortal injuries. Others may touch two live conductors, or one conductor and "earth", to die instantly by electrocution. On the positive side, many raptors now hunt from electricity poles and wires, and increasing numbers find them to be safe nesting sites. In treeless areas the poles may be the only perches and nest sites.

Raptors are capable of high-speed flight and are vulnerable to flying into the thin, almost invisible wires in their path. A worldwide study of raptor collisions with utility lines (including telephone lines) revealed that Peregrine Falcons (*Falco peregrinus*), Bald Eagles (*Haliaeetus albicilla*), Golden Eagles (*Aquila chrysaetos*), Red-tailed Hawks (*Buteo jamaicensis*) and Ospreys (*Pandion haliaetus*) accounted for 70 percent of the suspected collisions. Of 76 birds whose age was recorded, 55.3 percent were adults and 44.7 percent were subadults.

Electrocution of Golden Eagles in the western states of the USA stimulated research resulting in the first recommendations for correcting hazardous structures and for designing new safe ones. The problem concerns the wingspan of large raptors and the spacing of live conductors on the poles that carry them. Success has been achieved by retrospective modifications to increase clearances, remove earthed structures, or by fitting perches and shields to keep raptors away from danger areas.

In South Africa many endemic Cape Vultures (*Gyps coprotheres*) were electrocuted on 88 kV distribution lines. Perches fitted to the top part of the steel towers served to keep birds away from the danger area, and greatly reduced the number killed.

Many different species of birds build nests on electricity towers—they regard them as steel or wooden trees quite suitable for the purpose. For many decades electricity line maintenance staff systematically removed nests in the belief that they threaten the reliability of the power supply. This is rarely the case, and many electric utilities around the world have now adopted a more accommodating policy towards birds nesting on towers.

Large eagles will build strong nests that they maintain for years and defend against intruders. Long sticks brought during the construction phase may hang down and cause flashovers from conductor to tower. Simply trimming away such branches solves the problem for the electricity supplier. Destroying the nest results in ongoing headaches as the eagles attempt to build again.

African raptors recorded nesting on transmission line towers include Greater Kestrel (*Falco rupicoloides*), Common Kestrel, Lanner Falcon (*Falco biarmicus*), African Hawk Eagle (*Hieraaetus spilogaster*), Tawny Eagle (*Aquila rapax*), Black Eagle and Whitebacked Vulture (*Gyps africanus*). In the USA, nesting platforms designed by Morlan Nelson and fitted to electricity transmission line towers have been used for breeding by Golden Eagles, Red-tailed Hawks and Ospreys. The platforms with a sunshade provide conditions similar to those required by cliff-nesting raptors.

THE DEMISE OF THE CALIFORNIA CONDOR

NOEL SNYDER

The primary causes of the California Condor's *(Gymnogyps californianus)* decline were not known for many decades. Some observers suspected that many pairs were failing to breed, possibly because of human-caused declines in food supplies. Others suggested that the species was suffering mainly from shooting, human disturbance of nests and roosts, loss of habitat, and secondary poisoning by compound 1080 (sodium fluoroacetate) resulting from ground-squirrel control programs. Although good quantitative data to support these hypotheses were not available, conservation efforts proceeded on the assumption that these hypotheses might be true.

By the late 1970s it was becoming clear that existing approaches to Condor conservation were not reversing the decline. Obviously, much better information was needed on causes of the Condor's difficulties. A new intensive research program was begun in 1980, using expanded traditional observational approaches combined with new techniques, such as radio-telemetry and photographic census of the wild population of Condors.

Extensive searches for nesting pairs and continuous monitoring of the activities of these pairs, coupled with accurate photo-census information, finally allowed an evaluation of reproductive performance of the species. It was clear that the Condor was exhibiting reasonably good rates of reproductive effort and success. In contrast, photographic census data revealed that the survival rate of individuals was very poor. Clearly the main problem of the species was excessive mortality, but the exact causes of mortality were still known only very imperfectly. Fortunately, several dead Condors were recovered and given thorough postmortem analyses before the species was lost completely. Results led to a greatly improved understanding of mortality factors.

Of four birds autopsied after 1982, three had died of lead poisoning, apparently caused by ingestion of lead bullet fragments in their carrion food. Condors have been feeding on remains of hunter-shot mammals, such as deer and coyotes, for centuries. Thus, it seems likely that such poisoning has been a major continuing cause of the overall decline, even though it was not even suspected as major problem in earlier decades.

Other mortality factors, such as wanton shooting and collisions with overhead wires, have undoubtedly contributed to the decline, and probably all major causes have been direct or indirect effects of humans. Unfortunately, the major known mortality factors are all ones that will be difficult to reverse over most of the recent range of the species. The short-term survival of the species depends entirely on captive breeding.

François Gohier/Ardea London

CONSERVATION AND MANAGEMENT

STANLEY A. TEMPLE

Birds of prey have life styles that make them especially vulnerable to many of the environmental changes that accompany an expanding human population. Being predators, most raptors have predictable life-history traits: they are relatively large, they reproduce at relatively low rates, they tend to have relatively long lifespans, they exist at relatively low population densities, they are at the top of long food chains, their numbers are often limited by the availability of their prey, and they often have specialized requirements for habitats and nesting sites.

These same traits that adapt raptors so well for success under natural conditions often lead to population declines when humans and raptors interact. Human persecution can lead to elevated mortality, for which the limited reproductive output of many species cannot compensate. Habitat alterations can reduce the availability of prey or nesting sites. Toxic chemicals concentrated in food chains reach dangerously high levels in many raptors, causing mortality or reproductive dysfunctions.

The resulting population declines can lead to local extirpations or rangewide declines that make a species liable to extinction. Local declines or extirpations and the threat of total extinction are two of the primary reasons why raptors have received special conservation management. In addition, there is a growing public awareness that raptors are valuable and beautiful creatures that greatly enhance the integrity of the ecosystems they occupy. A rugged cliff without Peregrine Falcons (*Falco peregrinus*), a wild lake without Ospreys (*Pandion haliaetus*) and fish eagles, or a carcass on a savannah without attending vultures are deficient in a way that many conservation-minded individuals feel must be corrected through restoration efforts.

There can be little doubt that birds of prey, as a group, have fared poorly in the face of human development. Severe reductions in population size and local extirpations are the rule when natural habitats are invaded and developed. Only a handful of species have responded positively to human development by achieving higher densities in altered habitats. In view of this pattern, it is perhaps surprising that only one raptor, the Guadalupe Caracara (*Polyborus lutosus*), has become extinct since 1600, since which time most avian extinctions have been documented. Nonetheless, 43 of the 292 species of Falconiformes are now considered to be threatened with extinction, according to the most recent compilation by the International Council for Bird Preservation. Some of these rare and endangered raptors are managed specifically and effectively by conservationists, and several species once in serious trouble have responded so well to this management that their status is secure today. Peregrine Falcons, Bald Eagles, Ospreys and other species formerly on endangered species lists have recovered impressively.

▼ The mastery with which an African Fish Eagle (*Haliaeetus vocifer*) snatches a large fish from a seemingly pristine lake belies its vulnerability to many human-wrought changes in the environment. Pesticides have washed into many African lakes and concentrate in the eagles, causing thin-shelled eggs and reproductive failure.

Kevin Carlson/Aquila Photographics

Kenneth W. Fink/Ardea London

Jack & Lindsay Cupper/Auscape

THREATENED RAPTORS

Adapted from International Council for Bird Preservation, Technical Publication No. 8

Species	Range	Threats
California Condor (*Gymnogyps californianus*)	Western USA	Toxic chemicals, habitat loss
Black Honey Buzzard (*Henicopernis infuscata*)	New Britain Island, Papua New Guinea	Habitat loss
Red Kite (*Milvus milvus*)	Europe and North Africa	Persecution
Solomon Sea Eagle (*Haliaeetus sanfordi*)	Solomon Islands	Habitat loss
Madagascar Fish Eagle (*Haliaeetus vociferoides*)	Madagascar	Habitat loss
Pallas' Fish Eagle (*Haliaeetus leucoryphus*)	Central Asia	Habitat loss
White-tailed Sea Eagle (*Haliaeetus albicilla*)	Eurasia	Habitat loss, toxic chemicals, persecution
Steller's Sea Eagle (*Haliaeetus pelagicus*)	East Asia	Toxic chemicals, habitat loss
Cinereous Vulture (*Aegypius monachus*)	Eurasia	Habitat loss, persecution
Cape Griffon (*Gyps coprotheres*)	South Africa	Habitat loss
Kinabalu Serpent Eagle (*Spilornis kinabaluensis*)	Malaysia	Habitat loss
Andaman Serpent Eagle (*Spilornis elgini*)	Andaman Islands	Habitat loss
Madagascar Serpent Eagle (*Eutriorchis astur*)	Madagascar	Habitat loss
Imitator Sparrowhawk (*Accipiter imitator*)	Solomon Islands and Papua New Guinea	Unknown
Semicollared Hawk (*Accipiter collaris*)	Northern South America	Habitat loss
Dwarf Sparrowhawk (*Accipiter nanus*)	Sulawesi, Indonesia	Habitat loss
New Britain Collared Sparrowhawk (*Accipiter brachyurus*)	New Britain, Papua New Guinea	Habitat loss
Cuban Hawk (*Accipiter gundlachi*)	Cuba	Habitat loss, persecution
Red Goshawk (*Accipiter radiatus*)	Northern Australia	Habitat loss
Slate-colored Hawk (*Leucopternis schistacea*)	Amazonia	Habitat loss
Plumbeous Hawk (*Leucopternis plumbea*)	Northwestern South America	Unknown
White-necked Hawk (*Leucopternis lacernulata*)	Brazil	Habitat loss

◀ Top left: Cinereous Vulture (*Aegypius monachus*), Portugal. Center left: Harpy Eagle (*Harpia harpyja*), South America. Bottom left: Red Goshawk (*Accipiter radiatus*), Australia.

Species	Range	Threats
Gray-backed Hawk (*Leucopternis occidentalis*)	Ecuador	Habitat loss
Mantled Hawk (*Leucopternis polionota*)	East-central South America	Habitat loss
Black Solitary Eagle (*Harpyhaliaetus solitarius*)	Central America and western South America	Habitat loss
Crowned Solitary Eagle (*Harpyhaliaetus coronatus*)	Southeastern South America	Habitat loss, persecution
Ridgway's Hawk (*Buteo ridgwayi*)	Hispaniola	Habitat loss
Galapagos Hawk (*Buteo galapagoensis*)	Galapagos	Human disturbance, introduced organisms
Hawaiian Hawk (*Buteo solitarius*)	Hawaii	Habitat loss
Rufous-tailed Hawk (*Buteo ventralis*)	Patagonia	Unknown
Guiana Crested Eagle (*Morphnus guianensis*)	Central and South America	Habitat loss
Harpy Eagle (*Harpia harpyja*)	Central and South America	Habitat loss
New Guinea Eagle (*Harpyopsis novaeguineae*)	New Guinea	Habitat loss, persecution
Great Philippine Eagle (*Pithecophaga jefferyi*)	Philippines	Habitat loss
Imperial Eagle (*Aquila heliaca*)	Southern Eurasia	Habitat loss
Spanish Imperial Eagle (*Aquila adelbertii*)	Spain	Habitat loss
Javan Hawk Eagle (*Spizaetus bartelsi*)	Java, Indonesia	Habitat loss
Wallace's Hawk Eagle (*Spizaetus nanus*)	Southeast Asia, East Indies	Habitat loss
Slaty-backed Forest Falcon (*Micrastur mirandollei*)	Central and South America	Unknown
Buckley's Forest Falcon (*Micrastur buckleyi*)	Amazonia	Unknown
Lesser Kestrel (*Falco naumanni*)	Eurasia	Toxic chemicals, habitat loss
Mauritius Kestrel (*Falco punctatus*)	Mauritius	Habitat loss, introduced organisms
Gray Falcon (*Falco hypoleucos*)	Australia	Habitat loss
Orange-breasted Falcon (*Falco deiroleucus*)	Central and South America	Habitat loss, toxic chemicals

▶ Top right: Pallas' Fish Eagle (*Haliaeetus leucoryphus*), India. Center right: Great Philippine Eagle (*Pithecophaga jefferyi*), Philippines. Bottom right: Gray Falcon (*Falco hypoleucos*), Australia.

Frans Lanting/Minden Pictures

▲ Gyrfalcons were prized and protected in medieval times, and are again today. But conservation issues are now determined by an awareness of wildlife's intrinsic value.

▶ Legal protection is not always enough. Well-intentioned, rigidly enforced, protection of the California Condor allowed its virtual extinction. With only a handful of birds remaining, approval was given to take them into captivity. Successful breeding has given some hope of reintroduction.

▼ Trained by a falconer, a Lappet-faced Vulture holds its audience spellbound. Public education promotes appreciation of the splendor and worth of raptors.

Intensive conservation efforts focused specifically on raptors are a relatively recent phenomenon, even though the roots of these efforts can be traced back centuries. In all cases, conservation occurred only when raptors were valued by society. When Peregrine Falcons and Gyrfalcons (*Falco rusticolus*) were highly prized by European nobility for use in falconry, these birds received protection. Later, when falconry waned and shooting preserves expanded, large falcons were persecuted as threats to game birds. During recent decades rare birds of prey, like most other scarce but impressive wildlife species, have

begun to take on an intrinsic value of their own, not related directly to utilization by a specific group. With this appreciation of raptors has come protection and conservation management.

PROTECTION FROM PERSECUTION AND OVER-EXPLOITATION

Raptors have been persecuted as vermin with varying intensities in different parts of the world. When such persecution is severe, marked reductions in population size and even local extirpations are possible. This is especially true for some of the larger birds of prey whose low reproductive rates cannot compensate for the higher mortality rates that result from shooting, trapping, and poisoning campaigns.

Furthermore, some raptors have been and are exploited, creating the potential for a drain on some local populations. Live raptors are captured for use in falconry and for exhibition in zoos, and during the 1800s, when egg collecting was in vogue as a hobby, some species were subject to heavy local pressure from collectors. When local populations are over-harvested, declines and extirpation are possible if recruitment from other less-exploited populations cannot compensate for the removals of birds or eggs.

When local declines or extirpations can be blamed on persecution or over-exploitation, the most appropriate conservation activities are legal protection and education. By subjecting violators to penalties for killing or taking raptors, a reduction in the rates of loss can be achieved, and, assuming other factors are not involved, a recovery in numbers can be expected. Sometimes laws alone are ineffective in detering malicious individuals. It has proven necessary in some cases to actively guard raptors from some threats. Round-the-clock guards have been posted at some raptor nest sites, such as those of Ospreys, Red Kites (*Milvus milvus*), Peregrine Falcons, and White-tailed Sea Eagles (*Haliaeetus albicilla*), in order to keep egg collectors at bay.

Often legal protection must be accompanied by public education to dispel popular misconceptions and prejudices. Some individuals who had previously persecuted raptors can be dissuaded by exposure to the birds in an educational setting. Falconers, in particular, have won many converts by exposing the public to the beauty and value of a living raptor. Just demonstrating that someone cares about the welfare of raptors convinces others that mindless persecution is unjustifiable.

Legal protection is, however, only an effective conservation measure when persecution or over-harvest are the causes of declines. Not infrequently conservationists have mistakenly placed faith in legal protection when other factors were primarily responsible for problems. In these cases, even

Keith Scholey/Seaphot Ltd/Planet Earth Pictures

completely effective protection will not improve a population's status if, for example, its habitat has been altered or its food chain contaminated with toxic chemicals. In some instances, rigidly applied legal protection has actually been a detriment to effective conservation management.

For decades, the California Condor (*Gymnogyps californianus*) was protected from all human contact in the mistaken belief that direct human disturbance was causing decline. Unfortunately for the condors, they were legally off-limits to well-meaning biologists as well as to malicious individuals. The condor population plummeted while, for a long time, strict protection prevented the studies that would have identified the real causes of decline. Strict protection also precluded many types of conservation management, such as captive breeding.

Although legal protection from malicious persecution and over-harvest should, of course, be afforded to all wildlife species, including raptors, conservationists must realize that in today's world complex environmental problems often require complex solutions that go far beyond mere protection. The days in which a strictly protectionist, *laissez-faire* approach to managing raptors worked are for many species long past, and more innovative approaches must be used to maintain some species.

REDUCING INCIDENTAL THREATS

Whereas persecution and over-exploitation are direct and purposeful threats that can reduce populations, there are also many indirect and inadvertent threats that result from human activities. These indirect threats are the inevitable result of the pervasive presence of human beings and their technological artefacts. Conservationists must often deal with these threats to raptors, but the solutions to these problems can be difficult.

In some cases, human activities posing indirect threats to raptors can be regulated or controlled by legal means. It was possible to greatly limit the use of certain persistent toxic chemicals, such as DDT, by governmental regulation. The benefits of these regulations for raptors have been dramatic. In the decade following bans on chlorinated hydrocarbon pesticides, raptors that had declined after decades of pesticide-induced reproductive failures began spectacular recoveries. Ospreys in North America and Peregrine Falcons in the British Isles bounced back to regain or even exceed pre-pesticide population levels. Although there can be no doubt about the cause–effect relationship between chlorinated hydrocarbons and raptor declines, these chemicals still pose threats to raptors in Third World areas where their use continues.

Toxic chemicals are not the only by-products of our modern technology that have inadvertently

Kenneth W. Fink/Ardea London

Neillaine Price/Survival Anglia

▶ A conservation success. Osprey populations, once decimated by persecution and pesticides, have been returned to (or above) their former levels by active and intelligent protection and management.

harmed raptors. Electrical power-transmission lines are now ubiquitous features on the landscape. The poles and towers that support those lines are often fatally attractive to raptors that seek to perch or build their nests on them. Concerned about the electrocutions and collisions that claimed the lives of many raptors, conservationists have worked with power companies to redesign these structures so that the threats they pose can be reduced. Working with falconry-trained birds, researchers tested various designs to find the proper spacing and

configuration of wires that would allow birds to perch on poles without risk. In one study in western North America it was estimated that 95 percent of the raptor electrocutions could be eliminated by altering the design of only 2 percent of the poles in a region; these were poles that happened to be in particularly favored locations for large raptors.

Lead poisoning of raptors is an inadvertent problem that can result from decades of accumulated lead pellets in wetlands hunted for waterfowl. Lead pellets lying on the bottom of a wetland are ingested by waterfowl, which are then captured by raptors when they become ill or scavenged after they die. Other waterfowl, wounded by hunters, are also caught by raptors and provide another source of lead shot. Raptors, such as the Bald Eagles (*Haliaeetus leucocephalus*), that frequently feed on waterfowl are then, in turn, poisoned. It is hoped that a ban on the use of lead shot for waterfowl hunting and a switch to steel shot in the United States will eventually reduce the losses of both waterfowl and raptors. To a lesser extent lead bullets that remain in unretrieved carcasses of animals killed by hunters can poison scavengers. Lead poisoning of this type was important in recent losses of California Condors.

Although oiled seabirds are the most frequently publicized victims of oil spills, raptors can also be inadvertent victims. The tendency of raptors to be attracted to pools of oil that resemble bathing sites, or to attempt to scavenge previously mired animals, has led to impressive collections of fossilized raptor bones in natural oil seeps, such as the La Brea Tar Pits of California. Oil spills and

Dr Bernd U. Meyburg

Stephen J. Krasemann/Bruce Coleman Ltd

▲ Thriving in a modern world, Osprey nests grace electricity pylons. Power companies and conservationists work together to design powerlines safe for birds; often they provide secure structures for nesting.

▶ By attaching a nestbox to a billboard, conservationists hope to encourage kestrels into an area previously unused. Artificial nest structures are successful only where other resources, such as food, are not limiting.

Lori Lauber/Oxford Scientific Films

◄ Landing on a knoll of wildflowers, a Bald Eagle looks far from harm. Yet it may be one of many that feed on waterfowl, ill or dead from ingesting lead gunshot pellets built up over decades on the bottom of wetlands. A ban on the use of lead shot, and a switch to steel shot by hunters, should eventually reduce the numbers of deaths of both waterfowl and eagles due to lead poisoning.

pools around modern-day drilling sites have proven to be just as deadly, and regulations against open pools have surely prevented the inadvertent deaths of many raptors.

REMOVING NEST-SITE LIMITATIONS

Because some raptors have special requirements for their nest sites, the availability of suitable sites can effectively limit some populations. Cavity nesters and cliff nesters can be limited by nest-site availability. Conservationists have been quick to take advantage of this situation by providing nest-limited raptors with extra sites. By doing this they allow such raptor populations to expand in numbers or to nest in areas from which they were previously excluded.

Sometimes these supplemental nest sites are artificial structures that are surrogates for scarce natural nesting structures. Densities of several cavity-nesting kestrels have been increased by providing artificial nest boxes; when placed in areas of suitable habitat lacking cavities, these boxes have allowed kestrels to readily occupy these previously unused areas. By increasing the number of nesting ledges and holes in dirt banks along a river, Canadian biologists were able to increase the number of breeding Prairie Falcons (*Falco mexicanus*) in the area from 7 to 11. Ospreys have been encouraged to nest around newly created reservoirs that lacked nesting trees by providing artificial poles with platforms attached.

Although provision of additional nest sites has the potential to increase the proportion of birds

that can breed in a population with limited nest sites, it will not have the same effect in a population limited by the availability of some other essential resource. Although such birds may occupy artificial sites, they usually have done so by choosing the artificial site over a natural one; hence the breeding population has not expanded, but merely relocated.

Although creating artificial nest sites for raptors has a technological appeal, it is a poor substitute for preserving natural sites. Preventing nest-site destruction can keep populations from becoming nest-site limited, and raptor nest sites have received special protection in several areas. Cliff-side nesting sites of Peregrine Falcons, Gyrfalcons, Golden Eagles (*Aquila chrysaetos*), and Rough-legged Hawks (*Buteo lagopus*), for example, have received special protection from disturbance along the routes of Alaskan and Canadian oil pipelines. Cutting of potential nesting

Howard R. Postovit

▲ When mining was due to resume along a rock wall used in the interim by nesting Prairie Falcons, the chicks were moved to an improvised nest on a modified mobile light pole. Their parents continued to attend while the box was moved gradually, over several days, to a safe distance from the wall.

Helilo & Van Ingen/NHPA

◄ Its nest destroyed by a harvester, a Montagu's Harrier chick (*Circus pygargus*) is placed in an artificial nest. The adults will return to feed it. Informed intervention saved the chicks and ensured that they were raised in the best way possible, by their parents.

► Sound, well-researched management can be compatible with commercial interests. Conservationists were called in when coal-mining operations necessitated the removal of a tree used by nesting Golden Eagles (*Aquila chrysaetos*). They studied the resident eagles and identified an area heavily used by the pair, but not slated for mining. To encourage the pair to shift their breeding activities the nest was removed during the non-breeding season and relocated at the new site. The eagles accepted the new position and bred there in subsequent years.

Howard R. Postovit

trees for Bald Eagles and Ospreys is prohibited on government-owned forestland in North America. Potential effects on raptor nest sites are being considered a serious negative feature in a growing number of environmental impact assessments in the United States.

MANIPULATING FOOD SUPPLIES

Just as some populations are limited by availability of nest sites, many other raptor populations are limited in size by the availability of prey or carrion. Such food limitations seem especially frequent in predators, and they account for the dramatic fluctuations of some raptor populations that rely on cyclic prey, such as Goshawks (*Accipiter gentilis*) that feed on snowshoe hares or Rough-legged Hawks that feed on lemmings.

For many birds of prey the most serious consequence of habitat alterations caused by human development is a decline in their food supply. The conversion of natural grasslands to agricultural fields, or natural forests to forestry plantations, almost always reduces the available food supply for raptors, even though many of the physical features of the habitat might remain suitable. Comparisons of raptor numbers in natural and developed landscapes almost invariably reveal differences that are primarily due to changes in food supply.

Occasionally, human development actually enhances the food supply for some raptors, allowing their numbers to increase in altered habitats. Certain scavengers, such as Turkey Vultures (*Cathartes aura*) and Black Vultures (*Coragyps atratus*), reach impressive densities around Latin American cities where garbage dumps and other human waste provide a rich concentrated food source that greatly exceeds natural supplies of carrion. Similar concentrations of kites and Old World vultures occurred in past centuries in Europe before modern sanitation eliminated this food source and the scavengers that thrived on it.

Osprey numbers often increase dramatically around artificial reservoirs where fish populations grow rapidly in the years following damming and flooding. One of the attractions of large cities for Peregrine Falcons seems to be the large numbers of pigeons, the peregrine's favorite prey.

▼ Human waste has become carrion for a flock of Black Vultures, scavenging on a smouldering Ecuadorian rubbish tip. Such concentrated and abundant food has helped this vulture to expand in numbers and distribution.

S. C. Bisserot

In some instances, it is feasible to manipulate the food supply of a bird of prey for conservation purposes. Supplemental feeding to help a food-limited population is an effective but somewhat labor-intensive activity that has helped a few raptor species. In parts of Africa and Europe, "vulture restaurants" have been established to provide vultures with carcasses and slaughterhouse offal in areas where natural carrion is scarce. These artificial feeding stations are poor substitutes for a natural food supply, but they may make the difference between having scavengers in an area or losing them. They can also be useful in educating the public about scavengers and their value.

In some other cases it is not primarily the quantity of food but its quality or the characteristics of the feeding sites that are manipulated. In Sweden, White-tailed Sea Eagles, threatened by feeding on pesticide-contaminated prey, were enticed to feed on chemically safe slaughterhouse carcasses and offal. By consuming a "cleaner" diet, their body burdens of toxic chemicals were reduced and their survival and reproduction enhanced.

FEEDING SEA EAGLES IN WINTER

BJÖRN HELANDER

Winter-feeding has proved effective in the management of threatened eagle populations in temperate areas. In Sweden, the White-tailed Sea Eagle (*Haliaeetus albicilla*) was facing extinction in the 1970s, following two decades of strongly depressed reproduction due to the influence of persistent chemicals in the environment. The production of offspring was much too low to balance the mortality of adults, and a population crash seemed inevitable if the situation continued.

At this point, an extensive feeding program was started within the "Project Sea Eagle," run by the Swedish Society for the Conservation of Nature. One purpose of the program was to present uncontaminated meat to the birds, thereby limiting their intake of harmful pollutants and improving the chances of healthy reproduction. The other main purpose was to provide supplemental food to the birds during the cold season to improve the survival rate, mainly among the young, inexperienced birds. One hundred feeding stations in Sweden now provide a total of about 150 tonnes of food per winter to the eagles.

The effects of this feeding program on breeding success have been limited—some pairs improved their offspring production, while others remained barren. But juvenile survival increased strongly, eventually resulting in a stabilization in the breeding population as the surviving young birds reached maturity and began to form pairs.

Thus, it proved possible to compensate for the poor reproductive output by increasing the survival rate of the few young that were produced. The feeding program was started just in time and actually saved the White-tailed Sea Eagle population by the Baltic Sea from a catastrophic decline. Continued winter-feeding will also speed up the recovery of the population, as reproduction gradually improves along with a decrease in the levels of DDT and other pollutants in the environment.

Bjorn Helander

WHITE-TAILED SEA EAGLE REINTRODUCTION IN SCOTLAND

JOHN A. LOVE

Around 1916 the White-tailed Sea Eagle (*Haliaeetus albicilla*) became extinct in Britain. The bird had suffered heavily at human hands—being shot, trapped or poisoned, or else having its eggs stolen by collectors. Recolonizing by natural means has not been possible since populations elsewhere in Europe were similarly reduced by persecution or, more recently, by toxic chemicals. People have since tried to make amends. Three Sea Eagles were released in western Scotland in 1959 and four more on the Shetland Islands in 1968, but neither reintroduction attempt was successful. In 1975, the Nature Conservancy Council made a fresh attempt, this time liberating many more birds, from Norway, and over a longer time period.

Norway has retained a healthy population of Sea Eagles and, since the number of breeding pairs there has been increasing, the authorities proved willing to donate eagles to be freed in Scotland. The island of Rum, in the Inner Hebrides, was chosen as the release point. This island is a national nature reserve, in the heart of the Sea Eagle's former range and one of the last known breeding sites in Britain.

The eagles were removed from nests at about two months of age, a few weeks before they fledged. Such is the breeding density and success in northern Norway that different donor pairs were used each year, and only one chick from broods of two were taken. The eaglets were then flown to Scotland by the Royal Air Force and, within 10 or 12 hours, were safely ensconced in cages specially built in a remote part of Rum.

After a statutory five weeks in quarantine, the young eagles could be released. However, they were still provided with "natural" prey until they were able to hunt for themselves. Although no parental example proved necessary, the youngsters derived benefit from older, more experienced birds in the vicinity that had been set free a few years previously.

The project started in 1975 with the release of three juveniles, and up to ten were liberated each year (up to and including 1985)—a total of 82 altogether, approximately equal numbers of males and females. Sea Eagles take about five years to reach maturity, and by 1983 courtship display and nest-building had been recorded.

The first two clutches of eggs were laid that year, but it was not until 1985 that one pair had gained sufficient experience to hatch and fledge the first Scottish-bred eaglet. This pair repeated their success, but with twins, the following year and again in 1987. That year, too, a second pair reared a single eaglet. Unfortunately both these pairs failed in 1988 due to bad weather, but a new pair, breeding for the first time, fledged two young. This pair failed in 1989, but three other pairs (including a new pair) reared five young. This has brought the total of wild-bred Sea Eagles to thirteen. About six other pairs have proved capable of laying and incubating but have yet to hatch and rear young, and a further four or five pairs are holding a territory. Breeding output is still low, however, so the species has not yet established a viable population in Britain. The eyries are protected by the Royal Society for the Protection of Birds.

▲ By the early twentieth century, persecution had driven the White-tailed Sea Eagle to extinction in Britain. In the decade from 1975, conservationists released on the isle of Rum 82 young birds, flown in from a healthy population in Norway. Older eagles visited the cages of youngsters awaiting release and later provided examples as they learned to hunt. In 1985, 70 years after their demise, Sea Eagles once again bred in Britain.

In South Africa the endangered Cape Griffon (*Gyps coprotheres*) may be experiencing a problem with food quality, in this case a nutritional deficiency. Many nestling vultures have suffered from bone abnormalities associated with calcium deficiency. Apparently parent vultures now feed primarily on carcasses of domestic livestock rather than on the remnants of predator-killed ungulates, especially in areas where predators have been destroyed. Unlike carcasses of native ungulates that are usually torn apart by bone-crushing predators or scavengers and contain crushed bone fragments, carcasses of livestock have no bone fragments small enough for vultures to eat and deliver to their nestlings. A shortage of bone fragments in the nestling diet leads to bone abnormalities and poor survival. Vulture restaurants featuring bone fragments have been used to provide the calcium needed for normal nestling development.

Occasionally, it is not the quantity or quality of the food but where it is found that conservationists manipulate to the birds' benefit. When the available food supply is located in a situation that places raptors feeding there at risk, manipulating the food supply can encourage the birds to feed in safer locations. In recent years Californian Condors have been forced to leave safe nesting and roosting areas in wilderness mountain areas and descend to ranchlands in the foothills and valleys to feed on carcasses of livestock and unretrieved, hunter-killed deer. There is little carrion for the birds to eat in the mountains, where fire control has

Peter Steyn

permitted dense chapparal vegetation to overgrow previously open habitat. When condors venture into ranchland, they are subject to shooting, poisoning, colliding with power-transmission lines, and other unnatural hazards. In the future, when California Condors, all of which are now in captivity, are reintroduced to the wild, efforts will be made to keep the birds in safe wilderness areas by providing supplemental food there.

▲ Ornithologists noticed that Cape Griffon chicks had severe bone abnormalities and traced the cause to a lack of calcium in their diet. A scarcity of carcasses caught and torn apart by mammalian predators left few bone fragments for the vultures to carry back to their growing nestlings. Vulture restaurants, offering suitably sized pieces of bone, are helping to alleviate the problem.

C. M. Perrins/Oxford Scientific Films

◄ Mountainous wilderness, secure from the unnatural hazards of shooting, poisoning and collision with powerlines, was the original haunt of the California Condor. However, in some areas fire control encouraged the growth of a dense shrub layer, forcing the Condors down to forage in the open but perilous ranchlands. Any future attempt at reintroduction must incorporate the best of both worlds—a clean, safe habitat and a regular food supply.

PEREGRINE FALCON RECOVERY IN THE UNITED STATES

W. BURNHAM

During the 1950s and 1960s, falconers and biologists noticed a dramatic decline in many Peregrine Falcon (*Falco peregrinus*) populations. The decline was partly a result of reproductive failures involving thin-shelled, broken eggs, caused by DDT, and partly additional adult mortality caused by dieldrin, after these insecticides were ingested by the falcons in their prey. In the United States the decline was so severe that all known nesting Peregrines were lost east of the Mississippi River by the mid-1960s, and only a remnant population remained in some western states. The decline in the western population continued through the 1970s. For example, in the state of Colorado in 1974, ten falcons laid approximately 40 eggs, which resulted in only a single young. More northern populations in Alaska also declined, but probably to no more than half their original numbers.

By 1970 many scientists believed that the Peregrine Falcon would be extinct in North America by the end of the decade. That year Tom J. Cade, Professor of Ornithology at Cornell University, began a program which would not only affect the Peregrine, but other endangered species internationally, and give hope that extinction need not be inevitable. In an atmosphere of skepticism and doubt, Dr. Cade began a program to breed Peregrines in captivity, believing that the young could be released to the wild, remnant populations could be saved and bolstered, and lost populations could be re-established. This program was called "The Peregrine Fund." Its success was due partly to the successful breeding and release of Peregrines, and partly to the banning of the offending pesticides in the United States in the early 1970s.

Large-scale breeding of raptors in captivity was believed impossible by most aviculturists, but in 1973 twenty Peregrines of arctic (*tundrius*) and maritime (*pealei*) races were bred by The Peregrine Fund. Equally significant was the breeding of the first five Peregrines from the western race (*anatum*) by Professor James Enderson of The Colorado College. These successes were the beginning of productions which have exceeded 300 birds per year and by 1988 totaled over 3,500 Peregrines. In 1974 The Peregrine Fund established a western facility in Colorado, and Dr. William Burnham joined the organization to build the program to re-establish the remnant western populations. Dr. Enderson donated his falcons to The Peregrine Fund, as did many other falconers, forming the base stock for recovery. In 1980 Brian Walton and the Santa Cruz Predatory Bird Research Group joined the recovery effort to work in California and Nevada, receiving breeding stock from The Peregrine Fund. Peregrines were bred and recovery efforts managed from three regional facilities in New York, Colorado, and California.

Release of Peregrines was accomplished in two main ways. Where breeding pairs remained, their thin-shelled eggs were collected and replaced by three-week-old young falcons from captivity (fostering). Peregrines begin to fly at about 42–45 days of age. Where no falcons remained, or when more captive young were produced than could be accommodated in known wild nests, a technique called "hacking" was used. The term and much of the methodology were borrowed from falconry.

Falconers of medieval times who took nestlings freqently placed them on a castle tower or building, feeding them daily and allowing them to develop, learn to fly and hunt. The falconers then recaptured the young before they flew away and disappeared. The Peregrine Fund used a similar technique, building a specially designed square box (122 x 122 centimeters; 4 x 4 feet) with a barred front. The "hack box" was placed on a cliff, tower, or building where the young were contained for the last ten days before they began to fly. When they were old enough to fly, the barred front was removed and the young were continually monitored and fed daily until they became independent in four to six weeks. Released young were fed by adult Peregrines at breeding facilities before going to hack sites, and then they continued to be fed in such a way as to prevent them from associating food with humans and becoming tame.

More than 3,000 Peregrines have now been released by The Peregrine Fund into 28 states. In 1975 only 27 pairs were known

Frans Lanting/Minden Pictures

in those states, but over 300 pairs have now been located, and most result from releases and are reproducing normally. Although the effort is not yet finished, as the falcon is still absent from large areas of former range, the species is expected to make a full recovery before the turn of the century. In Alaska, after DDT levels dropped and where an adequate number of wild breeding Peregrines remained, reintroduction was not necessary, just as in Great Britain and other parts of Europe. On both continents the population in some areas has now increased to above known historical levels.

The story of the recovery of the Peregrine Falcon in the United States, although not yet complete, is one of the great wildlife successes of the twentieth century. Thanks to the falconers, the biologists, government and corporate leaders, and the thousands who have supported the efforts of The Peregrine Fund, once again people in the United States can share the feeling that R. B. Treleaven expressed: "There is no more exciting sound in all nature than the angry raucous rasp of a Peregrine challenging all who enter its domain, nor more magnificent sight than its dark silhouette emblazoned on a cloud, the unmistakable hallmark of nature's perfection."

Frans Lanting/Minden Pictures

▲ A massive and successful conservation initiative, nearly 4,000 Peregrine Falcons have been bred in captivity in the USA since 1973. Released into the wild many are raising chicks in eyries deserted for years. By 2000, the population of Peregrine Falcons is expected to be fully recovered, returned to parts of the USA left empty through pesticide use.

▼ To release young captive-bred Peregrine Falcons to the wild, the medieval technique of "hacking back" is used. Towering office blocks have replaced castle turrets. Nestlings are placed in a wire-fronted box to which they return for food for about six weeks as they gradually develop hunting skills.

MANIPULATING THE NESTING BIOLOGY OF RAPTORS

Many birds of prey normally reproduce at relatively slow rates. In some cases, this naturally low production of offspring is reduced further as a result of human factors. Increasing the birth rate of raptors through intensive management can help populations maintain their numbers.

Some manipulations of nesting biology increase the number of offspring produced by each managed pair, whereas others increase the proportion of pairs that nest successfully. In all cases, these management efforts are labor-intensive and justified only when the population concerned is critically endangered. They can, nonetheless, be very effective in encouraging population growth when reproduction is otherwise inadequate.

Like many birds, raptors lay a replacement clutch of eggs if their first clutch is lost early in incubation. Taking the first clutches of eggs to induce the production of a second clutch has been termed "double clutching," and this has been used to increase the reproductive output of selected pairs.

Peregrine Falcons in North America and Europe have been double-clutched in this way. Eggs from the first clutches were artificially incubated and the resulting young then fostered to wild pairs with small broods. One of the benefits of this procedure during the pesticide era was that thin-shelled eggs could be hatched at a higher rate in incubators than under parent birds. Many eggs too thin to support the weight of the incubating parent, or eggs that were already cracked or pitted, could be saved.

With Ospreys in eastern North America, double clutching was used in conjunction with a regional egg transfer. Ospreys in Chesapeake Bay that laid eggs with normal shells were double clutched. The eggs from first clutches were transferred to the nests of heavily contaminated New England Ospreys that were laying thin-shelled eggs and producing few young. The Chesapeake Bay eggs hatched at high rates under New England foster parents, while the Chesapeake Bay Ospreys laid replacement clutches and still produced normal numbers of young. The importance of this large-scale egg transfer became clear after only a few years: Most of the Ospreys breeding in New England in the post-pesticide era were products of the egg transfer program. Without the program the population would have been very much smaller.

Some large eagles regularly lay clutches of eggs that are larger than the number of young that are normally reared. Sometimes sibling aggression results in "Cain and Abel" struggles in which the smaller hatchlings are killed by their older siblings. In other cases competition for food between siblings results in mortality. In either case, if any of these extra young could be saved, the number of birds produced would be higher.

Lesser Spotted Eagles (*Aquila pomarina*) in Europe lay two eggs but normally rear only one young because of sibling aggression. Second hatched nestlings have been removed by biologists and temporarily cross-fostered to a Common Buzzard (*Buteo buteo*) or Black Kite (*Milvus migrans*) before being returned to their real parents' nest at an age when they were no longer aggressive. The parents were then able to raise both their young, effectively doubling their reproductive rate.

In North America, Bald Eagle nestlings have been removed from nests containing more than two young. These young are then fostered to unproductive eagles in other regions or hand-reared and released to the wild in areas where eagles have been extirpated.

Ospreys often build their large nests atop dead trees and some are lost because these trees are

▼ An Osprey perches on its seemingly precarious bundle of sticks atop a pylon; powerline authorities often remove such nests. Wasted nesting effort can be avoided by providing safe, sturdy artificial sites nearby. These have proved just as attractive to Ospreys, and in many cases nesting has been more successful than at natural sites.

blown down. Also, Osprey nests on power poles or other man-made structures are often removed so the nesting effort is wasted. By providing Ospreys in these situations with safe, sturdy, alternative sites on specially erected platforms, losses are reduced. In some areas of North America most Ospreys nest on these artificial platforms, and reproductive success is often higher than in populations nesting in more natural sites.

With captive breeding programs for some species producing impressive numbers of birds, it has been possible to use young bred in captivity to augment wild populations or to restore birds to areas where they had been extirpated. In some cases, young birds produced in captivity have been fostered to wild pairs. This procedure has helped bolster the breeding rate of remnant populations, such as the Peregrine Falcon population in the western United States, which has received hundreds of additional recruits from captive-breeding programs and is now on the increase.

More typically, captive-breeding programs have provided birds that are used to restore a population to parts of a range where extirpation has occurred. The most extensive program of this sort has involved the Peregrine Falcon in the eastern United States, where a pre-pesticide population of several hundred pairs had disappeared by 1965. Since 1975, over 1200 young produced in captivity have been returned to the wild. By 1989, these releases had given rise to a growing population of over 100 breeding pairs.

The success of restoration programs is dependent on large numbers of birds being released to the wild in such a way that their prospects for survival and reproduction are good. Making the transition from captivity to the wild has involved the use of "hacking," a falconry technique. Nestlings are reared in artificial nest boxes in the field and allowed to fly free at normal fledging age. The birds instinctively return to the "hack box" for food while they hone their flying and hunting skills. After several weeks, when they are able to hunt for themselves, they disperse from the release sites, and subsequently live as independent free-flying individuals.

Birds released in this manner have survived at near normal rates, and returned to establish territories and breed in the general vicinity of their release site. To date, captive breeding and the release of young birds through hacking have been employed successfully with a variety of raptors, ranging from Andean Condors (*Vultur gryphus*) to Mauritius Kestrels (*Falco punctatus*).

REHABILITATION OF INJURED RAPTORS

Many rare raptors, especially large ones, depend on relatively high survival of adults in order to maintain their populations. Any unnatural factor that raises mortality can cause population declines,

Peter Steyn

even though the birds may be reproducing at normal rates. Raptors such as large eagles, condors, and vultures typically have this life-history pattern.

For such species, preventing the loss of individuals through a variety of human causes, such as shooting, poisoning, collisions and so forth, can make an important contribution to population maintenance. Despite our efforts to prevent raptors from being harmed by people, many birds are still killed or injured. The injured ones can often be given a second chance through the efforts of a growing number of dedicated and skillful individuals who treat injured birds and, if possible, return them to the wild. The benefits of these rehabilitation programs are twofold. For certain raptors the return of rehabilitated individuals is important for wild populations. Secondly, the public education value of these humanitarian efforts is tremendous. The public generally sympathizes with the plight of these unfortunate birds and deplores those thoughtless individuals who injured them.

▲ Endangered by habitat destruction and monkeys, the Mauritius Kestrel numbered about six birds in 1974. Protection of nests and native forest, together with the release of captive-bred kestrels, has helped bring the population back from the brink of extinction.

▼ Restrained in an old stocking, a broken-winged Variable Goshawk awaits veterinary treatment, the first step towards return to the wild. The experience gained may help valuable individuals of rare species, and the effort reinforces the notion that raptors are worth conserving.

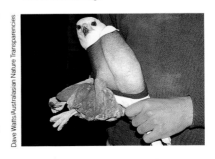

Dave Watts/Australasian Nature Transparencies

▲ Loss or degradation of habitat is the biggest threat to raptor populations. Consequently, preservation of tracts of land known to be important to wildlife assumes top conservation priority. The Snake River Birds of Prey Area is set aside and maintained by the United States government to preserve its impressive raptor community. Biologists, here ringing two Ferruginous Hawk chicks, monitor the 700 pairs of 15 species found within the Area.

PROVIDING HABITAT

As is the case with most wildlife, destruction or alteration of natural habitats is the most pervasive human activity that affects raptors. Protecting ecosystems that can accommodate raptor populations as part of an intact wildlife community is a high priority conservation activity, especially where large proportions of the local raptors are habitat specialists, as are many species in tropical forests.

The needs of raptors are sometimes specifically considered in strategies to protect natural ecosystems. In some cases, raptors receive special attention because they are large, space-demanding species, the habitat needs of which may be among the most extensive of any species in the community. A tropical forest nature preserve that can accommodate a viable population of Harpy Eagles (*Harpia harpyja*) will, for example, almost certainly accommodate viable populations of most other forest animals.

It is uncommon for a habitat preservation scheme to be planned primarily around raptors, but there are a few notable exceptions. The most impressive is the Snake River Birds of Prey Area maintained by the United States Federal government in southwestern Idaho. Containing some 247,000 hectares (610,000 acres) along 129 kilometers (80 miles) of the Snake River, the preserve is home to over 700 pairs of 15 raptor species, including an estimated 4 percent of the world's Prairie Falcons. The area's primary management objective is preservation of this impressive raptor community and the habitat it requires.

Even when protection of extensive areas is not feasible, critical habitat for raptors can still be preserved by more localized actions. Buffer zones have been established to keep disruptive human activities at bay at specific places and times when raptors would be disturbed. Buffer zones around nests of species, such as Bald Eagles and Peregrine Falcons, or around winter feeding sites, as in the Bald Eagle feeding areas on the Chilkat River in Alaska, have proven effective in protecting key pieces of habitat.

PROSPECTS

As society increasingly values birds of prey for their beauty and ecological roles, programs to conserve and manage these birds are sure to grow. The tremendous expansion in raptor management activities over the past 20 years shows no sign of

abating, and this trend is fortunate. The threats to raptors are complex and increasing. The crisis caused by toxic chemicals is, in many parts of the world, behind us, but in other areas, particularly in Third World countries, the problem persists. Habitat loss looms as a major threat to raptors, many of which are tropical forest specialists. As tropical deforestation proceeds apace, the number of tropical raptors on endangered species lists will continue to grow. Of the 30 birds of prey added to the ICBP's list of threatened birds since 1977, 21 are tropical raptors threatened by habitat loss.

We can take justifiable pride in accomplishments for raptor conservation over the past two decades. Populations of Peregrine Falcons, Ospreys, and Bald Eagles that were once endangered have now largely recovered, and the prospects for other species, such as the California Condor, Mauritius Kestrel, and Florida Everglade Kite (*Rostrhamus sociabilis plumbeus*) are much improved. The most impressive recoveries, however, have taken place in well-known species residing in the richest nations of the world, whereas the most discouraging declines are now occurring in the little known species that occur in the poorest of nations. If raptor conservationists are to repeat the successes of the recent past, they must promptly shift their regional emphasis, and join with other conservationists in the quest to preserve more habitat for wildlife. Tropical forest raptors and island raptors are obvious high priority candidates for attention.

▼ Once common and confiding, the Galapagos Hawk (*Buteo galapagoensis*) has suffered from shooting and feral cat predation at nests. About 150 pairs remain. Now protected, these hawks range over the Galapagos and are maintaining stable populations on certain islands. Conservation efforts are securing their future.

CHECKLIST OF LIVING DIURNAL RAPTORS
ORDER FALCONIFORMES

SUBORDER CATHARTAE—
CATHARTID VULTURES AND
TERATORNS

FAMILY TERATORNITHIDAE—TERATORNS (FOSSIL)
FAMILY CATHARTIDAE—CATHARTID VULTURES
(NEW WORLD VULTURES OR CONDORS)

Coragyps atratus . . . . Black Vulture
Cathartes aura . . . . Turkey Vulture
Cathartes burrovianus . . . . Savanna Vulture
    (Lesser Yellow-headed Vulture)
Cathartes melambrotus . . . . Wetmore Forest Vulture
    (Greater Yellow-headed Vulture)
Gymnogyps californianus . . . . California Condor
Vultur gryphus . . . . Andean Condor
Sarcoramphus papa . . . . King Vulture

SUBORDER ACCIPITRES—
OSPREYS, HAWKS, AND ALLIES

FAMILY ACCIPITRIDAE—
OSPREYS, HAWKS, KITES, AND ALLIES

SUBFAMILY PANDIONINAE—OSPREYS

Pandion haliaetus . . . . Osprey (Fish Hawk)

SUBFAMILY ACCIPITRINAE—
HAWKS, KITES, EAGLES, AND ALLIES

Aviceda cuculoides . . . . African Cuckoo Hawk
Aviceda madagascariensis . . . . Madagascar Cuckoo Hawk
Aviceda jerdoni . . . . Asian Baza (Jerdon's Baza)
Aviceda subcristata . . . . Crested Baza (Pacific Baza)
Aviceda leuphotes . . . . Black Baza
Leptodon cayanensis . . . . . . Gray-headed Kite (Cayenne Kite)
Chondrohierax uncinatus . . . . Hook-billed Kite
Henicopernis longicauda . . . . Long-tailed Honey Buzzard
    (Papuan Honey Buzzard)
Henicopernis infuscata . . . . Black Honey Buzzard
    (New Britain Honey Buzzard)
Pernis apivorus . . . . Western Honey Buzzard
Pernis ptilorhynchus . . . . Eastern Honey Buzzard
Pernis celebensis . . . . Barred Honey Buzzard
    (Crested Honey Buzzard)
Elanoides forficatus . . . . Swallow-tailed Kite
Machaerhamphus alcinus . . . . Bat Kite (Bat Hawk)
Gampsonyx swainsonii . . . . Pearl Kite
Elanus leucurus . . . . White-tailed Kite
Elanus caeruleus . . . . Black-shouldered Kite
Elanus notatus . . . . Black-winged Kite
Elanus scriptus . . . . Letter-winged Kite

Chelictinia riocourii	Scissor-tailed Kite
Rostrhamus sociabilis	Snail Kite (Everglade Kite)
Rostrhamus hamatus	Slender-billed Kite
Harpagus bidentatus	Double-toothed Kite
Harpagus diodon	Rufous-thighed Kite
Ictinia plumbea	Plumbeous Kite
Ictinia mississippiensis	Mississippi Kite
Lophoictinia isura	Square-tailed Kite
Hamirostra melanosternon	Black-breasted Kite
Milvus milvus	Red Kite
Milvus migrans	Black Kite
	(Yellow-billed Kite—Africa; Pariah Kite—India)
Haliastur sphenurus	Whistling Kite
Haliastur indus	Brahminy Kite
Haliaeetus leucogaster	White-bellied Sea Eagle
	(White-breasted Sea Eagle)
Haliaeetus sanfordi	Solomon Sea Eagle (Sanford's Sea Eagle)
Haliaeetus vocifer	African Fish Eagle
Haliaeetus vociferoides	Madagascar Fish Eagle
Haliaeetus leucoryphus	Pallas' Fish Eagle (Band-tailed Fish Eagle)
Haliaeetus albicilla	White-tailed (Sea) Eagle (Gray Sea Eagle)
Haliaeetus leucocephalus	Bald Eagle (White-headed Eagle)
Haliaeetus pelagicus	Steller's Sea Eagle
Ichthyophaga humilis	Lesser Fishing Eagle
Ichthyophaga ichthyaetus	Greater Fishing Eagle
	(Gray-headed Fishing Eagle)
Aegypius monachus	Cinereous Vulture
Aegypius tracheliotos	Lappet-faced Vulture (Nubian Vulture)
Aegypius occipitalis	White-headed Vulture
Aegypius calvus	Red-headed Vulture (Pondicherry Vulture)
Necrosyrtes monachus	Hooded Vulture
Gyps fulvus	Eurasian Griffon
Gyps indicus	Long-billed Griffon
Gyps himalayensis	Himalayan Griffon
Gyps rueppellii	Rüppell's Griffon
Gyps coprotheres	Cape Griffon (Cape Vulture)
Gyps bengalensis	Asian White-backed Vulture
Gyps africanus	African White-backed Vulture
Neophron percnopterus	Egyptian Vulture
	(White Scavenger Vulture—India)
Gypaetus barbatus	Bearded Vulture (Lammergeyer)
Gypohierax angolensis	Palmnut Vulture (Vulturine Fish Eagle)
Circaetus gallicus	Short-toed Eagle
Circaetus cinereus	Brown Snake Eagle
Circaetus fasciolatus	East African Snake Eagle
	(Southern Banded Snake Eagle)
Circaetus cinerascens	Banded Snake Eagle
Terathopius ecaudatus	Bateleur (Eagle)
Spilornis cheela	Crested Serpent Eagle
Spilornis kinabaluensis	Kinabalu Serpent Eagle
Spilornis minimus	Nicobar Serpent Eagle
Spilornis elgini	Andaman Serpent Eagle
Dryotriorchis spectabilis	Congo Serpent Eagle
	(African Serpent Eagle)
Eutriorchis astur	Madagascar Serpent Eagle
Polyboroides typus	African Harrier Hawk (Gymnogene)
Polyboroides radiatus	Madagascar Harrier Hawk
Melierax poliopterus	Eastern Chanting Goshawk
	(Somali Chanting Goshawk)
Melierax metabates	Dark Chanting Goshawk
Melierax canorus	Pale Chanting Goshawk
Melierax gabar	Gabar Goshawk
Kaupifalco monogrammicus	Lizard Buzzard
Butastur rufipennis	Grasshopper Buzzard
Butastur teesa	White-eyed Buzzard
Butastur liventer	Rufous-winged Buzzard

Butastur indicus	Gray-faced Buzzard
Circus assimilis	Spotted Harrier
Circus maurus	Black Harrier
Circus cyaneus	Northern Harrier
	(Marsh Hawk—America; Hen Harrier—England)
Circus cinereus	Cinereous Harrier
Circus macrourus	Pallid Harrier
Circus melanoleucos	Pied Harrier
Circus pygargus	Montagu's Harrier
Circus aeruginosus	Western Marsh Harrier
Circus spilonotus	Eastern Marsh Harrier
Circus approximans	Swamp Harrier (Pacific Marsh Harrier)
Circus ranivorus	African Marsh Harrier
Circus maillardi	Malagasy Marsh Harrier
Circus buffoni	Long-winged Harrier
Accipiter poliogaster	Gray-bellied Hawk
Accipiter trivirgatus	Asian Crested Goshawk
Accipiter griseiceps	Celebes Crested Goshawk
Accipiter tachiro	African Goshawk
Accipiter castanilius	Chestnut-flanked Sparrowhawk
	(Chestnut-bellied Sparrowhawk)
Accipiter brevipes	Levant Sparrowhawk
	(Short-toed Sparrowhawk)
Accipiter badius	Shikra (Little Banded Sparrowhawk)
Accipiter butleri	Nicobar Sparrowhawk
Accipiter soloensis	Gray Frog Hawk (Chinese Sparrowhawk)
Accipiter francesii	Malagasay Sparrowhawk
	(Frances' Sparrowhawk)
Accipiter trinotatus	Spot-tailed Sparrowhawk
Accipiter fasciatus	Brown Goshawk (Australasian Goshawk)
Accipiter novaehollandiae	Variable Goshawk
	(Gray Goshawk, White Goshawk)
Accipiter melanochlamys	Black-mantled Goshawk
Accipiter albogularis	Pied Sparrowhawk (Pied Goshawk)
Accipiter rufitorques	Fiji Goshawk
Accipiter haplochrous	New Caledonia Sparrowhawk
	(New Caledonia Goshawk)
Accipiter henicogrammus	Moluccan Barred Sparrowhawk
	(Gray's Sparrowhawk)
Accipiter luteoschistaceus	Blue and Gray Sparrowhawk
Accipiter imitator	Imitator Sparrowhawk
Accipiter poliocephalus	Gray-headed Sparrowhawk
Accipiter princeps	Gray-headed Goshawk
Accipiter superciliosus	Tiny Hawk
Accipiter collaris	Semicollared Hawk
Accipiter erythropus	Red-thighed Sparrowhawk
Accipiter minullus	Little Sparrowhawk
Accipiter gularis	Japanese Sparrowhawk
Accipiter virgatus	Besra (Sparrowhawk)
Accipiter nanus	Dwarf Sparrowhawk
Accipiter cirrhocephalus	Australasian Collared Sparrowhawk
Accipiter brachyurus	New Britain Collared Sparrowhawk
Accipiter erythrauchen	Moluccan Collared Sparrowhawk
Accipiter rhodogaster	Vinous-breasted Sparrowhawk
Accipiter madagascariensis	Madagascar Sparrowhawk
Accipiter ovampensis	Ovampo Sparrowhawk
Accipiter nisus	Eurasian Sparrowhawk
Accipiter rufiventris	Rufous-breasted Sparrowhawk
Accipiter striatus	Sharp-shinned Hawk
Accipiter cooperii	Cooper's Hawk
Accipiter gundlachi	Cuban Hawk (Gundlach's Hawk)
Accipiter bicolor	Bicolored Hawk
Accipiter melanoleucus	Black and White Goshawk
	(Great Sparrowhawk; Black Sparrowhawk)
Accipiter henstii	Madagascar Goshawk (Henst's Goshawk)
Accipiter gentilis	Northern Goshawk

Accipiter meyerianus . . . . Papuan Goshawk (Meyer's Goshawk)
Accipiter buergersii . . . . Chestnut-mantled Goshawk
Accipiter radiatus . . . . Red Goshawk
Accipiter doriae . . . . Doria's Goshawk
Urotriorchis macrourus . . . . Long-tailed Hawk
Geranospiza caerulescens . . . . Crane Hawk
Leucopternis schistacea . . . . Slate-colored Hawk
Leucopternis plumbea . . . . Plumbeous Hawk
Leucopternis princeps . . . . Barred Hawk
(Black-chested Hawk)
Leucopternis melanops . . . . Black-faced Hawk (Masked Hawk)
Leucopternis kuhli . . . . White-browed Hawk
Leucopternis lacernulata . . . . White-necked Hawk
Leucopternis semiplumbea . . . . Semiplumbeous Hawk
Leucopternis albicollis . . . . White Hawk
Leucopternis occidentalis . . . . Gray-backed Hawk
Leucopternis polionota . . . . Mantled Hawk
Asturina nitida . . . . Gray Hawk
Buteogallus aequinoctialis . . . . Rufous Crab Hawk
Buteogallus subtilis . Pacific Black Hawk (Mangrove Black Hawk)
Buteogallus anthracinus Common Black Hawk (Lesser Black Hawk)
Buteogallus urubitinga . . . . Great Black Hawk
Buteogallus meridionalis . . . . Savanna Hawk
Parabuteo unicinctus . . . . . Harris' Hawk (Bay-winged Hawk)
Busarellus nigricollis . . . . Black-collared Hawk
(Collared Fishing Hawk)
Geranoaetus melanoleucus . . . . Black-chested Eagle
(Black-chested or Gray Buzzard Eagle)
Harpyhaliaetus solitarius . . . . Black Solitary Eagle
Harpyhaliaetus coronatus . . . . Crowned Solitary Eagle
Buteo magnirostris . . . . Roadside Hawk
Buteo leucorrhous . White-rumped Hawk (Rufous-thighed Hawk)
Buteo lineatus . . . . Red-shouldered Hawk
Buteo ridgwayi . . . . Ridgway's Hawk (Hispaniolan Hawk)
Buteo platypterus . . . . Broad-winged Hawk
Buteo brachyurus . . . . Short-tailed Hawk
Buteo swainsoni . . . . Swainson's Hawk
Buteo galapagoensis . . . . Galapagos Hawk
Buteo albicaudatus . . . . White-tailed Hawk
Buteo polyosoma . . . . Red-backed Hawk
Buteo poecilochrous . . . . Puna Hawk (Variable Hawk)
Buteo albonatatus . . . . Zone-tailed Hawk
Buteo solitarius . . . . Hawaiian Hawk
Buteo jamaicensis . . . . Red-tailed Hawk
Buteo ventralis . . . . Rufous-tailed Hawk
Buteo buteo . . . . Eurasian Buzzard
Buteo oreophilus . . . . Woodland Buzzard (Mountain Buzzard)
Buteo brachypterus . . . . Madagascar Buzzard
Buteo rufinus . . . . Long-legged Buzzard
Buteo hemilasius . . . . Upland Buzzard
Buteo regalis . . . . Ferruginous Hawk
Buteo lagopus . . . Rough-legged Hawk (Rough-legged Buzzard)
Buteo auguralis . . . . . Red-necked Buzzard (Red-tailed Buzzard)
Buteo augur . . . . Augur Buzzard
Buteo rufofuscus . . . . Jackal Buzzard
Morphnus guianensis . . . . Guiana Crested Eagle
Harpia harpyja . . . . Harpy Eagle
Harpyopsis novaeguineae . . . . New Guinea Eagle
Pithecophaga jefferyi . . . . Great Philippine Eagle
(Monkey-eating Eagle)
Ictinaetus malayensis . . . . Asian Black Eagle
Aquila pomarina . . . . Lesser Spotted Eagle
Aquila clanga . . . . Greater Spotted Eagle
Aquila rapax . . . . Tawny Eagle
(Africa, India); Steppe Eagle (temperate Asia; southern
Asia and Africa, as migrant)

Aquila heliaca . . . . Imperial Eagle
Aquila gurneyi . . . . Gurney's Eagle
Aquila chrysaetos . . . . Golden Eagle
Aquila audax . . . . Wedge-tailed Eagle
Aquila verreauxii . . . . . Verreaux's Eagle (African Black Eagle)
Hieraaetus wahlbergi . . . . Wahlberg's Eagle
Hieraaetus fasciatus . . . . Bonelli's Eagle
Hieraaetus spilogaster . . . . African Hawk Eagle
Hieraaetus pennatus . . . . Booted Eagle
Hieraaetus morphnoides . . . . Little Eagle
Hieraaetus ayresii . . . . Ayres' Hawk Eagle
Hieraaetus kienerii . . . . Rufous-bellied Eagle
Hieraaetus bellicosus . . . . Martial Eagle
Spizastur melanoleucus . . . . Black and White Hawk Eagle
Spizaetus occipitalis . . . . Long-crested Eagle
Spizaetus africanus . . . . Cassin's Hawk Eagle
Spizaetus cirrhatus Crested Hawk Eagle (Changeable Hawk Eagle)
Spizaetus nipalensis . . . . Mountain Hawk Eagle
Spizaetus bartelsi . . . . Javan Hawk Eagle
Spizaetus lanceolatus . . . . Celebes Hawk Eagle
Spizaetus philippensis . . . . Philippine Hawk Eagle
Spizaetus alboniger . . . . Blyth's Hawk Eagle
Spizaetus nanus . . . . Wallace's Hawk Eagle
Spizaetus coronatus . . . . African Crowned Eagle
Spizaetus ornatus . . . . Ornate Hawk Eagle
Spizaetus tyrannus . . . . . Black Hawk Eagle (Tyrant Hawk Eagle)
Spizaetus isidori . . . . . Black and Chestnut Eagle (Isidor's Eagle)

SUBORDER SAGITTARII—
SECRETARYBIRDS
FAMILY SAGITTARIIDAE—SECRETARYBIRDS

Sagittarius serpentarius . . . . Secretarybird

SUBORDER FALCONAE—CARACARAS
AND FALCONS
FAMILY FALCONIDAE—CARACARAS AND FALCONS

SUBFAMILY POLYBORINAE—CARACARAS, LAUGHING
FALCONS, AND FOREST FALCONS

Daptrius ater . . . . . Black Caracara (Yellow-throated Caracara)
Daptrius americanus . . . . Red-throated Caracara
Phalcoboenus carunculatus . . . . Carunculated Caracara
Phalcoboenus megalopterus . . . . Mountain Caracara
Phalcoboenus australis . . . . Striated Caracara
Polyborus plancus . . . . Crested Caracara
Milvago chimachima . . . . Yellow-headed Caracara
Milvago chimango . . . . Chimango Caracara
Herpetotheres cachinnans . . . . Laughing Falcon
Micrastur ruficollis . . . . Barred Forest Falcon
Micrastur gilvicollis . . . . Lined Forest Falcon
Micrastur mirandollei . . . . Slaty-backed Forest Falcon
Micrastur semitorquatus . . . . Collared Forest Falcon
Micrastur buckleyi . . . . Buckley's Forest Falcon
Spiziapteryx circumcinctus . . . . Spot-winged Falcon

SUBFAMILY FALCONINAE—FALCONS AND FALCONETS

Polihierax semitorquatus . . . . African Pygmy Falcon
Polihierax insignis . . . . White-rumped Pygmy Falcon
Microhierax caerulescens Collared Falconet (Red-legged Falconet)
Microhierax fringillarius . . . . Black-thighed Falconet
(Black-sided Falconet)
Microhierax latifrons . . . . Bornean Falconet
Microhierax erythrogonys . . . . Philippine Falconet
Microhierax melanoleucos . . . . Pied Falconet
Falco naumanni . . . . Lesser Kestrel
Falco sparverius . . . . American Kestrel (Sparrow Hawk)
Falco tinnunculus . . . . Old World Kestrel
Falco newtoni . . . . Madagascar Kestrel
Falco punctatus . . . . Mauritius Kestrel
Falco araea . . . . Seychelles Kestrel
Falco moluccensis . . . . Moluccan Kestrel
Falco cenchroides . . . . . . Australian Kestrel (Nankeen Kestrel)
Falco rupicoloides . . . . . . White-eyed Kestrel (Greater Kestrel)
Falco alopex . . . . Fox Kestrel
Falco ardosiaceus . . . . Gray Kestrel
Falco dickinsoni . . . Dickinson's Kestrel (White-rumped Kestrel)
Falco zoniventris . . . . Banded Kestrel (Barred Kestrel)

Falco chicquera . . . . Red-headed Falcon (Red-necked Falcon)
Falco vespertinus . . . . Western Red-footed Falcon
Falco amurensis . . . . Eastern Red-footed Falcon (Amur Falcon)
Falco eleonorae . . . . Eleonora's Falcon
Falco concolor . . . . Sooty Falcon
Falco femoralis . . . . Aplomado Falcon
Falco columbarius . . . . Merlin (Pigeon Hawk)
Falco rufigularis . . . . Bat Falcon
Falco subbuteo . . . . Northern Hobby (Eurasian Hobby)
Falco cuvierii . . . . African Hobby
Falco severus . . . . Oriental Hobby
Falco longipennis . . . . Australian Hobby (Little Falcon)
Falco novaeseelandiae . . . . New Zealand Hobby
(New Zealand Falcon)
Falco berigora . . . . Brown Falcon
Falco hypoleucos . . . . Gray Falcon
Falco subniger . . . . Black Falcon
Falco mexicanus . . . . Prairie Falcon
Falco jugger . . . . Laggar Falcon
Falco biarmicus . . . . Lanner Falcon
Falco cherrug . . . . Saker Falcon
Falco rusticolus . . . . Gyrfalcon
Falco peregrinus . . . . Peregrine Falcon (Duck Hawk)
Falco pelegrinoides . . . . Barbary Falcon (Shaheen)
Falco deiroleucus . . . . Orange-breasted Falcon
Falco fasciinucha . . . . Taita Falcon

FURTHER READING

Much of the information in this book derives from original research undertaken by the contributors. Regional guides on the local birds of prey written by ornithologists are readily available in libraries and bookshops. However, the following publications may be of value to readers who would like to explore more fully the fascinating world of birds of prey.

Amadon, D., and Bull. J. 1988. "Hawks and Owls of the World: A Distributional and Taxonomic List". The Genus *Otus*, by J. T. Marshall and B. F. King, in *Proceedings of the Western Foundation of Vertebrate Zoology*, **3** (4), July 1988.

Austin, O. L. Jnr. 1975. *Birds of the World*. Hamlyn Publishing Group, London.

Birds of the World. IPC Magazines, London.

Brown, L. 1976. *Birds of Prey: Their Biology and Ecology*. Hamlyn Publishing Group, London.

Brown, L., and Amadon, D. 1968. *Eagles, Hawks and Falcons of the World*. Leslie Brown and The Hamlyn Publishing Group, London.

Cade, T. J. 1982. *The Falcons of the World*. Collins, London.

Cade, T. J. 1988. *Peregrine Falcon Populations: Their Management and Recovery*. The Peregrine Fund Inc., Boise, Idaho.

Donne, P., Sibley, D., and Surton, C. 1988. *Hawks in Flight*. Houghton Mifflin Co., Boston.

Grossman, M. L., and Hamlet, J. 1988. *Birds of Prey of the World*. Bonanza Books, New York.

Hollands, D. 1984. *Eagles, Hawks and Falcons of Australia*. Nelson, Melbourne.

Kerlinger, P. 1989. *Flight Strategies of Migrating Hawks*. University of Chicago Press, Chicago.

Lloyd, Derek, and Lloyd, Glenys. 1969. *Birds of Prey*. Hamlyn Publishing Group, London.

Newton, I. 1979. *Population Ecology of Raptors*. Buteo Books, South Dakota, and Poyser, Calton, England.

Newton, I. 1986. *The Sparrowhawk*. Poyser, Calton, England.

Perrins, C. 1976. *Bird Life: An Introduction to the World of Birds*. Elsevier, Oxford.

Pickford, Peter, and Pickford, Beverley. 1989. *African Birds of Prey*. New Holland (Publishers), London.

Steyn, P. 1982. *Birds of Prey of Southern Africa*. David Philip Publisher (Pty) Ltd, Claremont, Cape.

Weick, F. 1980. *Birds of Prey of the World*. Verlag Paul Dailey, Berlin.

ACKNOWLEDGMENTS

The publishers would like to thank the following people for their assistance in the preparation of the book:
Lloyd F. Kiff, Western Foundation of Vertebrate Zoology, Los Angeles, for initial advice on contributors and current research; Simone Perryman and Helen Cooney for editorial and administrative assistance; Walter Bowles, Australian Museum, Sydney, Peter Mitchell, Macquarie University, Sydney, Jack Pettigrew, University of Queensland, Graeme Phipps, Taronga Zoological Park, Sydney, and Steven Symonds, Commonwealth Bureau of Meteorology, Sydney, for assistance in the preparation of illustrations.

WHAT IS A RAPTOR?
Page 25, Foot structure and prey type
Illustrations adapted from L. Brown, *Birds of Prey: Their Biology and Ecology*, Hamlyn Publishing Group, London, 1976, p. 100; and F. Weick, *Birds of Prey of the World*, Verlag Paul Dailey, Berlin, 1980, pp. 40, 41, 55.
Page 27, Wingspans
Adapted from J. M. Mendelsohn, A. C. Kemp, H.C. Biggs, R. Biggs and C. J. Brown, "Wing Areas, Wing Loadings and Wing Spans of 66 Species of African Raptors", in *Ostrich* 60, p. 39; and C. Perrins, *Bird Life: An Introduction to the World of Birds*, Elsevier, Oxford, 1976, p. 32.

KINDS OF RAPTORS
References for the illustrations in this chapter came from many sources, but the following are given special acknowledgment:
Pages 33-51, Silhouettes
Shelly Grossman, in M. L. Grossman and J. Hamlet, *Birds of Prey of the World*, Bonanza Books, New York, 1988.
Page 33, Andean Condor
Birds of the World, IPC Magazines, London, p. 346.
Page 34, Osprey
Hans and Judy Beste/Ardea London.
Page 35, Crested Baza
David Hollands, in D. Hollands, *Eagles, Hawks and Falcons of Australia*, Nelson, Melbourne, 1984, p. 13.
Page 35, Hook-billed Kite
L. Brown and D. Amadon, *Eagles, Hawks and Falcons of the World*, Leslie Brown and the Hamlyn Publishing Group, London, 1968, p. 217.
Page 36, Black-shouldered Kite
Peter Steyn/Ardea London.
Page 36, Snail Kite
Haroldo Palo/Natural History Photographic Agency.
Page 37, Swallow-tailed Kite
L. Brown and D. Amadon, *Eagles, Hawks and Falcons of the World*, p. 214.
Page 37, Pearl Kite
L. Brown and D. Amadon, *Eagles, Hawks and Falcons of the World*, p. 235.
Page 38, Brahminy Kite
Jean-Paul Ferrero/Auscape International.
Page 39, Black Kite
Hans Reinhard/Bruce Coleman Ltd.
Page 40, Lappet-faced Vulture
Leonard Lee Rue III/Tom Stack & Associates.
Page 41, Eurasian Griffon
Udo Hirsch/Bruce Coleman Ltd.
Page 42, Bateleur
Barrie Wilkins/Bruce Coleman Ltd.
Page 42, Palmnut Vulture
Kenneth W. Fink/Ardea London.
Page 43, Bearded Vulture
St Meyers/Zentrale Farbbild Agentur.
Page 44, African Harrier Hawk
Alan Weaving/Ardea London.
Page 44, Eastern Chanting Goshawk
Peter Davey/Bruce Coleman Ltd
Page 45, Spotted Harrier
Hans and Judy Beste/Auscape International.
Page 45, Crested Serpent Eagle
L. Brown and D. Amadon, *Eagles, Hawks and Falcons of the World*, p. 361.
Page 46, Slate-colored Hawk
Birds of the World, IPC Magazines, London, p. 488.

Page 46, Rough-legged Hawk
Shelly Grossman, in M. L. Grossman and J. Hamlet, *Birds of Prey of the World*, p. 269.
Page 48, Ornate Hawk Eagle
L. Brown and D. Amadon, *Eagles, Hawks and Falcons of the World*, p. 705.
Page 48, Bonelli's Eagle
Shelly Grossman, in M. L. Grossman and J. Hamlet, *Birds of Prey of the World*, p. 311.
Page 50, Lined Forest Falcon
Gunther Ziesler/Bruce Coleman Ltd.
Page 50, African Pygmy Falcon
Birds of the World, IPC Magazines, London.
Page 51, Striated Caracara
Brian Hawkes/Natural History Photographic Agency.
Page 51, White-eyed Kestrel
John Visser/Bruce Coleman Ltd.

HABITATS AND POPULATIONS
Page 80, Size of territory,
M. L. Grossman and J. Hamlet, *Birds of Prey of the World*, Bonanza Books, New York, 1988, pp. 262, 315, 400; and I. Newton, *Population Ecology of Raptors*, Buteo Books, South Dakota, and Poyser, Calton, England, 1979, p. 63.
Pages 80-81, Vegetation zones
Adapted from *National Geographic Atlas of the World*, National Geographic Society, Washington, DC., 1975, p. 9; *The Macquarie Illustrated World Atlas*, Macquarie Library, Sydney, 1984, p. 75; and *The Times Concise Atlas of the World*, Times Books, London, 1985, pp. 14-15.

SOCIAL BEHAVIOR
Page 114, Dimorphism and diet
I. Newton, *Population Ecology of Raptors*, Buteo Books, South Dakota, and Poyser, Calton, England, 1979, p. 20.
Page 117, Territoriality of Eurasian Sparrowhawks
I. Newton, *Population Ecology of Raptors*, p. 59.

REPRODUCTION
Pages 132-133, Breeding displays
L. Brown, and D. Amadon, *Eagles, Hawks and Falcons of the World*, Leslie Brown and the Hamlyn Publishing Group, London, 1968, pp. 95, 96, 100.
Page 134, Mid-air passing of food
Adapted from *Birds of the World*, IPC Magazines, London, p. 605; and I. Newton, *The Sparrowhawk*, Poyser, Calton, England, 1986, p. 158.
Page 135, Copulation
Adapted from T. J. Cade, *The Falcons of the World*, Collins, London, 1982, p.44.

MIGRATION AND MOVEMENTS
Page 152-153, Migration paths
Additional reference from Derek and Glenys Lloyd, *Birds of Prey*, Hamlyn Publishing Group, London, 1969.
Page 162, Two types of flying
P. Donne, D. Sibley and C. Switch, *Hawks in Flight*, Houghton Mifflin, Boston, 1988, pp. 54, 58, 80, 163; and P. Kerlinger, *Flight Strategies of Migrating Hawks*, University of Chicago Press, Chicago, 1989, Chapter 6.

HUMAN IMPACTS ON RAPTORS
Page 200, British index of Sparrowhawks
I. Newton, *Population Ecology of Raptors*, Buteo Books, South Dakota, and Poyser, Calton, England, 1979, p. 221.
Page 203, Food chain
T. J. Cade, *Peregrine Falcon Populations: Their Management and Recovery*, The Peregrine Fund Inc., Boise, Idaho, 1988, p. 352.
Page 204, Eggshell thinning
T. J. Cade, *Peregrine Falcon Populations: Their Management and Recovery*, p. 346.

NOTES ON CONTRIBUTORS

JAMES C. BEDNARZ

James Bednarz has conducted research on raptors for more than twelve years on locations throughout North America. He completed his doctorate and post-doctorate studies on the social biology of the Harris' Hawk while at the University of New Mexico. Currently, he serves as Director of Higher Education and Research at Hawk Mountain Sanctuary in Pennsylvania. He has published more than twenty-five scientific papers on raptor behavior and ecology. His recent research has focused on the social behavior of raptors, migration behavior and strategies, and conservation biology.

MICHAEL G. BROOKER

After joining the CSIRO Division of Animal Genetics in 1961, Michael Brooker worked with the sheep breeding program until 1969 when he transferred to the Division of Wildlife and Ecology to study the ecology of the Wedge-tailed Eagle in Western Australia with Michael Ridpath. Subsequent projects have included five fauna surveys in New South Wales and the Northern Territory, the ecology of wetlands, the breeding biology of some passerines (*Amytornis, Acanthiza, Malurus*), the biology of cuckoos, the effect of fire on the flora and fauna in heathlands, and the dynamics of remnants of native vegetation in the wheat belt of Western Australia.

C. J. BROWN

Christopher Brown spent three years in the Drakensberg and Maluti mountains of southern Africa, studying the biology of the Bearded Vulture and other large birds of prey for the Natal Parks Board. In 1983 he took the post of ornithologist in the Namibian Directorate of Nature Conservation based in Windhoek. He is responsible for the conservation of all birds in the country at the local and national levels. Dr. Brown's main research interest remains with birds of prey, and he is currently working on declining populations of Martial and Tawny Eagles on farmlands, and Lappet-faced Vultures in the Namib Desert. He is the editor of the scientific journal, *Madoqua*, which publishes in the field of arid zone biology and nature conservation research.

WILLIAM A. BURNHAM

Dr. Bill Burnham has, since 1986, served as President of The Peregrine Fund, a non-profit international conservation organization dedicated to preserving birds of prey. His interest in raptors originated through falconry which he has practiced for more than twenty-five years. His research has taken him to the tropics, as well as the arctic and temperate regions of the world. He has published over thirty scientific papers. Dr. Burnham is an adjunctive professor at Boise State University and is advising students working internationally.

WILLIAM S. CLARK

Bill Clark's lifelong interest in birds of prey began as a hobby and became a profession. He has coordinated the Raptor Migration Banding Project at Cape May, New Jersey, for the past twenty-three years, and served for five years as Director of the NWF's Raptor Information Center. He has written numerous articles on raptor migration, conservation and field identification, and co-authored a North American raptor field guide. Currently, Bill Clark operates Raptours, a tour company specializing in watching raptors, and he regularly lectures and conducts workshops on birds of prey.

JOHN E. COOPER

After qualifying at Bristol University in 1966, John Cooper obtained the Diploma in Tropical Veterinary Medicine at Edinburgh University in 1968, was elected a Fellow of the Institute of Biology in 1980, was awarded a Fellowship of the Royal College of Veterinary Surgeons, for work on avian diseases, in 1986, and in 1989 was admitted as a Member of the Royal College of Pathologists. His interests are disease and pathology of non-domesticated species, especially birds, reptiles and amphibians; health and welfare of laboratory animals; zoonoses; tropical diseases; and the role of animals in educational establishments. Currently Veterinary Conservator and Senior Lecturer in Comparative Pathology, Royal College of Surgeons of England, he is the author of many papers and books.

BJÖRN HELANDER

Born in Stockholm, Dr. Helander studied zoology at the University of Stockholm and gained his doctorate in 1983. In the early 1960s he became interested in Sea Eagles, and since 1968 has been responsible for annual censuses of this species, run by the Swedish Society for the Conservation of Nature. Since 1971, he has been the leader of the Swedish "Project Sea Eagle", a combined research and conservation progam. At present, he is Conservation Officer for the Swedish Society for the Conservation of Nature. As well, he is involved in a monitoring program for seals and Sea Eagles run by the Swedish Museum of Natural History and the National Environment Protection Board.

CHARLES J. HENNY

Dr. Henny studied at Oregon State University and, since 1970, has been Research Scientist with the US Fish and Wildlife Service. He has conducted field studies at many places in the USA, Canada and Mexico. He has been particularly interested in the Osprey, Eastern Screech Owl and the American Kestrel. Research interests include population dynamics with an emphasis in recent years on the impact of environmental pollutants on raptors.

DAVID C. HOUSTON

After studying zoology at Bristol University, Dr. Houston began research on vultures at the Serengeti Research Institute in Tanzania, East Africa, to investigate the interaction between scavenging birds and large mammalian predators. He has continued working on scavenging birds and the role they play in wildlife communities, especially the activities of vultures. Currently Senior Lecturer in the Department of Zoology, University of Glasgow, he has recently been working on the feeding ecology of South American vultures, particularly their role as scavengers in tropical rainforests.

ALAN KEMP

Born in Gweru, Zimbabwe, Dr. Kemp attended Peterhouse School in that country, where natural history, falconry and egg-collecting were encouraged. Qualifying as a zoologist at Rhodes University, Grahamstown, South Africa, he worked as research assistant to Professor Tom Cade of Cornell University (New York). This involved three years of field work in the Kruger National Park, on raptors, mainly vultures and Gabar Goshawks, and doctoral research on hornbills. Since then he has been at the Transvaal Museum, doing broad systematic studies on raptors, including owls, on hornbills, and on biogeographic interpretations. Dr. Kemp has travelled widely in southern Africa, and to museums and study areas in Kenya, Australia, Malaysia, India, Mauritius, Seychelles, Europe and North America.

ROBERT E. KENWARD

Dr. Kenward grew up on a farm in southern England before taking Honours and Doctoral degrees at Oxford University, including a thesis on goshawk predation for the Edward Grey Institute of Field Ornithology. He was subsequently responsible for radio-tagging 400 goshawks to study their behavior and population dynamics in Sweden. Employed since 1978 by the Natural Environment Research Council's Institute of Terrestrial Ecology, he is based at Furzebrook Research Station in Dorset, after six years at Monk's Wood Experimental Station in Cambridgeshire. He is a coordinator for the World Working Group on Birds of Prey, and has written a textbook on radio-tagging as well as more than forty other scientific publications.

JOHN LEDGER

Dr. Ledger is a graduate of the University of the Witwatersrand, and specialized in medical entomology at the South African Institute for Medical Research. He has been interested in raptors from his schooldays, and in 1973 founded the Vulture Study Group with Dr. Peter Mundy. John Ledger has been director of the Endangered Wildlife Trust since 1985; he has also been wildlife consultant to Eskom, the electric utility of South Africa, since 1978.

YOSSI LESHEM

Yossi Leshem studied zoology and genetics at Hebrew University, Jerusalem, and presented a thesis on the breeding biology of Bonelli's Eagle in Israel to the University of Tel-Aviv for his master's degree. His present research is on the spring and autumn migration of soaring birds over Israel and the influence of climatic factors on migration. He is Director of the Israel Raptor Information Center.

JOHN A. LOVE

Interested in natural history since his boyhood in Inverness, John Love graduated from Aberdeen University. His intimate involvement with the recent reintroduction of the White-tailed Sea Eagle united his love for his native Highlands, his interest in seabirds, and his fascination with birds of prey. For ten years he lived on the Isle of Rum in the Inner Hebrides, managing the sea eagle project. In 1983 Cambridge University Press published his *Return of the Sea Eagle*. John Love is on part-time contract to the Nature Conservancy Council and spends the rest of his time lecturing, illustrating and writing.

B. RILEY McCLELLAND

Dr. McClelland has served on the faculty at the University of Montana for sixteen years. He teaches courses in bird conservation and park resource management. He has also worked for the US National Park Service for thirty-three years, recently concurrently with his faculty position. His work with birds has focused on woodpeckers and raptors. He and his wife Pat have studied Bald Eagles in Glacier National Park, Montana, since 1965. This research has included several graduate students and has ranged throughout western North America, using radio-telemetry to track the migrations of eagles from Glacier.

PETER MUNDY

Born in London, Dr. Mundy went to Nigeria as a schoolteacher in 1969. There he met birds, and in particular vultures, and in 1972 went to Rhodesia (now Zimbabwe) to study vultures for a doctorate. In 1973 he was co-founder of the Vulture Study Group which continues working for the conservation of these birds in southern Africa and elsewhere. With the group, he is involved in the biannual production of the journal *Vulture News*. In his current position as government ornithologist for Zimbabwe, he is particularly concerned with the protection of bustards, cranes, falcons, lovebirds and other species, and also with policies on Quelea bird control.

IAN NEWTON

Educated at the Universities of Bristol and Oxford, Dr. Newton now works for the Natural Environment Research Council in Britain. He has twenty-five years' experience on birds, including seed-eating finches, waterfowl and birds of prey. His main interests are in population ecology, and the effects of pesticides and other toxic chemicals on bird populations. He has written more than 150 scientific papers and three books, including *Population Ecology of Raptors* which has become the standard reference for raptor researchers worldwide. His work includes studies of peregrines, buzzards, kites and sparrowhawks. Widely travelled, Dr. Newton has served on many committees concerned with ornithological research and conservation. He holds the medal of the British Ornithologists Union, awarded for "eminent services to ornithology".

LYNN W. OLIPHANT

Dr. Oliphant grew up in the outskirts of Detroit, Michigan, and studied biology at Wayne University. He then moved with his wife to Seattle, Washington, to continue graduate work, specializing in cellular ultrastructure. The coastal Black Merlins that wintered in Seattle often threatened to turn his head from the electron microscope. Moving to Saskatoon about the same time the Merlins invaded that city, he has followed the population through its major period of growth; since then he has become involved in captive breeding and reintroduction of Peregrines. He is currently Professor of Veterinary Anatomy at the University of Saskatchewan.

JERRY OLSEN

Jerry Olsen has studied raptors for thirty years, first in Washington State, USA, and then in Australia. His interests include the biology of Black and Peregrine Falcons near Port Augusta, South Australia; captive breeding; using falcons in control of airport gulls; the effect of weather on breeding raptors; studies of prey; risk of hunting accidents. He has helped to make six films on raptors, including the award-winning "Hunters of the Skies", and has also written many articles and three books. He lectures in Counselling and Special Education at the University of Canberra. His research time is divided between studies of troubled children and birds of prey.

PENNY OLSEN

Penny Olsen has been studying birds of prey for fifteen years. She and her husband, Jerry, live on a farm near Canberra with about thirty raptors unable to be released. They have rehabilitated about 200 sick, orphaned or injured birds and returned them to the wild. Penny has been President of the Australasian Raptor Association, is on the International Committee of the Raptor Research Foundation, and is a member of the ICBP's World Working Group on Birds of Prey. She has written about fifty research papers and forty more-popular articles. A contributor to three books, including *Australia Land of Birds*, she is co-author of *Birds of Prey and Gamebirds of Australia* and an as-yet untitled book on Australia's falcons.

KENTON E. RIDDLE

Dr. Riddle has been a falconer for thirty-eight years. His post-graduate research work was done at the Yerkes Primate Research Center, Emory University, Georgia, USA, and for eleven years he was Associate Professor of Veterinary Medicine and Surgery at the University of Texas. He has done extensive field work in Greenland, Alaska and the Texas Gulf coast, involving trapping, banding and blood-sampling of arctic Peregrine Falcons. Toxicological analysis of blood and other tissues resulted in numerous publications of data on environmentally relevant toxins. Dr. Riddle designed a unique veterinary research hospital for falcons, and directs research and management of a large collection of hunting falcons belonging to the ruling family of Abu Dhabi.

STANLEY E. SENNER

A native of Kansas, Stanley Senner has devoted his professional career to conservation of wildlife and their habitats. His training is in biology, with emphasis on birds. Over the past fifteen years he has worked as a policy advocate for a national conservation organization, as a staff member for a committee of the US House of Representatives, and as a research biologist at the Institute of Arctic Biology. Currently he is executive director of the Hawk Mountain Sanctuary Association, a non-profit organization with a program in education, research, and policy that is national and international in scope. His primary interests are the ecology and conservation of migratory birds and management of publicly owned lands for the benefit of wildlife.

NEAL GRIFFITH SMITH

Dr. Smith was born in New York, and his Ph.D. thesis concerned species-isolating mechanisms in *Larus* gulls in the Canadian Arctic. Joining the Smithsonian Tropical Resarch Institute in 1963, he was based in Panama and worked throughout Central and South America, conducting research on brood parasitism by a cowbird on a group of socially nesting icterids. This work also concerned the nature of the association of these icterids to wasps, bees and parasitic flies. He has studied hawk migration in that area, first as a ground observer, and later from powered and glider aircraft. He has spent time in Egypt, Israel and Turkey, doing a comparative study of soaring migration.

NOEL F. R. SNYDER

A native of Pennsylvania, Dr. Snyder completed a B.S. degree in biology at Swarthmore College and a B.M. at the Curtis Institute of Music. His research for his Ph.D. in evolutionary biology from Cornell University was on alarm behavior of aquatic snails. From 1962 to 1972 he was an assistant professor at the University of South Florida and carried out research on the behavior of various invertebrate species, as well as on the behavior and ecology of

accipitrine hawks in the southwestern states. In 1972 he joined the Endangered Wildlife Research Program of the US Fish and Wildlife Service, directing the Puerto Rican Parrot field program. During 1978–79 he investigated the ecology of Florida Snail Kites and was leader of the California Condor field research program from 1980 to 1986. At present he is working at the Arizona Game and Fish Department and has initiated a program to re-establish the Thick-billed Parrot in the United States.

PETER STEYN

Born in Cape Town, South Africa, Peter Steyn was educated there at Diocesan College and the University of Cape Town. In 1971 he went to Rhodesia (now Zimbabwe) where he taught for ten years. He then left teaching to follow a career as a freelance ornithologist/wildlife photographer/safari guide/lecturer. Peter has photographed birds since the age of 14 and has specialized in birds of prey. He has travelled widely, including both the Arctic and Antarctic, and has written numerous scientific papers and popular illustrated articles on birds, as well as four books, *Eagle Days*, *Wankie Birds*, *Birds of Prey of Southern Africa* and *A Delight of Owls*.

STANLEY A. TEMPLE

Dr. Temple's special area of interest is the ecology and management of endangered species, especially birds. He has worked extensively with birds of prey, including some of the world's rarest and most threatened species, such as the Californian Condor, Mauritius Kestrel, Peregrine Falcon, Seychelles Kestrel and Andean Condor. He has written more than 140 technical publications on wildlife ecology, including a book on the management of endangered birds. He teaches courses at Cornell University on wildlife ecology and management, and endangered species, and has received several awards for the excellence of his teaching and research accomplishments. As part of his lifelong interest in birds of prey, he is an active falconer.

JEAN-MARC THIOLLAY

After working for ten years in active field ornithology in Europe, Dr. Thiollay turned his attention to tropical birds. He has worked in West Africa, East and North Africa, Nepal, Southeast Asia, Central America (mainly Mexico) and South America (mostly French Guiana). Raptors, of both savannas and rainforests, have always been his preferred topic, and he is currently working on the maintenance of the high species diversity in tropical forests. He is the author of over 150 publications in many ornithological and ecological journals and books.

ANDREW VILLAGE

Dr. Village works for the Institute of Terrestrial Ecology at Monks Wood, Huntingdon, UK. He studied for a Ph.D. at Edinburgh University, researching the ecology of European Kestrels and owls in conifer plantations. During 1980–89, he studied kestrels in farmland habitats in eastern England. His main interest is in population ecology and the regulation of numbers.

HARTMUT S. WALTER

Born in Germany, Dr. Walter studied zoology at the University of Bonn. He chose Eleonora's Falcon as his dissertation topic after an extensive study of the Mediterranean avifauna in Sardinia. After a post-doctorate fellowship in California, he began to work for African wildlife conservation from UNESCO's Nairobi Science Office. For the past eighteen years, he has been based at UCLA in Los Angeles, where he teaches courses in biogeography, ecological restoration and conservation geography. His love for birds, particularly social raptors, has carried him around the world.

INDEX